"[*Among the White Moon Faces*] transports the reader to another time
and place, with fascinating characters and a suspense that keeps
the pages turning. . . . [Lim] recounts her journey with a poet's eye for
detail and a storyteller's gift for narrative."
—Ms.

"Lim's descriptions are both lyrical and precise whether they are
of the heat, bougainvillea and crowds of her home in Malacca or
the wintery climate, the packaged food, the self-conscious
bohemianism of New England."
—Publishers Weekly

"A frank and beautifully written story of a life that is touched
and shaped by the people and communities around her, and who,
in that process, touch and shape those lives and communities
in return. Splendid reading!"
—Midwest Book Review

"In using vivid imagery and word pictures to describe the details
of her life, Lim conveys more meaning than the actual printed
text on the page. . . . Shirley Lim's book is a testament to her
strength as a woman, poet, mother, teacher, wife, feminist,
scholar, and Asian-American activist."
—Sojourner: The Women's Forum

"Immigrants come to America bearing many fabulous gifts;
among the most precious of these are their stories, which span decades,
oceans, and continents, opening our minds and hearts to human
possibilities we might otherwise never imagine. Shirley Geok-lin Lim's
story is just such a gift."
—Elaine Kim, coeditor of Making Waves: Writings By and About Asian American Women

"A wonderfully accessible journey into rites of passage—girl to
woman to parent, student to teacher, victim to survivor."
—Asian American Press

The Cross-Cultural Memoir Series introduces original, significant memoirs from women whose compelling histories map the sources of our differences: generations, national boundaries, race, ethnicity, class, and sexual orientation. The series features stories of contemporary women's lives, providing a record of social transformation, growth in consciousness, and the passionate commitment of individuals who make far-reaching change possible.

## THE CROSS-CULTURAL MEMOIR SERIES

*Juggling: A Memoir of Work, Family, and Feminism*
by Jane S. Gould

*Fault Lines* by Meena Alexander

*The Seasons: Death and Transfiguration* by Jo Sinclair

*I Dwell in Possibility* by Toni McNaron

*Lion Woman's Legacy: An Armenian American Memoir*
by Arlene Voski Avakian

*A Lifetime of Labor: The Autobiography of Alice H. Cook*

*Come Out the Wilderness: Memoir of a Black Woman Artist*
by Estella Conwill Májozo

*Under the Rose: A Confession* by Flavia Alaya

*Life Prints: A Memoir of Healing and Discovery*
by Mary Grimley Mason

# AMONG THE WHITE MOON FACES

## An Asian-American Memoir of Homelands

*Shirley Geok-lin Lim*

The Feminist Press

at The City University of New York

Published by The Feminist Press
at The City University of New York
The Graduate Center
365 Fifth Avenue
New York, NY 10016

First paperback edition, 1997

*Library of Congress Cataloging-in-Publication Data*

Lim Shirley.
    Among the white moon faces : an Asian-American memoir
of homelands / Shirley Geok-lin Lim.
        p. cm.—(The Cross-cultural memoir series)
    ISBN-13: 978-155861-179-5 (pbk.)
    ISBN-10: 1-55861-179-7 (pbk.)
      1. Lim, Shirley—Biography. 2. Women poets, American—20th
    Century—Biography. 3. Asian American women—Biography.
      I. Title. II. Series.
PS 3562.I459Z463   1996
811'.54–dc20.
[B]                                        95–25428
                                            CIP

This publication is made possible, in part, by public funds from the National Endowment
of the Arts and the New York State Council on the Arts. The Feminist Press is also grateful
for a grant from the John D. and Catherine T. MacArthur Foundation. The Feminist Press
would like to thank Joanne Markell, Barbara Sicherman, and Genevieve Vaughan for their
generosity.

Text design by Tina R. Malaney

Third reprint.

*To Richard, Florence, and Ursula*
*and for Chin Som and Chye Neo*

## ACKNOWLEDGMENTS

My thanks to the Feminist Press sisters who worked with me, Alyssa Colton, Susannah Driver, Sue Cozzi, and others; to Sue Lanser for her reader's heart; and as always to my family, Charles Bazerman and Gershom Kean Bazerman.

# CONTENTS

Midlife stalled, I look for women.
Where are they, my mothers and sisters?
I listen for their voices in poems.
Help me, I have fallen asleep, fallen
With sleepers. These women have murdered
Themselves, violent, wrenched from home.

Grandmother was barren. She died,
Tubes in nose and green shanky arm,
Hair yellow, a dirty dye, patches
Like fungus on a stricken pine.

I read terrible stories—
Hate, rage, futilities of will—
And look for women, the small
Sufficient swans, showers of stars.

# Prologue

The first time I heard Shakespeare quoted, it was as a joke. Malayans speaking pidgin English would dolefully break out into Elizabethan lines, "Romeo, Romeo, wherefore art thou, Romeo?" before bursting into chortles and sly looks. *"Aiyah! Dia Romeo, lah!"*—"He's a Romeo!"—I heard said over and over again of any number of men, including my father, Baba. "Romeo" was a name recognized equally by English, Malay, Indian, and Chinese speakers. As a child I thought it meant the kind of thing men did to women; not so much in the dark that no one could see it, but sufficiently outside the pale that it was marked with an English word. That thing was a male effect—erotic heat combined with suave flirtation, distributed promiscuously, promising a social spectacle and unhappiness for women.

"Romeo" was both an English and a Malayan word. "Hey, Romeo!" the young men said of each other as they slicked Brylcreem into their glossy black hair and preened before mirrors. The performance of the Romeo was their version of Western romantic love. It had nothing to do with tragedy or social divisions, and everything to do with the zany male freedom permitted under Westernization. It included a swagger, winks, laughs, gossip, increased tolerance, as well as disapproval and scandal. The Romeo dressed to kill, a butterfly sipping on the honey of fresh blossoms, salaciously deliberate about his intentions. Although there was a Romeo around every corner for as long as I could remember, I did not learn of Juliet's existence until I finally read the play at fourteen. By then, my imagination had hardened over the exclusion. For me, there were no Malayan Juliets, and sexual males were always Westernized.

This was Shakespeare in my tropics, and romantic love, and the English

1

language: mashed and chewed, then served up in a pattering patois which was our very own. Our very own confusion.

I didn't know about Juliet, but I knew my name. On my birth certificate, my name appears as Lim Geok Lin, a name selected from the list that Grandfather had prepared for his sons' children. It is a name intended to humble, to make a child common and same, like the seeds of the hot basil plant that puff up as hundreds of dandelion-whirly-heads in sugared drinks. The significant name, appearing first, belongs to the family, its *xing:* Lim. There are millions of Lims on this planet, spelled Lin, Ling, Lum, Lam, Leng, and so forth, depending on the anglophone bureaucrat who first transcribed the phoneme. Drawn as two figures for "man," a double male, formed from the hieroglyphs for two upright trees resembling two pines or firs, the Chinese name is the same despite its English-translated differences.

To be sure of my existence, however, Baba gave me other names. So everyone would know that I was from the female third generation of Grandfather's line, I was named "Geok," the second name giving descent position. Every granddaughter wrote her name as "Geok," the Hokkien version of that most common of Chinese female names, "Jade." Tens of millions of Chinese baby girls over the millennia have been optimistically named "Jade," the stone treasured above all stones, smooth as deep running water fossilized in a moment of alchemical mystery, whose changeful colors, from greenish white to leaf-gold to the darkest hue of rich moss, were believed to signal the health of the wearer.

My name birthed me in a culture so ancient and enduring "I" might as well have not been born. Instead, "we" were daughters, members of a family that placed its hope in sons. Something condescending and dismissive, careless and anonymous, accented the tones in which we were addressed. Girls were interchangeable. They fetched, obeyed, served, poured tea, balanced their baby brothers and sisters on their hips while they stood in the outer circles of older women. Unnecessary as individuals, girls need concern nobody, unlike sons, especially first sons, on whose goodwill mothers measured their future. My girl cousins and I, collectively named Precious Jade, were destined someday to leave our parents' homes, claimed by strangers, like jewels given up to the emperor of patriarchs. No wonder we were valued generically as girls and seldom as individuals.

Like my cousins I received a personal name, my *ming.* So as not to confuse me with Geok Lan, Geok Phan, Geok Pei, Geok Mui, or any other Geok, I was named Geok Lin. All my girl cousins answered to their Chinese *ming.* Ah Lan. Ah Mui. Ah Pei. But I was always "Shirley" to everyone. "Ah Shirley," my aunts called me.

Shirley, after Shirley Temple. Because we both had dimples. Because Baba had loved her in the movies in the 1930s. I knew the story of my name. "It's your dimples," Baba told me from the beginning. "You look just like Shirley Temple." I thought Shirley Temple was an untidy child, burnt brown, with straight black hair, a Hollywood star whose fame ensured my own as a Chinese girl.

The first time I saw the child actress in the 1934 movie "Bright Eyes," decades later in a television clip on New York public television, she was tap dancing in shiny black patent leather shoes, her ringlets bouncing to the music. I know the details now: golden hair, blue eyes, Mary Janes on her feet. We could not have been more different as babies and little girls. But growing up I was assured that I was like Shirley Temple; a child star, reborn in Malacca, the glory atoms just the same.

It remains a mystery to me what strange racial yearnings moved Baba to name me after a blond child. I'd like to think he was not tied to the fixities of race and class, that this presumption was less colonized mimicry than bold experiment. Looking at the dozens of nieces duplicated for a domestic future, did he rebel for me? Although, unarguably, he had written in his neat English script my Chinese name on my birth certificate, he never called me anything but Shirley, a Hollywood name for a daughter for whom he wished, despite everything his heritage dictated, a life freer than his own.

I was confused when I first went to school and the Irish nuns called for "Geok Lin." For the first few years I had to remember that I was "Geok Lin" in English school and "Shirley" in my home. It did not occur to me then that my scrambled names were a particular problem. Language mixes and mix-ups were Malayan everyday reality. Your own name tripped on your tongue, a series of hesitations, till you stopped noticing the hesitations, and the name flowed as yours, as a series of names.

When I was baptized at the age of eleven, Father Lourdes said I had to choose a Catholic name, the name of a saint. Baba had shown no interest one way or another when I told him that I wanted to become a Catholic. He signed a form agreeing to my baptism with no discussion; it could have been a form for participation in a School Day parade. The looming question that almost turned me away from the moment of baptism was, what would I call myself? Unlike Baba I knew that baptism intended a serious change of identity. At eleven I didn't know who I wanted to be. Saint Martha? Saint Lucy? Saint Bernadette? Saint Josephine? If I was going to change from Shirley to Martha, I wanted to know what I was exchanging my star status for. Who were these saints and what kinds of lives had they led?

In the sales annex of the convent school, I looked through the holy pictures, glossy cards which featured images of sainted women on one side and brief biographies on the other. The nuns' favorite presents to successful students, these holy pictures showed white women in long robes clasping their hands upward with piteous expressions. The stories were equally unvarying: saints died to preserve Christianity and their virginity. I chose Agnes, a virgin condemned to be devoured by lions because she had refused the seduction of a Roman tyrant. Agnes had a young noble face cast toward a stream of sunlight, and she rested her hands casually on the manes of a couple of lions who lay by her sandaled feet like overgrown house cats. I knew no one named Agnes in Malacca. It would seem a difficult name for my aunts to pronounce: Ah Agnes. For a few months after my baptism the nuns called for Agnes, had to call for Agnes again and again, before I recognized it as my name.

Then in a year there was confirmation. "You must choose a confirmation name," Father Lourdes said. More sophisticated, I checked out the Hollywood actresses whose looks I liked. Jennifer Jones matched with a Saint Jennifer, but Jennifer Jones had breasts, dark hair, a sultry look. Unlike Saint Jennifer of the holy picture, she was a moving image, a woman larger than life on the screen in the Rex Cinema. I wrote my name down as Agnes Jennifer on the cover of my school exercise books. Jenny was a friendlier version, but I already knew of at least three Jennies in Malacca; it would be too confusing to take their names.

I tried writing my names down: Shirley Agnes Jennifer Lim Geok Lin. But after months of trying one or another, only Shirley stuck. It was the name Baba had given me out of his fantasy of the West, what he saw when he saw me for the first time, his only daughter, with dimples, in a Hollywood halo. Shirley was Baba's version of the beloved girl-child, played back without the Mary Janes, without the blue eyes and golden ringlets, without anything Western in it for a Malayan daughter except the language of the West.

Whether I have had too many names or never received my right name still isn't clear to me. Malayans, imagining Romeo as a comic outlaw, transformed the play into a comedy of sexual manners because the tragedy of naming was so much a part of everyday life that we could not see it. Names also stuck on us: Chinese names, Malay names, Tamil names, English names, Portuguese names, Dutch names, Hollywood names, Roman names, Catholic names, Hindu names. They stuck, and they peeled off, became tangled like strings of DNA matter. Too many names, too many identities, too many languages.

But it was never certain that this confusion should lead to comedy or tragedy. For my mother's people, the *peranakans*—a distinctive Malayan-born people of Chinese descent assimilated into Malay and Western cultures—mockery and laughter accompanied our mélange of Chinese, Malay, Indian, Portuguese, British, and American cultural practices. Laughter acknowledged we were never pure. We spoke a little of this, a little of that, stole favorite foods from every group, paid for Taoist chants, and dressed from Western fashion magazines, copying manners we fancied. One of the earliest peranakan writers in English, Ee Tiang Hong, titled his first book of poems *I of the Many Faces*. He meant the title as an angst-loaded lamentation, but angst also is one of the many stances of the peranakans, one of their elaborate cultural plays between Chinese and Malay, Asian and Western. They, we were neither one nor the other: true peranakan copies, mixes, looking like nothing else in the world than ourselves

I begin my memoir in the United States at a moment when a female heroic of autonomy and resistance seems to have lost some of its persuasive edge. Perhaps that is why now more than ever we need to reconsider Virginia Woolf's plea that women think back through their mothers. For many of us, it is the story of our mothers that makes a female heroic so necessary, yet also so impossible. In my first life, growing up as a Malaysian woman, I only could write of Asian women whose identities intertwined with mine: mother, aunts, cousins, rivals, and friends. In my second life as an immigrant Asian American, I find that Western women have also helped me plot my life, as I write forward: women of all colors—workers, neighbors, colleagues, mentors, and sisters. This book is for all these women in my life.

# PART ONE

CHAPTER ONE

# Splendor and Squalor

*Years later, I lie awake*
*In the deep enclosing heart of a household.*
*Years later than in a crib*
*Floating among the white moon faces that beam and grasp.*

*Years later, flecking the eyes,*
*Faces like spheres wheeling, savoring myself.*
*Years later, I awake to see*
*Dust falling in the dark, in the house.*

I know no other childhood than mine, and that I had left secret as something both treasured, the one talent that my parents unwittingly have provided me, and shameful, how these same parents have as unwittingly mutilated me. Moving myself from Malacca, a small town two degrees north of the equator, to New England, then to Brooklyn and to the rich New York suburb of Westchester County, and now to Southern California, I have attempted to move myself as far away from destitution as an ordinary human creature can. In the move from hunger to plenty, poverty to comfort, I have become transformed, and yet have remained a renegade. The unmovable self situated in the quicksand of memory, like those primeval creatures fixed in tar pits, that childhood twelve thousand miles and four decades away, is a fugitive presence which has not yet fossilized. Buried in the details of an American career, my life as a non-American persists, a parallel universe played out in dreams, in journeys home to Malaysia and Singapore, and in a continuous undercurrent of feelings directed to people I have known, feared, loved, and deserted for this American success.

The irony about a certain kind of immigrant is how little she can enjoy of the very things she chases. Even as she runs away from her first life, this other life that begins to accrue around her remains oddly secondary, unrooted in the sensuality of infancy and the intensities of first memory. Before I could learn to love America, I had to learn to love the land of unconditional choice. The searing light of necessity includes my mother and father, characters whom I never would have chosen had I choice over my history.

Before there is memory of speech, there is memory of the senses. Cold water from a giant tap running down an open drain that is greenish slime under my naked feet. My mother's hands are soaping my straight brown body. I am three. My trunk is neither skinny nor chubby. It runs in a smooth curve to disappear in a small cleft between my two legs. I am laughing as her large palms slide over my soapy skin which offers her no resistance, which slips out of her hands even as she tries to grasp me. I do not see her face, only her square body seated on a short stool and a flowered *samfoo* that is soaked in patches.

The same open area, the same large green-brass tap above my head, only this time I am crying. My anus hurts me. My mother is whittling a sliver of soap. I watch the white piece of Lifebuoy grow sharper and sharper, like a splinter, a thorn, a needle. She makes me squat down, bare-assed, pushes my body forward, and inserts the sliver up my anus. The soap is soft, it squishes, but it goes up and hurts. This is my mother's cure for constipation. I cry but I do not resist her. I do not slide away but tense and take in the thorn. I have learned to obey my mother.

Both scenes occur in my grandfather's house. The house is full of the children who belong to his sons. It is already overflowing with my brothers and cousins. But all I remember of this early childhood are my aunts. They bulk like shadows to the pre-verbal child, very real and scary. One aunt is tall and stringy; her face, all planes and bolted bones, stares and scowls, her voice a loud screech. Another aunt is round; everything about her curves and presses out; her chest is a cushion, her stomach a ball, her face a full moon, and her smile grows larger and larger like a mouth that will eat you. I am afraid of them both. They wear black trousers and dull sateen *samfoo* tops, gray embossed with silver or light blue filigree. Their hair is very black, oiled to a high sheen, pulled tight off their faces into round buns, secured by long elaborate gold pins.

I do not remember my mother's figure in this infant's memory of my grandfather's house. She is an outsider, and silent in their presence. This is not her house as it is their house, although my father is a son here. In my infant memory my mother is never a Chinese woman the way my aunts, speaking in Hokkien, will always be Chinese.

Hokkien, a version of Southern Xiamen, the Min dialect from the Fujien Province, is the harsh voluble dialect of the Nanyang, the South Seas Chinese, directive, scolding, a public communication of internal states that by being spoken must be taken in by all. I heard Hokkien as an infant and resisted it, because my mother did not speak it to me. This language of the South Chinese people will always be an ambivalent language for me, calling into question the notion of a mother tongue tied to a racial origin. As a child of a Hokkien community, I should have felt that propulsive abrasive dialect in my genes. Instead, when I speak Hokkien, it is at the level of a five-year-old, the age at which I moved out of my grandfather's house on Heeren Street into my father's shoe store on Kampong Pantai. Hokkien remains for me an imperfectly learned system of grammar comprised of the reduced nouns and verbs of a child's necessary society—*chia puai* (eat rice); *ai koon* (want to sleep); *kwah* (cold); *ai kehi* (want to go); *pai* (bad); *bai-bai* (pray); *baba* (father); *mahmah* (mother). It remains at a more powerful level a language of exclusion, the speech act which disowns me in my very place of birth.

Chinese-speaking Malayans called me a "Kelangkia-kwei,"—or a Malay devil—because I could not or would not speak Hokkien. Instead I spoke Malay, my mother's language. My peranakan mother had nursed me in Malay, the language of assimilated Chinese who had lived in the peninsula, jutting southeast of Asia, since the first Chinese contact with the Malacca Sultanate in the fifteenth century. And once I was six and in a British school, I would speak chiefly English, in which I became "fluent," like a drop of rain returning to a river, or a fish thrown back into a sea.

Hokkien had never been a language of familiarity, affection, and home for me. Like the South Seas Chinese paternal house I was born in, Hokkien laid out a foreign territory, for I was of the South Seas Chinese but not one of them. Hokkien was the sounds of strong shadowy women, women who circled but did not welcome me, while in my grandfather's house my enclosing mother dimmed into two hands washing, holding, penetrating me, neither a face nor a shadow.

Then, when Baba opened his shoe shop, we had our own house. Here, in my memory, my mother becomes a woman. She chattered to us, her two sons, her daughter, her baby boy, in Malay. I do not remember moving to the shophouse on Kampong Pantai. It was as if I woke up from a dark and discordant infancy into a world of pleasure in which my mother was the major agent.

In my mother's presence there is memory of talk, not labor. Mother ordered my brothers around. She scolded us for getting ourselves wet or dirty or tired. She joked with her sisters on the manners, the bodies, and crude lusts of their acquaintances. Her *baba* Malay—the Malay spoken by assimilated Chinese—the idiomatic turns of her ethnic identity, was a waterfall whose drops showered me with sensuous music. She was funny, knowing, elegantly obscene. I remember the rhythms of her phrasings, gentle drumbeats that ended with a mocking laugh, short scolds that faded away, assuming assent.

In my mother's house, she was a *nonya*, a Malayan-native Chinese woman, whose voice ran soft-accented, filled with exclamations. Scatological phrases, wickedly funny and nasty comments on neighbors and relatives, numerous commands, an infinite list of do's and don'ts, her Malay speech was all social, all appearance and lively, never solo, always interweaving among familiar partners. How could she have talked alone to herself in *baba* speech? It would have been impossible. Even when alone, it would be speech addressed to kin, a form of *sembahyang,* prayers before the ancestral altar, to dead yet watchful fathers and mothers.

I listened and must have chattered in response. From a very early age, I was called teasingly by family and strangers a *manek manek,* a gossipy grandmother or an elderly woman who loves talk, her own and others'. I must have chattered in Malay, for just as the Hokkien-speaking elders named me as a Malay, so the Malay-speakers placed me as an ancestral talker. But I have little memory of what I said or of this precocious childhood tongue I associate with my mother's house. In memory it is my mother's speech but not mine; it was of my childhood but I do not speak it now.

My mother wore *nonya* clothing, the *sarong kebaya*. Her stiffly starched sarongs wrapped elegantly around her waist fell with two pleats in the front. Her sarongs were gold and brown, purple and brown, emerald and brown, crimson and brown, sky blue and brown. Ironed till they gleamed, they were stacked in the armoire like a queen's treasure. She wore white lace chemises under her *kebaya* tops. The breast-hugging, waist-nipping *kebayas* were of transparent material, the most expensive georgette. They were pale blue, mauve, lavender, white, yellow-green, pricked and patterned with little flowers or tiny geometric designs. They were closed in the front by triple pins or brooches, and these borders were always elaborately worked with a needle into delicate lacy designs, like scallops and shell shapes, or leaf and vine patterns. Women with time on their hands, needing food and money, meticulously picked the fragile threads apart and reworked them into an imitation of the free natural world around them. Each *kebaya* was a woman's work of art, and my mother changed her *sarong kebaya* daily as a curator changes an exhibition.

She was good-humored in this act, surrounded by many strange containers. One was filled with sweet-smelling talc and a pink powder puff like a rose that she dipped into white powder and lavishly daubed over her half-dressed body, under her armpits, around her neck and chest, and quickly dabbed between her legs like a furtive signal. Another was a blue-colored jar filled with a sugary white cream. She took a two-fingertip scoop of the shiny cream and rubbed it over her face, a face that I can still see, pale, smooth, and unmarred. She polished her clear fair face with this cream, over her forehead, her gently rounded cheeks, and the sloping chin. Her face shone like an angel's streaked with silver, and when she wiped the silvery streaks off, the skin glowed faintly like a sweet fruit. Later, I would discover that the blue jar was Pond's Cold Cream, the tub of powder, Yardley Talc. She was immersed in Western beauty, a Jean Harlow on the banks of a slowly silting Malacca River, born into a world history she did not understand.

More than store-bought magic, she was also my mother of peranakan female power. Like a native goddess she presided over an extended family— younger sisters Amy and Lei came to live with her, and younger brothers Ling, Charlie, and Mun passed through her home on their way to adult separation. She was surrounded by rituals that worshipped her being. The ritual of the peranakan female face began with white refined rice ground to a fine powder. This *bedak* was dampened with rainwater to form a smooth paste that my mother smeared over her face. The rice paste caked and dried like a crackled crepe. It filled in the fine pores on her nose and cheeks, the tiny lines around her eyes and forehead; it turned gritty like bleached beach sand. Washed away, it left her face glimmering like a piece of new silk.

My mother was the goddess of smells. She perfumed herself with eau de cologne from cut-glass bottles that were imported from the Rhine Valley in Germany. She knotted one end of a sheer cambric handkerchief and sprinkled the cologne on the knot. I kept the handkerchief in my plaid smock pocket and took it out throughout the day to sniff the knotted end. The scent was intoxicatingly fresh. It was my mother's Hollywood smell.

Some days she dressed us both elaborately, herself in a golden brown sarong and gleaming puce *kebaya,* and I in a three-tiered, ruffled, and sashed organdy dress with a gold-threaded scarlet ribbon in my hair. We rode in a trishaw to a plain structure, its doorway flanked by banana palms. The walled courtyard led to an interior room; through the door there was darkness and a flickering oil lamp. Gradually my eyes adjusted to the darkness. The small room was empty except for an altar facing the door, and on the altar was a *lingam,* a black stone stump garlanded with wreaths of orange marigolds and white jasmines. A man as dark as the room, barechested and with a white cotton *dhoti* wrapped around his hips, his face marked with lines of ash, a thumbprint of red in the center of his forehead, took my mother's money. He gave her a small comb of *pisang emas*—perhaps ten to fifteen finger-sized bananas—and a clump of incense like a pebble of gray rock candy.

Later that evening she burned the incense on a brass saucer. As the smoke rose with a pleasantly acrid scent she walked from room to room, waving the saucer till the entire house was impregnated with smoke, the smell of frankincense, and the spirits that banish fear, pain, and illness. The gray smoke wavered across the rooms and shrouded me. My mother worked with deities to cast out the envious eye, the ill-wisher, and the intruding hungry ghosts attracted by the plenty in her home. This burning incense was the smell of my mother's faith.

My mother lived through her senses. I do not believe she was capable of thinking abstractly. Her actions even late in her life were driven by needs—for food, shelter, security, affection. When needy mothers love, there is a shameful nakedness about their emotions, a return to flagrant self-love, that embarrasses. Their heat is distancing: we are driven to reject them before they can eat us up. Because my mother abandoned us when I was eight, I was never certain that she loved her children till later in life, when she needed us. Living through her senses, she could not lie about her needs. In this way, my mother's actions were always honest.

When she lived with us, my mother did not read except for magazines on Hollywood stars. Father was enthralled by the movies that frequently came into our town, and he bought expensive copies of *Silver Screen* and *Motion Picture*, fan magazines imported from wildly distant cities like Chicago and Burbank. I grew up in the company of glossy photographs of Leslie Caron, Doris Day, Fred Astaire, Ginger Rogers, Douglas Fairbanks, even Roy Rogers and Dale Evans, and those magnificent creatures Trigger, Lassie, and Francis the Talking Mule.

Other than these Hollywood familiars, we had few photographs and no pictures hanging on our walls. Framed certificates testifying to Father's success in passing the Senior Cambridge Examinations and in achieving the status of a Queen's Scout hung along the upper floor's corridors. So Father's identity was literally imprinted on the walls of our home. But Emak's presence wavered in our senses, entangled among our synapses, roused involuntarily by a scent from a perfume counter, a passing sadness at the sight of white-colored blossoms, an undercurrent of loneliness in a church or temple where old incense still lingers in the empty pews.

My mother's aesthetic sense was insensible to anything as abstract as a picture or a photograph. It must have been Father who cherished the photographs of actors and actresses, which came all the way from California, to be gazed upon by my five-year-old self. These portraits were as remote from me as the statues of Ganesha, the elephant-headed god, whose temple my mother visited, as remote as the gold-leafed, soot-covered seated figures of Kuan Yin, Goddess of Mercy, and Kwan Ti, God of Literature, War, and Justice, that rested on the tall altars where we placed joss-sticks twice a year in the Cheng Hoon Teng Temple—the Temple of The Green Merciful Clouds. Hollywood, Hindu, and Chinese spirits circled the maternal air, fit denizens whose presence in our lives gave comfort, interest, and security when we chose to remember them. But except for ancestral worship days and forays to temples, Mother lived chiefly from day to day without spirits.

In the background another woman ruled, a doughy-complexioned, large-boned woman in a cotton *samfoo*. Ah Chan washed our clothes, cooked our meals, and cleaned the bedrooms upstairs. Ah Chan came in the mornings and left every evening. She was and was not one of us.

Ah Chan made it possible for Mother always to be carefully dressed. She ironed our clothes to a high starched gloss. Often she sat on the little stool by the open-air bathroom area next to the kitchen, where she had a large zinc-plated tub full of water and dirty clothes. Or she stood in front of the baked clay charcoal braziers, raising a shower of ash with each blast of her breath, stirring the blackened wok with a huge cast-iron ladle. Ah Chan swept the rooms upstairs with a soft straw-plaited broom, pushing the skirt of straw from one corner of a room to the other. Stocky, broad, silent, she was always doing something. I never heard her speak.

Ah Chan's daughter, Peng, older than I was yet also a young girl, came to our house in the afternoons to help her mother with the laundry, ironing, cooking, and washing up. I did not play with Peng, for she was the servant's daughter and, like her mother, she remained busy and silent.

My earliest remembered dreams are of Ah Chan. Behind my shut eyelids white spots move and dance. Gradually, then faster and faster, the spots rotate and magnify till they each resolve into a round shining face with two bright black eyes and a beaming smile. They are all faces of the same woman. Her smile brightens till the myriad rows of white teeth shine and blind me, although my eyes are tightly shut. I am terrified of this female vision, these expanding faces with their pasted elongating grins spinning bodiless everywhere. Why should Ah Chan terrify me when she continues to remain in the background, seemingly screened and unheard?

Memory fixes two versions of Ah Chan, the maternal servant. In one she is stoically silent. Constantly moving, she works at small domestic chores, a necessary machine in the household. In the other version, a nightmare of beatific power, her face multiplies and expands to claim the entire ground of my vision. I wake up with my five-year-old heart racing. Awake I am careful to stay with my mother or to play in a room away from Ah Chan's presence.

Before there was trouble there were years I remember as happy, when we ventured out as a family to visit Grandma, Grand Auntie, and Mother's and Father's friends. In the evenings or on Sundays after Father had taken out the plank panels, fitted them into the metal tracks, and closed up his store which sold Bata shoes, we squeezed into his dark green Morris Minor and drove slowly up the coast with its old colonial houses, or to Bandar Pasir where friends lived in new housing estates.

It was a ritual my mother called *makan angin:* to eat the wind, to move as leisure. Not as a challenge or as a means to an end, which are Western notions of travel, but as easy pleasure. It held nothing of the association of speed that "wind" arouses in the West, but rather of slowness, a way of drawing life out so that time is used maximally. *Makan angin* makes sense only in a society in which time is valueless, a burden to be released with least financial loss and most pleasure. It speaks for lives that have not understood necessity or luxury, and that drift in dailiness, seeking escape from boredom of the senses through the senses.

The Tan family lived in a grand rambling house in Klebang. The circular driveway enclosed a flowered plot that was circled with yellow and blue tiles. Bachelor buttons, cockscombs, and zinnias glowed orange, blood red, and plum purple in the evenings when we visited. I wandered by the garden dazed by growing things. Pink clusters of sweet william flourished above me, and a thickly-branched *jambu-ayer* offered green–pink watery guavas. Inside the polished planked living room, the adults sat on rattan armchairs. Who knew what they said to each other, why the Tans felt it necessary to welcome us, what my parents intended by these visits?

I do not remember these relatives or friends visiting us except for Chinese New Year. There was something different about my parents: their restlessness to be out of the shophouse, shuttling their children, first three, made up of Beng, Chien, and myself, and gradually including Jen and Wun, all of us putt-putting into an unpaved driveway, stopping by to visit for an hour or two. Was there a pathos to this unreciprocated ritual? Even as a five-year-old child I understood social place. We were a piece of Malacca society but not secured in it.

Or less secured than the Malacca families we visited. My envy of intact families begins with those Sunday afternoons when, like a gypsy troupe or a circus mob, we stopped before a private home. Not a shophouse like ours, nor an ancestral house with five or six families in it like Grandfather's, but a house with a garden, a living room, a dining room, and bedrooms, possessing the banal regularity of the Western home.

So we made our way to another Lim home, no relative of ours but another businessman like my father, who sold books, magazines, stationery, and school supplies. The family had once lived above their shop the way we were living above the shoe store, but, newly prosperous, they were able to move into a bungalow in Bandar Hilir. The parents bustled each time we dropped by, and we never stayed long.

Their house seemed to have been constructed completely of cement. The rooms led one to another with no logic of space, no markers for inner and outer lives. They had two girls and only one son, their most valuable possession, whom they called Kau Sai, or Dogshit, for fear of the envious spirits. We thought Kau Sai was as obnoxious as his name, given to deceive the gods. The children, usually kept busy with tuition classes, piano lessons, and homework, played with their toys when we visited, disregarding our envious looks.

Perhaps we felt temporary and unimportant because we no longer lived in Grandfather's house, like the families of First Uncle, Second Uncle, Third Uncle, and Sixth Uncle. This ancestral home was a long, many-roomed, merchant's house Grandfather had built for his children. Grandfather had come to Malaya as a young man from a village near Amoy, in the Fujien province. He came as a coolie immigrant with no education or social rank, one of thousands of poor males from southern maritime China who poured into the British-controlled Straits Settlements at the beginning of the twentieth century. A common laborer, he carried sacks of charcoal wood, rice, dried foodstuffs, and agricultural imports from the cargo ships anchored off the narrow mouth of the Malacca River, onto the light boats that navigated the mud flats to unload on the quays. Through industriousness and foresight, he managed to save sufficient money to set up a chandler's shop beside the river mouth.

As a young child, I visited Grandfather's shop, a large room that opened immediately onto the street. Untidy and crowded, it was a child's fantasy of strange things, boxes and barrels that overflowed with nails, bolts, screws, brass fittings, washers, various thicknesses of ropes, steel wires, and other clunky metal fixtures. He must have done well, for he went on to buy farmland which he rented out. Grandfather weathered the world depression of 1929–32, and his store and farms prospered with the establishment of Malacca as a careening station, in the wake of British colonial and naval expansion in the Malayan peninsula.

With seven sons, the coolie transformed now into a merchant, a *towkay*, Grandfather built a handsome house on one end of Heeren Street, named after the Dutch burghers who had first settled along the coast by the mouth of the Malacca River. In the early twentieth century Heeren Street was where Malacca society lived. There, merchants like Grandfather built solid deep houses, ornately tiled, floored with quarried marble and fired red clay. I was born in such a house.

All my life I have dreamed about Grandfather's house, sometimes that I had bought the old house and was repairing it. These dreams are rarer now; more often I dream that I am exploring its rooms again. The rooms open up one into another, and old fragments of carved screens, an etched glass pane, antique spaces of yellowing marble and worn teak flooring flow in a visual stream. I am almost always delighted to rediscover its grandeur. A pride not of possession but of identity pushes the exploration. The images trigger a strong visceral sensation of identity. I know this material world, and know myself through it. The spaces are dream spaces, distorted, like the looming image of a cavernous hall for the altar room, or seeing an enormous room from under the altar table, as a child might have done, crouching in play, a long time ago. The dreams are usually pleasant, yet I am sad when I wake up.

I do not remember speech between my grandfather and myself, as if my early childhood were spent in a dumbshow, a silence of mutually uncomprehending animals. I see Grandfather in our home on Kampong Pantai. He is burnt brown, not so much scrawny as stringy, like dried toughened meat. His head is shaved and short gray bristles cover his scalp like pinpricks. His face is narrow, his cheeks drawn. He sits on the chair, an exhausted man, neither smiling nor talking. I know he is *Ah Kong*, but what does *Ah Kong* mean? With so many sons and grandsons already in the world, I must have struck him as insignificant. He is mute in my memory, giving nothing of himself except his utter weariness. He sits like a man who is only a dried burned body.

My other memory is of Grandfather's portrait which I first saw during his funeral, and then for a number of years on the altar table facing the front door, where anyone entering the house on Heeren Street would have to see it. Tinted in shades of gray, it shows the unsmiling face of a man in his early sixties, somber yet not grim, as if a history of hardship and sorrow were masked in the stoical mien and deliberately erased. It is not a face of suffering but of suffering blanked out.

This is how I envision the history of the Chinese pioneers to Malaya, the men who lived for three bowls of rice a day, and then for their sons, so that their sons would be able to feast on pork fat and white chicken meat. My grandfather's life repeats the myth of immigrant Chinese heroes, but his sons, my uncles, to whom he refused to show his sufferings, were beginning to fall away, even before he died, from the lives he had struggled to achieve for them. This truth may explain the exhaustion I saw in the man on the chair. It explains the hysteria that came over the extended family when he died.

My mother took us to a tailor's shop in the back streets of Malacca and had us measured for mourning clothes. We needed sufficient black clothes for six months, and because we had to wear black immediately, some of our other clothes were sent to be dyed. For a week until the tailor was able to complete the newly fashioned mourning clothes for us, we wore these stiff dyed cloths. They were more of an indigo than inky black. The dye penetrated the fibers and made them hard, as in a form of rigor mortis, and the seams of my blouse sat on my body like rulers. Through the day I walked in an ambience of indigo stink. It circled my head as the dye diffused with my body's heat, and its odor rose, wafted from my armpits and pores. I smelled like a corpse being prepared for burial, so that, although I was not permitted to see my grandfather's enormous teak coffin as it rested for five days on trestles in the front hall of his house, I was reminded every moment that a death had occurred.

On the day of the funeral, we joined our uncles, aunts, cousins, and numerous related people in accompanying the coffin as it moved out of the house to Bukit China, or Chinese Hill, the oldest and largest cemetery for Chinese in Malaya. We began the funeral procession at Grandfather's house. The coffin, carved with upturned ends like a pagoda roof, was hoisted with ropes and pulleys onto a lorry, and blanketed with wreaths and embroidered banners. Then, his portrait, set in an oval frame, was tied to the hood of the lorry. The scent of the cream and pink-centered frangipani wreaths masked our sweat and indigo heat, as we followed the lorry on foot, crying and lamenting. Hoods of sack cloth covered our heads, and we shuffled in straw sandals to show how his death had stripped us to destitution. First Aunt, half-carried by the other women through the hot streets, screamed the loudest.

The procession filled an entire street, the flower-bedecked lorry trailed by dozens of weeping adults and children, and they in turn followed by a solemn brass band, with drums, trumpets, and Chinese flutes blowing dirges. Behind the band fluttered banners carried streaming from a single pole or spanning the breadth of the street between two men. The banners of bright crimson, purple, midnight blue, and garish green satiny stuff were emblazoned with the names of associations and shops that had done business with Grandfather. Men in blue shirts and trousers ran up and down offering yellow "charm" papers, blessed by the Buddhist temple, to the passers-by. Grandfather's funeral was a civic occasion as much as it was a private grief, and as we dragged our fraying sandals behind the slow jerking lorry, the streets rang with the shouts of the banner carriers, and with the cries of the water carriers as they hurried from group to group dispensing bamboo joints of cool water from their covered buckets.

A photograph captures this single moment, when I felt Malacca not as a town but as a familiar spirit, a space extending from the family, and familiarity encompassing territory intimately inside my memory. In the photograph, the coffin-loaded lorry occupies center stage. The sons, faces visible under their sack-cloth hoods, kneel in front of the lorry and stare into the camera. Grandchildren stand on the sides, fanning outwards with mothers and related womenfolk behind us. There are so many grandchildren that the photograph, forming a broad, flattened rectangle, appears to have netted me within the psychic space of the extended family, that veining trajectory of multiple cousins, blooming for a shortened history in our lives.

This moment imprinted on me the sense of Malacca as my home, a sense I have never been able to recover anywhere else in the world. To have felt the familiar once is always to feel its absence after. The town through whose streets I mourned publicly, dressed in black, sack, and straw, weeping with kinfolk, united under one common portrait, is what my nerves understand as home. It doesn't matter that the family is lost, and that the town has been changed long ago by politics and economics. Every other place is foreign after this moment.

Father came from a family of six boys and one girl. He was the only son to have taken a peranakan woman as his wife. He broke away from being Chinese, and as soon as his children started school, he began to speak to them in English. As the fifth son, he had been left to his own devices, and, finding his pleasures in films and Western music, he constructed a life out of Western products. These included books. Before poverty stripped him down to essential pleasures, he read widely if with little depth. Newspapers, magazines, and omnibuses of *Reader's Digest* novels filled our home. He must have spent recklessly on subscriptions. We received *National Geographic* and two film magazines; later, as his tastes grew cruder, we received the *British Tatler* and *Tid-Bit*. He ordered copies of British funnies for my brothers, so that we were raised on popular British humor, with Desperate Dan, Billy Bunter, Dennis the Menace, and Gnasher.

When I study the few photographs I have of him as a young man, it becomes clear how differently he saw himself from his older Chinese-educated brothers. My father is almost always smiling in his photographs, as if there were an injunction against solemnity or misery in his world. In this way his image is already un-Chinese. The convention of individual portraits, a seriously considered expenditure when it wasn't an extravagance, taken perhaps only once in a lifetime, was that of the gaze across the centuries. One was looking at masses of one's great-grandchildren and expecting their worship. It was as human deities that Chinese parents looked into the camera, lofty, and as always under the eye of eternity, with a tragic cast. But my father's image for the future-capturing camera defies this Chinese deification. He sees before him the bent, tilted, shoulder-slanted pose of the Hollywood stars, the Howard Keels and Douglas Fairbanks of the non-Chinese world. His boyish head is always askew in the frame. He tilts it back as if to invite admiration. He has a smile that can charm any woman, even a five-year-old child. Sometimes he is posed with other men, but he is always in the center and at front. His pants are broad linen slacks, and he wears a cardigan whose sleeves are casually draped over his shoulders and tied loosely around his neck. In one photograph he wears a Panama hat and cradles a mandolin. He could have been a Chino in Cuba.

Where did my handsome father get his Western ways?

Father's imagination was possessed by Western images. He had a Gramophone that needed to be cranked up, and after he placed the needle in the groove of the heavy dinner-plate-sized records, music poured out of a mouthpiece curved elegantly like a horn of plenty. A little puppy with a brown-splashed ear guarded the instrument, and a man sang, "Oh Rosemarie, I love you, I'm always dreaming of you." A bright female voice promised, "Mangoes, papayas, chestnuts in the fire, the food is so good that you'll wanna stay!" My favorite was "The Mockingbird's Song," a tune which veered in my memory as the sound of happiness in the melancholic years that soon followed.

There was a time when Father and Mother enjoyed taking us to the Great World Amusement Park, a fenced-in area adjacent to the Rex Cinema. We bought entrance tickets for admission and filed through a narrow gate. Once inside, an entire brightly lit world surrounded us. Shops full of records, magazines, dolls, and knickknacks beckoned. A carousel of metal horses with large painted eyes and flying manes swirled giddily. A screen kept us from seeing into the darkened dance hall where sailors and playboys paid taxi-girls a dollar a dance. We could hear the brassy music of the Malay *joget* or the slow thump of fox trots through the open yet hidden door. Food stands offered exotic cut apples, pears, and red plums from Australia. We sat around the rickety wooden tables of an open-air coffee shop, drinking colored syrups and listening to an ancient Chinese musician as he sawed on his two-stringed *erhu*. With an artist's pride, he placed a dried plum on our table, and in exchange we gave him some coins. He did not play for money, and we acknowledged this in accepting his plum for our coins.

Passing by the record shop we stopped to let Father browse. A large doll with bright yellow hair and blue irises stood propped by its box. "Look," the salesman said, "if you lay the doll down, it closes its eyes." Perhaps Father saw the way I held it, with incredulity and delight. A white and pink doll with the plumpest arms, and legs that moved the way the German soldiers marched in the movies! I went home that evening with my first doll, an alien almost half as big as I, so wonderful that it was placed in its box high on the highest cupboard, to be brought down only on special afternoons for me to play with gingerly.

Father was an inveterate movie fan. Although films from Hong Kong and Bombay also showed daily in Malacca, he seldom saw a movie that was not in English and imported from Britain or the United States.

There were at least three movie houses in Malacca in the 1940s and '50s: the Rex, the Lido, and Capitol. The names of these pleasure houses, owned by the Shaw Brothers who lived in Singapore and Hong Kong, blazed above two-storied buildings. These imperial Latin names hardly signified the cheap shambling structures in which light poured out through a peephole and filled a screen with new images of the West: white cavalry chasing after wild Indians; Errol Flynn with a kerchief round his forehead hoisting himself up a mast, pirate's shirt blowing in the wind and pressing against his giant pectorals, waving a cutlass and challenging a dozen sailors to a fight.

The cinema facades were festooned with giant posters advertising the latest Hollywood extravaganzas. A mustachioed Clark Gable, hair slicked back and head lowered, eyes half-closed, gazed into the green irises of a flaming red-haired beauty, her skin tinted pink, who tilted her giant head and lips to greet him. This fantastic American idealized passion, posed with broad male-clothed shoulders and bare woman's flesh, covered the Rex Cinema's facade for months. It dominated the entire open square where singlet-clad peddlers sold slices of pineapple, Chinese pears, apples, and *chiku,* packages of melon seeds, dried salted olives, sugared plums, and barbecued squid. We would stand over the dazzling array of snacks for long minutes, agonizing over what we should buy with our five-cent treat. We could already taste the tropical treasures in our eager mouths, together with the American imaginary—the luxurious orchestra sweep, panoramic scenes, close-ups of white male and female beauty—to be ingested in cool darkness and silence. We emerged from the cinema hall gorged with Western images, our ears ringing with the accumulated noise of the finale, our children's eyes blinking in the afternoon glare in which suddenly everything appeared dull, flat, and small.

Since Father's shop, which sold only fashionable, brand-name Bata shoes, was carried in the Rex Cinema's opening advertisements, we were given free admission to every show. Even after Father went bankrupt and lost the shop, the regular ushers knew us so well that they continued to allow us in without tickets. Some weeks we saw three or four movies at the Rex. On weekends Beng, Chien, Jen, little Wun, and I set off in a trishaw, the smaller boys balanced on the older, and myself, a small six-year-old, squatting, scrunched by the floor. We caught the 11 A.M. matinee, then the 2 A.M. main feature, and reeled home at five in the evening, drugged and speechless after so much spectacle.

A vivid memory at ages five and six is of being wakened by my mother who wraps me in a blanket. She carries me to the Morris Minor and my father drives us to the Rex Cinema. We climb up the stairs to the more expensive balcony seats where I doze in the midst of flashing pictures and glitzy amplified music. This ritual of the midnight show is repeated frequently. My brothers must have been left alone in the shophouse while my parents silently smuggled me out. But why me? Do they provide this midnight treat on alternative nights to my brothers? Or am I special, the only girl and my father's favorite child, the one he double-dates with my mother?

The pictures I absorbed in those late night moments now form part of my involuntary imagination. A Busby Berkeley musical with Esther Williams diving and backstroking, her strong muscular body pushing through the water. Then she stands perched on a carousel composed of long-legged sleek women, smiling and waving, a surprisingly asexual figure of womanhood. A clunky metal figure ominously emerges out of a metal hulk, the light dims, the music threatens. This image frightens me and I keep recalling it for years. Decades later, in New York, I learn that this is a shot from *The Day the Earth Stood Still,* a science-fiction fantasy that I believed a part of my Malacca world. I remember a musical with prancing men and pert women dressed in long flouncy gowns. That, I find in Boston, was *Seven Brides for Seven Brothers.* Each midnight show, I wake up in time to watch the finale and see the screen filled with loudly singing, gesturing, good-looking people.

I didn't ask in the morning about the dazed fantasies. I was too busy filling in the blanks of the day with sensory motions and with explorations of my body. The second story of bedrooms and a corridor play-area had a smooth polished wood floor, planked and deeply grained. Bored and delighted at the same time, I lay on the floor, feeling its cool surface on my cheek, and traced the wood grains with my fingers. I sat by the glassless window in my parents' bedroom that faced the street, a wooden balustrade like a fence marking the division between bedroom and open air. I held onto the round bars of the balustrade, pushed my head as far as it could go between two of the bars, and studied the street below. It was dazzling hot and sunny outside. A car drove slowly past, a trishaw moved languorously in search of a passenger. Across the street was a row of other shop fronts: the goldsmith's shop showed only a dark interior, although the steel accordion gates were pushed back all the way. A lorry was parked before the sundry shop, but no one was unloading anything. The street lay silent like a somnambulist's vision.

My father's shop had a prominent place on the street, but the street always appeared quiet and empty. Sometimes I went through the curtain that separated the family rooms from the sales area and found him sitting on a stool, slipping a customer's foot into a shoe with a shoehorn. He wore dark-rimmed glasses and appeared serious, a different person in his workplace, a person who frowned impatiently. After the customer left he wrapped the shoes back in their paper tissues, placed them in their boxes, and put away the boxes precisely in their places on the shelves, like a stack of catalogued books. He swept the floor and neatly rearranged the cushioned chairs. With a feather duster, a huge cluster of black and brown rooster feathers, he dusted the counters and chairs.

He was compact, efficient, and angry. When his anger erupted, he would seize the feather duster, chase after my brothers, and thrash them with the rattan handle, gripping the feathers so tightly that they shredded and fell like pieces of my brothers' bodies. The rattan whipped through the air with a singing tone, and red welts appeared on my brothers' bare legs and arms. They raised their arms to shield their heads. When they rolled themselves into balls, the rattan cut them on their backs and shoulders. I watched terrified, guilty: was it because of me that they were being caned? Had I cried, complained, or pointed a finger at them? I was aware that my father's arm, striking again and again at my brothers, could as well be aimed at me. I stayed in the corner of the room, unable to move away from his fury. Sometimes he yelled at me, "You stay here and watch this. Don't think I won't cane you either!" I knew he would also beat me some day.

We were not allowed in the shop except on Sundays when I could stand on a cushioned chair and jump off, imitating my brothers. Once, I fell clumsily, my elbow wrenched out of its socket. I screamed with pain; the elbow bone stuck out of the skin like a sharp stick. Nevertheless, I was determined to follow my brothers, to act as they did. To be one of them, I had to keep up with them. And they were a bunch of demons. They shrieked and ran like crazed animals all over the neighborhood.

Indoors they had to be quieter, and they delighted in games that excluded me. I stood by the closed door of their bedroom; they were whispering, conspiring about a game that I was not permitted to play. I pushed at the door, but they had blocked it with the full weight of their four male bodies. I begged them to let me in, I wanted to play with them, but they refused with gleeful laughs. I cried, exhausted. Why was I outside the magic of their play? I knew it was because I was a girl. What did it mean, that I was a girl? It meant that I was slower than all of them, although my youngest brother, four years younger, was barely a toddler. I was unwanted and unloved by my brothers.

My oldest brother, Beng, the prized first-born, was the one who disliked me most. In my earliest memory, he was gruff and distant. He was comfortable in Malay, and over and over again I heard him say of me, *"Benchi!"* signifying antipathy, even hatred. I understood he disapproved of me because I was a girl. The house was full of brothers, except for me, third-born. I was a despised female, but I was also the only girl whose tears, whines, requests, whims, and fancies my father responded to unashamedly. The only daughter overtook the first-born son in a family with too many boys. This childish anger that Beng showed me never shook my sense of being special, but it made me timid of the feelings of rivals.

Yet I held an unequal position over my brothers. All my brothers spoke of my father's favoritism toward me as a fact of life, and I assumed that I deserved my father's favors. Because my father treated me as a gift, a treasured child, I felt myself to be a gift, and that I held treasures within me.

Being a girl also made me precocious and edgy, asking not "Who am I?" but "How can I prove that I am not who I am?" From the moment my father dealt with me more gently than with my brothers, and I understood my oldest brother when he muttered *"Benchi,"* from the moment I stood outside a door and felt my sex make me unwelcome, I decided my brothers' acceptance was preferable to my father's favoritism. I rejected the identity of girl. Since I could not have both, I chose equality as a boy over privilege as a girl.

My parents explained to their friends with exasperation that I was a tomboy, born in the year of the monkey. But I was not born one. It did not come naturally to me to run fast, to jump from high walls, to speed on a bicycle, or to stay out late alone at night. I would not have wandered from place to place, except for the promise, barely sensed, that something was to be picked up, learned, found, discovered, given, taken, ingested, desired, something that I couldn't find in my home, that I would be stronger, better, improved, changed, transformed in a stranger's house.

I was given the trappings of a girl-child: like an antiquated pleasure machine, my memory churns out images of tea-sets, blond dolls, doll wicker furniture, frilly dresses, red tartan ribbons, and my power as the only girl. Lying on a rattan chaise lounge, with a high fever, I was a very small and sick four-year-old. But Baba hovered over me; he had bought grapes, rare delicious globes. Emak stripped the green skins from them. The flesh was translucent, pale jade, veined, and firm. Delirious with happiness, I held each cool fat fruit in my fevered mouth.

In a later image, I sat on the floor gravely arranging the plastic teacups and saucers, holding each teacup in turn by its little handle. Today, this child playing house is a mystery to me. What was she thinking of as she sipped the air and set the emptied cup on its daisied saucer? What company did she enjoy this solitary hot afternoon while her brothers were away in school? There was a stillness in this child, attentively at work with imaginary companions, that absorbs me now. Was she imitating her mother and the many aunts she had met? But Malacca society ran on glasses of Sarsi and Greenspot, frizzy, sugared pop, colored violent blood-brown and orange, rather than on cups of tea and cream. Tea in Malacca was Chinese tea, poured into small handleless cups that you clasped in one hand. Where had this girl-child learned to drink tea in the British way, grasping the handle gingerly between thumb and middle finger and sticking her pinkie out like a society woman? The illustration on the box that held the tea set showed a blond child, also on the floor, drinking tea with her equally blond dollies. The girl had studied the picture. She was more like this blond girl than like her aunts or even her mother. Her doll with the straw-textured blond curls sat upright across from her, the hard blue eyes wide open. The girl played not so much with the tea set as with the picture on the box. It was quite satisfactory.

But finally it was not as good as the real thing, which was my brothers' play. The boys played at fighting with each other, noisily and excessively. All kinds of sounds came from them—bangs, rattles, yells, screams, shouts, yipes, hollers, short murderous silences, stampings, thumps, pings, singing. It seemed to me that none of the boys were ever alone. They were always whispering together, laughing, planning something, sharing a joke, exchanging a look, chasing each other, pushing, shoving, howling, pinching, punching, kicking, blaming each other. I whined because they would not tell me what they were doing, but that was their favorite game, conspiring to keep me out. And when I had begged enough, they let me run with them in their chases, but they ignored me. It was too easy to catch up with me. I cried and whimpered when I was hit, which was after all the aim of their games, to see how often they could hit each other.

And I? My chest hurt as I flew down the narrow sidewalks, trying not to stumble against the dustcans and baskets of garbage left by the sundry shops next to our home. My breath hammering against my ribs, I scrunched down inside a dry drain, fearing to be discovered, fearing my brothers' physical play, listening to their hoots as they galloped up and down above me. I wanted desperately to be up there, out in the open, whacking them as hard with an open palm as they were dealing each other. But I was grateful to be hiding, to be silent, secret, left alone, and safe. The minutes passed, and I leaped from the drain, scrambled in front of the three boys, raced panic-stricken, and touched the pillar that spelled home.

It was my brothers' enmity that made me refuse to be a girl. To be a girl, as I saw through their mocking distance, was to be weak, useless, and worse, bored. It was to stay in one place and gossip for hours the way my mother sat gossiping with my aunts and grandaunts.

My mother's parents had lived in Malacca State all their lives. Their parents were descendants of Chinese traders who had migrated to Malaya as early as the fifteenth century and who had married local Malay women. My mother's father had been a station master at Tampin, a civil servant for the British administration. He had moved his family, four boys and five girls, to a house in Klebang outside the town of Malacca, survived the Japanese Occupation, then died suddenly of a bad heart, leaving behind five children still at home. His wife died soon after, and Mother found herself hosting one teenage sibling after another as they passed from her older brother's hands to hers and then to Singapore where two married sisters were able to set them up with opportunities and jobs.

A series of aunts came through our home. First, Aunt Amy, sweet-faced, gentle, always with a smile that meant nothing except how good she felt to be simply wherever she was. If my mother was wickedly funny and driven by the needs of her senses, Aunt Amy was amusing and grateful to receive whatever was given to her. Her strange contentment made happiness inevitable for her, while my mother's uncontainable needs marked her for misery. Aunt Amy was a bowl of brown-sugared oatmeal, delicious yet surprisingly good for you. Her warm and easy temperament gave her the halo of good looks. When Aunt Amy left for Singapore, Auntie Lei, Mother's youngest sister, came to live with us.

Auntie Lei was a short woman, darker-complexioned than the rest of her siblings, and fiercely passionate, almost as I imagine I might have appeared at sixteen. She had a willful vivid face, not pretty at all but catching because the eyes were so restless, the compact shape of the skull and cheeks seemingly too small for the furrowed countenance, the concentrated inward focus of a furious self. Her slight body was dense with resistance; she was like an animal that would not be housebroken. She quarreled continuously with my mother, kept her distance from the rest of us, and finally ran away with a fair-skinned young man whose languid manners promised a life of poverty.

I watched these aunts, intimate, fleeting, subordinate in my mother's household, the only women of my blood I would know from the inside. They offered two different selves, but each inescapable from *kismat,* or fate, as Emak loved to say. Aunt Amy was tamed for pleasure; whatever entered her mouth turned sweet if insipid. The youngest sister, however, was ruled by passions. Intense, brooding, her eyes tugged inwards, she was blind to self-interest and to safety. They were both of marriageable age, but, orphaned and dowryless, with no parents to negotiate their value, they were social waste, excess, unhoused women to be taken in by their married sisters as unpaid domestic help. Aunt Amy willingly waited in another sister's home in Singapore in hopes of a meager marriage; Lei, sexuality brooding in her sullen body, defied social approval and gradually disappeared into the Malacca underclass. Appearing more and more worn through the years, her face never lost its countenance of discontented sexuality, as if in the narrow squalor she had chosen she had kept unscattered that appetite of the sixteen-year-old.

Uncle Ling came through, then Uncle Charlie, to be followed by Amy, Lei, and Mun. Ling and Charlie stayed only briefly, but long enough for me to remember Ling's good nature mixed with a cruelty that had him throwing me into the waves. I screamed with panic as he seized and tossed me casually like a sack of charcoal into the deep water into which I gurgled and could not find my footing. I was perhaps four, a child who could drape her entire body over a blown-up plastic tube and imagine it to be a ship, but who also had a mind that could understand cruelty and be afraid of it. My grandparents' orphans introduced me to tragedy, and I learned in self-defense to stand apart, not to be like Mother and her sisters, who wept helplessly and who ran away and gave themselves to helpless men, nor like her brothers who were forced to depend on reluctant relatives.

So much family! Uncles, brothers, cousins! But all were only one step from strangers. Baba and Emak were the bedrock, that which could not be lost, although they might lose each other and themselves. But by the time I was six, even they were changing into strangers moving away from me.

Baba's temper grew more uncertain and unchecked, and Emak became pregnant again. The house was permeated with the scents of chicken and pork liver in Chinese wine boiled with ginger and ginseng root. One night I saw her using the flowered porcelain-covered metal chamber pot placed in the corridor connecting the three bedrooms. No one went to the bathroom downstairs after we went to bed; life was lived upstairs after 8 P.M. She was huge, her belly floating in the dark like a boat. The night sarong barely needed to be folded over.

Weeks later we were told that we had another brother named Wilson, but that our *Tua Ee,* our maternal First Grandaunt, would be taking care of him. Lei told us that a fortuneteller had predicted that Wilson would be a difficult child who would bring disaster to his parents, and that he would have to be given away. *Tua Ee* took him in although she already had three sons of her own and an adopted daughter. Our baby brother came and left without our ever seeing him.

CHAPTER TWO

# War and Marriage

W hen I was six and comic-crazy, running out of the house to stand by the Indian newsstand and browse through the comics clipped to the stand's ropes for an hour or more (the Indian newsman later charged me five cents for the privilege of reading each time I came by), something was misfiring at home. First, Father went to the hospital. He was pale when I visited him after the operation for appendicitis. The cold glass of fresh-squeezed orange juice on the bedside table confused me. Why was it there? Why hadn't he drunk it? Then I was sent to play in the sun room, where I found omnibuses of *Reader's Digest* novels shelved and free for the taking. Superboy and the Phantom obsessed me then; still, I was impressed by these books, free to the public, not in a stand or store beyond one's ordinary reach.

Father's hospital stay introduced me to Auntie May, a young buck-toothed nurse. After his return from the hospital, some evenings he took me, without my mother, for a car ride. We drove to the hospital which was about ten miles out of town. We picked up Auntie May, who sat with my father in the front passenger seat while I sat in the back, contented with the breeze blowing through the open window. She was kind to me in an absent-minded manner. We children called every adult "aunt" and "uncle," and Auntie May seemed like a real aunt to me in her odd familiarity. I was comfortable with her presence, and believed we three belonged together in a special way.

When these evening drives ended, Father began to take the family out to Coronation Park, a couple of miles across town along the shoreline. There, as the evening swiftly gave way to tropical night, my brothers and I tumbled about in the cooling grass, chased each other through the spookily darkening space, and ate boiled peanuts, fried legumes, and steamed chickpeas that Father bought from the peddlers who lined the roads under the flaring fluorescent street lamps.

Sundays were the best days of our life together. Father worked six days a week and late on Saturday night when families shopped for shoes and entertainment. But as a British colony, Malacca observed the blue laws. My parents were Westernized although not Christianized. When many of their friends were dressing for church, and our relatives were resting at home, we were packing up for a picnic by the sea. We fought over the Sunday newspaper, particularly who got to read the Sunday comics first. Then, all seven of us squeezed into the car and drove to Tanjong Bidarah, stopping to buy some coconut-steamed rice—*nasi lemak*—for lunch.

The sea was always a visual shock to me, the waves of the Malacca Straits slapping gently and unceasingly against a sloping gritty beach. Something about the sun shining on such immensity excited me. I was afraid of the water but in love with its sensation. I had just read in John Masefield's poem, "The sea, the sea, the open sea, the fresh, the wild, the ever-free," and I lay in the water as it ran down the sand ridges and murmured over and over again to myself, "The sea is my mother, the sea is my mother."

And so I wanted to believe. Was it because my own mother had already withdrawn from us that I loved the sea so extravagantly? I have no memory as a child of the kind of warm physical affection with my mother that I felt with my Primary One teacher, Sister Josie. Emak appears in my child's album as a self-absorbed driven creature, continuously pregnant—six babies with only a year or so between each of them.

My mother may have resolved on escape long before she left us, but she shared nothing of herself with us in those final years. She was already absent, a weeping woman stripped slowly to some unknown other whose ultimate departure came to me as no surprise. My images of her in the painful years of uprooting, in 1952 and 1953, are dulled, as if the imagination had leaped forward and already registered Mother as gone, not so much lost or misplaced as deliberately disappeared.

Maternal abandonment is unthinkable in human culture. Maternal malice marks a boundary humans can hardly bear to speak of, reformulating it instead into the wicked stepmother found in the Grimm brothers' fairy tales and numerous Asian folk tales. How then to understand my own mother, mother of six children, who picked herself up off the ground where my father had knocked her down, and left us forever?

Months of momentous crossings led up to that sudden evening when she vanished. One afternoon in the room behind the front shop, in the zone between home and store, I came across them yelling at each other. He had the red glare in his eyes, that crazed look of going over an edge that came over him when the rattan cane would come singing through the air again and again and again. She who had turned soft and fat after the sixth baby was stock-hard, facing him implacably. I went between them and caught them both in each hand. "Don't, don't," I cried and must have shamed them because they stopped, fell silent, and moved away. I remember the risk I felt, and the pride that I had reconciled them.

Of course I had done nothing of the kind. As they spun apart, my mother must have withdrawn into a shell of rage and hatred that reached out to include "his" children. For we were our father's children more than hers. At some point, after the drives with Auntie May ended, he had focused his life on us.

I remember one splendid Sunday morning when we four children, Beng, Chien, Jen, and myself, clung to each other's shoulders, and Beng hung on to Father's, who swam out to the horizon, unafraid that the four of us might drop out of each other's grip into the salty waves. Father was a strong swimmer. As a boy he had jumped off the bridge into the Malacca River in weekend play, and his love of the sea blinded him to the danger he was leading us through. The water rushed like a living current over us; we were suspended above the drowning element by the power of my father's body.

Were we seven, six, five, three? All four of us did not add up to my father's years, although he was still a young man. Remembering his body, I need to count to materialize it out of the myth of muscle and salt water. A man of twenty-eight, lean, muscular, bearing on his shoulders the exposed naked slippery bodies of four children, each destined to grow larger than he, whose little fish bodies he could have so easily shrugged off, dropped over the horizon's edge, to return unencumbered, a free male. Instead I feel his calves kick, his arms arc and flash in a flight through welcome space. His teeth gleam white, a father shark, as he turns his handsome head, laughing at our squeals, taking pride in our fearless faith.

Because my father loved his children, I have kept faith with him, through the years of living with his pursuit of women, his gambling, and his rages. The bond I sewed tight between my father and me was illicit. In a Chinese family, perhaps in every family, daughters must be wary of their love for their fathers. We are constrained as daughters; the ties that strain us to our fathers are tense with those constraints. A vast but fearfully crossable boundary must separate girl-child from male parent. I wonder if all daughters suffer a revulsion about their fathers' bodies, instinctively reacting to save themselves from unacknowledged dangers.

As a child I adored my father's body. When I slept with my parents, before even more children arrived to remove me to a newly purchased iron-frame bunk bed, it was my father's body I reached out to touch when I roused in the night. He was warm and solid; it made me happy to touch his flesh lightly with my fingers, then drift back into sleep. So in that serpent-like familial swim, with a brother gripping me around my neck, clinging to another brother as he clung to another who clung to my father's confident body, all of us children extruded from my father like grown sperm, links in an unbreakable, undrownable chain, the meaning of my father's life made manifest to him.

My father was so ordinary that his name appeared in his lifetime in only those two pieces of paper testifying to his King Scout status and his passing the Overseas Senior Cambridge Exams. After the age of nineteen, he left the world of testimonials, of the seen and acknowledged, and entered a world of breeding, of feeding hungry mouths, of struggle and failure, small pleasures, and modest hopes. His life has remained undocumented, unrecorded, and therefore unvalued and unsaved. I write to make my father's life useful. To do that, I have to explain my love for him.

My father beat me on many occasions. Every time he slapped me, raised the cane and cut me on my legs, my shoulders, my back so that the raised welts were also deeply grooved and bloodied, I hated him. My eyes would blank and hurt and in my ears I heard the chant, "I hate you, I hate you."

That silent chant gave me an enormous sense of secret power. I never begged him to stop beating me, never cried, although my throat burned with stifled feeling, and my head spun from the violence of his slaps. The rattan's whipping cuts were like knife-tongues of fire that licked the flesh and stayed and stayed. I hated him as much for humiliating me as for the pain. I felt public shame, for he beat me in front of anyone, my brothers, the neighbors, visitors, and relatives. I never asked then what drove him to these maddened episodes. I knew it wasn't me. He beat me viciously once for dropping a spoon and breaking it; on another occasion, when he thought a hawker had cheated me.

The only time I felt private shame when he beat me was the first time. A five-year-old stay-at-home, I was fascinated by my older brothers' sophistication, the new they brought home each day from school. They said different words, played different games, and owned large shiny books with photographs and drawings and stories in them. I felt my chest tighten with the desire to possess what was in their mouths and heads. My brothers shared a secret joke that galvanized them with mirth. I stood outside the circle of two and spied. They whispered, pretending not to see me. They formed circles with the thumb and first finger of their left hands and stabbed the round air with fingers of their right hands, a secret sign that haloed them as partners and insiders. It was an understanding that they shared, and they slyly glanced at me to see if I had caught it from them, then yelled, "Go away!"

I ran outside into the evening air with their secret. I was elated, for I understood the sign, I knew how to form that circle and how to penetrate it. I ran to my father who was just closing up the shop. He was moving yet another wood plank into its grooved position, completing the wooden wall that shut the shop each night and transformed it into a home. There was no one else for me to play with; I tugged at his arm and showed him the secret I had just mastered.

But his face reddened. His eyes took on that crazed glower, only this time, for the first time, it was directed at me. I was horrified, but it was too late. He put the plank against the wall, went inside, dragging me with him, and caned me. I do not remember how many times the feather duster descended. Perhaps, because it was the first time, the switch came down for only three cuts; perhaps it was more. After that evening I knew I could not count on my father's love.

Later, as I approached ten and eleven, I understood the meaning of the sign, and the memory of his rage shamed me. The shame is unspeakable. I am covered with confusion. Did I, five years old, know the power of the sign? What secret was I breaking open as I tugged at his arm, smiling? Why am I still ashamed? Am I shamed by his uncontrolled use of power over my small female body, his displaced, repressed fears? Or by my child's desire for him, the man whom I had approached as my playmate, my partner, with whom I wanted to share the secret of the circle?

When my father beat me for the first time, the horror that filled me as I sobbed through that evening was not simple horror at pain, the sting of the rattan switch on my buttocks. It was also the horror at the knowledge of the break, that he had forcibly set me aside from himself, asserting a presence so alien that it could turn the lithe pliable rod on my flesh and cut me. My father became a fearful stranger to me then; as he gripped my arm, cursing in the growing darkness, and brought the rattan down on me, he appeared simultaneously to melt away, to lose his familiar contours, and to harden, to loom as a featureless man to whom my screams and tears signified nothing. My lifelong sense of the evening as the hour of abandonment, when one looks out into the world and is overcome by one's aloneness, begins with the beating.

And the shame. For I understood clearly that it was what I had done that had changed this man from father to monster. Something in my desire for him, that tug on his arm, the sharing of a sign, had toppled something in him. His rage was inexplicable otherwise. The shame was like a hot stone I had swallowed, different from the pain of the caning. It was inside my body, it went bruising, slowly, down my chest, and settled in my stomach. For days after, I felt slow, draggy, as if the stone were weighing me down. The buoyancy of the five-year-old girl looking up into her father's eyes as she showed him the sign she had just learned from her brothers never returned. I can mark that moment as the consciousness of another self, a sullen within, hating the father who beat me.

Hate does not explain love, but it sharpens love, in as much as it gives us the power to see the fragilities of the object of our hate. From the moment my father beat me, I became aware of his weakness rather than of his power. While I feared the pain of his canings, I never came to fear him; instead I came to acknowledge the depth of my responses and the interiority of my feelings. His blows drove me inwards into misery that cannot be spoken. I felt the power of my unhappiness, and therefore the power of my personhood. I learned to love my father again because I pitied him, and I pitied him because he gave me the power to hate him.

I did not learn to love my mother, who left us when I was eight, though she is perhaps more to be pitied than my father. As a grown woman, I know that her life was harder than his, the odds in her struggles for a good life unfairly stacked against her. But as her daughter, when I think about her, I feel instead a stubborn resistance against pity and forgiveness, an adolescent resentment that will not grow up.

There was a time when I must have loved her. Doesn't every infant, cradled in human arms, sucking on a mother's breast, fix its loving gaze upon the eyes above? Yet I have no memory of that primal bonding, no memory of hugs, kisses, physical affection, the kind of comfortable, safe bodily pleasure taken and felt in the presence of a loved other.

In a black-and-white family portrait taken when I was five and touched up by the unknown photographer with paint, my mother, seated, wears a light-colored *samfoo*. My father sits close to her, his head leaning as if drawn in affection towards her. She is already round-faced, a little chubby in the fashionable print. I stand by her arm, my cheeks and lips painted red, in a tiered, outrageously flowered print dress, my little legs and arms like awkward stems on a droopy blossom. An absurd purse is looped around my arm, and a large bow shoots off the back of my head. Everything on me looks too big, too loose, too floppy. Beng and Chien stand by my father in shorts and white shirts, their skinny legs smartly turned out in pulled-up socks and polished shoes, and Jen sits solemn-faced on a metal pony. Except for my leaning father, we all face the camera straight as soldiers. Those studio portraits for which we sat every Chinese New Year posed us together as a family—permanent, transfixed, the moment held in mercury and paint innocently displayed in a way that I do not remember us at all.

I remember us as brushing images, as gazes, sensations, and stories. I remember my mother as a woman I gazed on. Pondering this childhood sensation of gazing upon the maternal face, rather than of living within the maternal breast, I wonder if the break was mine, coming from an infant's original coldness to the mother. Or did the break originate in my mother, unable to or refusing to nurse the infant, to whom she hovers, as a face, but never satisfies and fills up, as a breast?

Yet she also loved me, at least later in life. When I was sixteen and visited her in Singapore for the first time, she took a day off from work to spend the morning at Robinson's, then the largest department store in Singapore, where she had recently worked. "Eleanor, Eleanor!" the well-dressed and made-up women at the counters called, and it took me long minutes before I understood that they were calling her by an English name she had taken in Singapore.

We walked through the crowds and stopped at Helena Rubinstein, Estee Lauder, chinaware, and pajamas, where she introduced me to women who looked like each other. "This is my daughter," she repeated, "Shirley," as if this Eleanor, who hadn't seen me in eight years, were introducing me to herself over and over again, or as if my meeting her friends of the past eight years filled in the void of time between us.

Her pride, so evident during that social ritual, which continued in the afternoon and evening with taxi rides to numerous of her brothers' and sisters' homes, was a kind of love. But as my father's daughter, I knew love as familial and daily proximity, not as social ritual. Leaving Malacca for Singapore, abandoning family for society, my mother was always to remain estranged to me.

My parents married just before the outbreak of the Pacific War. I remember a photograph of two very young people dressed in the ancient heavy silk robes of the traditional peranakan wedding. She wears an ornately embroidered headdress that sweeps almost a foot above her smooth pinched face; its crimson tassels fall about her face like fuchsia blossoms. Her blouse is covered by a cape encrusted with silver and gold embroidery. On her feet, traditional embroidered silk shoes with curved tips peep out from under the long skirt. Father is uncharacteristically serious. On his head a conical straw and bead-plaited hat sits like a food cover. His costume is a long Chinese gown, like a mandarin's robe. The wedding portrait shows every sign of social respectability: their solemn seated pose, and especially their dress, the traditional wedding costumes that testify to the young couple's acceptance of the conventions of Malaccan peranakan society.

The elaborate robes also indicate that their wedding took place in a time of civil peace and plenty, when the British ruled Malacca as part of a tripartite state called the Straits Settlements that included Penang and Singapore. Baba and Emak, both born in the state of Malacca, were British subjects—as I was—

a position that conferred enviable status in a society of immigrants, transients, and undocumented laborers from China, India, and the Indonesian islands. In the late 1930s, there were almost two million Chinese living in the different political territories of the Malayan peninsula, and only a minority of them were Straits-born, a term that I was to hear pronounced with pride all through my growing years.

Baba grew up as an irresponsible child, loving Western popular culture, within a Confucianist-gated community. Unreflecting, he lived his early years as if *senang*—ease or leisure—were his human right. My father's charm lay in his reminder that struggle ought to be unnatural. It was also, for his children, the cause of our danger; for our needs and his *senang* were mortally conflicted. It was to this unsettled, pleasure-loving man that my mother was to graft her life at the age of seventeen.

He must have appeared to her as an ideal suitor. He was two years older than she, and had five more years of British schooling. With a Standard Six certificate, she could read, write, calculate, and was better educated than many of the women in town. She stayed home after the Standard Six examinations, cooking, keeping house for her parents, and waiting for a husband to declare himself. There were five girls and four boys in her family: five disastrous burdens and three of the boys too young for anything but school. A station master's eldest daughter had social standing. Her father's position as a British civil servant and her well-married aunts gave her a class association in the town that was above her actual precarious condition. My father's position as Fifth Son of a *towkay* similarly disguised his uncertain financial standing.

Theirs was not a traditionally arranged marriage, in which the woman is given to a man she has never met. My father not only had chosen her himself but had played the mandolin for her. I see him, this young passionate man who had just successfully completed his Senior Cambridge Examinations, who was wondering what life he would make for himself, biking to her parents' house in Klebang, balancing the small curved polished instrument on his handlebars. Standing in the sandy front yard of the wooden house with his best friend beside him, he glanced nervously at the moon in the clear night sky and then recklessly plucked the strings of the mandolin. It was only a joke he was pursuing, a story to tell his bachelor friends, for the marriage had already been arranged. He had seen her; she was pretty, quiet, and a wonderful cook.

My mother should have been warned by his mandolin, by the moon above her garden, by his breaking the propriety of peranakan behavior for a romantic tale. My father's unconventionality, in the face of small-town Malacca where everybody knew everybody's actions, was not to be trusted.

Married in the peace and security of the British Straits Settlements, she never had time to learn to trust him. On December 8, 1941, just a few months after the birth of their first son, the troops of the Japanese Imperial Army landed on the undefended northeast beaches of the Malayan peninsula. On swift light bicycles, carrying grenades and fast-firing weapons, thousands of green-uniformed soldiers rode south down the British-built roads, capturing without resistance Kota Bahru, Penang, Kuala Lumpur, Malacca, Johore, and finally Singapore, which the British had boasted of as the impregnable fortress of their empire. At the end of these ten amazing weeks, the British High Commissioner surrendered and withdrew the Royal Armed Forces from the entire peninsula. The mighty Royal Navy pulled out of Singapore port, ferrying British administrators and families in ignominious retreat to Australia.

It wasn't only the rumors of Japanese barbarity that struck my parents' early years of marriage. As a young child I heard, as a buzz of historical static, about the continuous daily horrors of the Japanese Occupation of Malaya from December 1941 to 1945, deeds less recounted than exclaimed over as sharp unexpected elements bursting like repressed trauma into a reconstructed normality.

The Japanese forces patrolled by the *Kempeitai* began a three-year era of pillage, killings, and terrorism at the time that my oldest brother was born. Word went around in February 1942 of the massacre of five thousand Chinese in Singapore. My mother's faith in her husband's power to defend her and to provide for their first-born must have been shattered as the Chinese Malayan male population shrank and went into hiding from the Asians in green uniform. The second child came when rice was rationed, no milk was available, meat was scarce, and the townspeople ate tapioca and yams, root vegetables with little protein value. By the time my mother was carrying me, the Japanese Imperial Army, at the point of defeat, was also at its most brutal. With two sons to feed and clothe, my parents were living with my grandfather at Heeren Street, and had yet to set up their own home. Jobless, my father had no way to feed his family without the handouts from his father.

I was conceived and born toward the end of the bleakest period of the war. Only in 1943 were the Allied Forces able to begin counterattacks in India, Burma, and the Philippines. These attacks seriously damaged Japan's war resources. Rice, which had always been an imported staple food for the Malayan population, became even less available. Sugar, milk, meat, and rice had been rationed when the Occupation began, but in 1943 shortages of food led to fears of starvation and to acute hunger and malnutrition. Hunger was most prevalent among the Chinese townspeople; the Malays who were rural folk still grew their own food.

Moreover, the imprisonment, torture, and massacre of Chinese Malayans, especially young men, continued unabated. The Japanese forces, having faced years of military struggle in their attempts to conquer China, equated every Chinese Malayan with the Chinese people, whose nationalist opposition had so enraged them that in a racialist bloody orgy the Japanese Imperial Army had massacred three hundred thousand Chinese in Nanjing in 1937. My fourth uncle, the brilliant brother who was planning to study medicine at the King Edward VII College of Medicine in Singapore before the outbreak of the Pacific War, broke the curfew one night. He never returned home. Family story has it that his body was found floating in the Malacca River, his decapitated head attached to the neck only by a skein of skin.

How did my grandfather protect the lives of his other sons? Where did he hide the men? How much did he pay to buy off the Japanese commandants, the *Kempeitai*? Wives and daughters had been raped and their wombs ripped by bayonets. Young men had obeyed or fled, and had been gunned down or decapitated. After the Japanese Imperial Army withdrew from Malaya in late August 1945, what sorrows lay in the ill-lit and shadowy rooms of 99 Heeren Street, in the memories of the executed brilliant son, of the savings extorted for a few illicit *katties* of rice and some store of crackers for the grandchildren, and of the hopes for a Chinese-peranakan union through my parents' socially matched marriage? What was exchanged for those few precious tins of condensed milk on which my mother fed her babies? How much more was given up to save his daughters-in-law from the attentions of Japanese soldiers and his sons from the forced recruitment of young Chinese males into the jungle to plant tapioca and yams when the supplies of rice and foodstuffs from Burma were cut off?

My birth, at the end of 1944, at the peak of Japanese torturous repression, and of food shortages and mass starvation, could have brought no rejoicing. Can an infant carry memories of hunger and terror, the whisper of rumors, the blackout of censorship? Can she imbibe the early darkness of days without electrical energy, the lackadaisical quiet of a mother's malnutrition, leading to the absence of the maternal breast?

The Japanese Occupation was not a story my parents dwelled upon, yet it marked our beginnings as a family. What might my mother have felt at the news of a third pregnancy? Was I an unwanted baby? The absence of physical intimacy, the coldness I felt even as a very young child toward my mother, may be, in part, derived from the history of war-time maternity.

The Chinese Malayan history of the Japanese Occupation—the experiences of over three million people—was almost immediately suppressed. The British, slowly returning a couple of months after the Japanese forces had left Malaya, ignored the horrors of Chinese Malayan wartime suffering and the courage of Chinese Malayan guerrilla fighters. Within a few months, a different war narrative replaced that of British defeat at the hands of Asian armies: the Chinese Malayans who had remained loyal to the British and fought the Japanese swiftly became the new Asian enemy. When a small group of poorly armed volunteer militia, the Malayan People's Anti-Japanese Army (MPAJA), gave rise to the Malayan Communist Party, a revolutionary party that pressed for political representation and independence, they came to be defined as no less "alien" than the Japanese invaders. These guerrillas threatened British colonial government and economy, and quickly became identified with the "Red Scare," Communists allegedly armed by the People's Republic of China and the Soviet Union. And thus Chinese immigrants and Straits-born Chinese, associated through race with disorders and terrorism, also had their "Chineseness" marked as evil.

In 1948, when I was three and when the Chinese in Malaya were 45 percent of the population in contrast to the Malays' 43 percent, the British High Commissioner, Sir Edward Gent, declared a State of Emergency in the Federation of Malaya. This policy resulted eventually in mass dislocations, in the military-patrolled resettlement of Chinese Malayans, in the complete suspension of civil liberties, and in the establishment of a police state empowered to search, detain, and deport suspected Communist members and sympathizers. The Malayan Emergency provided the model for all other state powers in the twentieth century for battling insurgency movements through the surveillance, control, and suppression of entire populations.

By the time I entered elementary school in 1951 at the age of six, the stories I grew up with were those of Chinese bandits and outlaws. *The Straits Times* carried stories of murders of British planters, Chinese *towkays*, village headsmen, simple farmers and rubber tappers. Sir Henry Gurney was assassinated by Chinese terrorists who burst out of the jungle then faded back, secure, into its concealing growth. Every movie we saw was preceded by British newsreels, and the Emergency in the Malayan colony was often featured. We watched urban Malaya in black and white, a sinister landscape of Chinese facades that wavered on the screen even as the British voice-over intoned, "In Malaya, Sir Henry Gurney was gunned down in cold blood by the cowardly Chinese Communists." A pan to rows of rubber trees rushing past the camera: "In this tropical country, the Communists, led by Chin Peng, have the population living in fear, but the British Army, under the leadership of Sir Gerald Templer, is successfully pushing them back into the jungles." On screen a thin white man in army khakis, carrying a baton, walks slowly past rows of khaki-clad soldiers.

Sir Gerald Templer was our hailed savior. Waving energetically, I stood in the hot sun with all the schoolchildren of Malacca lining the streets to welcome him as he drove swiftly past to fill in Sir Gurney's position in 1951. The Chinese Communists' imminent defeat signaled the continued glory of British imperial power.

I learned to hate Chinese Communists, men with faces like my father's or my uncles', whose pictures the *Straits Times* frequently published, with their despised Chinese names in large captions—Lai Teck, Liew Yit Fan, Lau Yew, Chin Peng. I could not distinguish among ordinary Chinese Malayans, the Kuomintang members—Chinese who considered themselves citizens of China—and the Communists—Chinese Malayans who claimed to be struggling for national sovereignty. Although the Kuomintang and the Communists were attacking each other, they were both marked by an alien hieroglyphic script, both equally hostile to peranakans, whom they looked down on as degraded people, people who had lost their identity when they stopped speaking Chinese. I grew up afraid of Chinese speakers, having been taught by the British that they were unpatriotic, brutal, and murderous. A Malayan child, I understood Chinese identity as being synonymous with Chinese chauvinism.

Because loyal Chinese Malayans could not be told apart from Chinese Communists, the non-Malayans, in 1948 the British colonial administration also required the mass registration of the Malayan population. At every road block, every unexpected encounter, and every state-regulated event, such as registering your child for school, you were asked to show your identity card. "I.C., I.C.," the clerks, police, and civil bureaucrats demanded, an acronym that I understood as "I see (you)!" in English and "*Ai sei!*" or "You are dead!" in Hokkien. Many evenings, groups of Malay constables, *mata-mata,* would suddenly come out from behind the shadows of shrubbery, their pistols resting casually on their hips. "Check!" they would say, and you would fumble clumsily for your card, your fear in the darkness as complete as their confidence.

I remember sitting in my father's Morris Minor, headed towards Tampin which was only about twenty miles away, passing through a number of checkpoints. At each checkpoint, soldiers hoisting long gleaming rifles searched our passenger seats and the car trunk, glanced at our blue identity cards, then waved us onward. Did we look suspicious? We hoped our faces resembled the scowling portraits on our identity cards. We worried a young soldier might be aggrieved by our festive family mood and shoot us. We pretended to be subdued; we became really subdued. It was confusing to find that we could not be distinguished from the bloodthirsty enemy, that to the soldiers with the gleaming rifles we might very well be the enemy.

Our identity cards became as much a part of our persons as our eyes or hands. We did not venture from home without it, for to be caught by the police without an identity card was already evidence of breaking the law. It wasn't enough that Chinese Communists had been driven out of certain "safe" areas of the peninsula, which therefore needed to be patrolled only by the Malay constabulary. By 1953, Malacca was declared the first "white area," officially free of the pollution of Communist insurgency, and all Emergency Regulations were lifted from the state. But large sections of "red areas" remained in the surrounding states. When I was twelve, I was still carrying the blue identity card wherever I went, still fearful of being stopped by a police check.

# CHAPTER THREE

# Geographies of Relocation

S trangers were in the house. They were moving furniture, snatching at our clothes in the *almeira,* cursing loudly. The entire kitchen was stripped. My father stood helplessly to one corner, watching the men at their work. My mother was somewhere packing, crying about her lost bangles. For as long as I could remember she had half a dozen or more elaborately wrought gold bangles on her wrists. They jingled like bells as she walked or waved her hands in conversation. She had had to give them up, and so her eyes were red, her hair unpinned.

In the afternoon the lorry was packed with a few pieces of the furniture that we were allowed to keep—the yellow painted iron bunk bed, the queen-sized wooden headboard and bed, the smaller *almeira* with the mirror insert—and with a few blankets and pillows, dishes and pots, our school uniforms and some clothes and towels, our school books and bags, my doll that closed and opened its tufted lids over plastic blue eyes. Everything else belonged to the creditors. I was eight years old, and even I could understand that, although I did not understand why it happened or what would happen to us next.

Finally, with all of us in it, the lorry drove us away from our house on Kampong Pantai. I sat on the mattress that had been secured by ropes on top of the possessions, feeling brave and lonely and strange. I promised myself that I would never forget this adventure. I watched the streets as the lorry drove on; the houses appeared already changed, as if in a foreign town.

We had been given the front room on the second floor, the dirty brown one facing the noisy street, of Grandfather's house, now the property of all the sons. Between this front room and First Uncle's rooms to the right was an open space, then the balustrades fencing the stairwell and the twisting wooden flight of stairs with its black polished carved spindles and the curving arm that reached like a flowing spiral of wood to the ground floor inner parlor. A large air-well filled the parlor with sunlight or damp night air, and a corridor on the left connected our room and First Uncle's rooms to Third and Sixth Uncles' rooms at the back of the house. The bunk bed had been placed in the open space, and Mother's *almeira,* the bed, and mattresses for the children were arranged in the bedroom.

I lay on the lower level of the bunk bed in the brown evening. For the first time in my life I felt hunger. My stomach growled and I pressed back against the lumpy mattress with a lassitude that came from being alone and from not having eaten all day. What an odd sensation hunger was! An emptiness, it left me giddy and weak. Nothing mattered much. Time seemed to have slowed down, and I was sitting or lying somewhere outside it, watching its motions. I did not cry because there was no one to see me cry. I wondered if anyone would find me here. I was neither sad nor happy, merely conscious of breathing by myself with a faintness that was new to me.

After that evening I remained hungry for almost two years. Caught in a pyramid scam, Father owed large sums of money. He had lost his business and everything we possessed as a family, and forced to declare himself bankrupt. Even his future earnings belonged to his creditors. For a long while we lived on his very small salary—what didn't go to the creditors—as a salesclerk for a new Bata shoes shop on Riverside Road. Destitute and homeless, we lived in that brown bedroom in Grandfather's house for over a year.

For the first few months Mother appeared to manage. I walked two miles to school and nibbled at crackers for breakfast, not the fancy Huntley's Biscuits that came crackling fresh from their green-papered tins, but hard soda biscuits from local factories. Five cents bought ten of them in the corner Chinese store that sold them separately out of tall, square-shouldered cans. There was no lunch, but at dinner we ate the broken rice that cost much less than the rounded, polished grains preferred by the Chinese. I never complained about the dishes—*kangkong* (swamp vegetables), *ikan bilis* (dried anchovies), *kiam chye* (salted cabbage)—that appeared on the round wooden table for barely a few minutes before vanishing into the bowls and mouths of my ravenous brothers.

We knew there was no money. No one needed to tell us this. We were reminded of it each time Mother gave us a five-cent coin for soda biscuits with a particular furtive glance so as to impress on us how difficult it was to arrive at that coin. When she gave us ten cents to buy the *ikan bilis* for dinner, we knew how far ten cents had to stretch and how precious that little coin was for all of us.

Yet I do not remember being deeply unhappy about my constant hunger or about Mother's anxious doling of coins. Returning to Heeren Street was entering another country, marking the conclusion of childhood and the growth of independence for me. Impoverished as we had suddenly become, my parents could not afford the luxury of a girl-child. The fancy clothes, the attention, the demands that I act like a girl were abandoned as poverty rolled its monolithic impression on them.

With poverty came space. I was no longer confined to a house and my mother's company. Now I roamed the streets with my brothers and cousins. In packs of seven, eight, or nine we ran up Heeren Street, past the shuttered, respectable *baba* houses with their flowered tile walls and carved blackwood doors to the Chinese middle school whose playground was open to our forays. From there one could jump down to the beach, for the Straits of Malacca lay immediately behind Heeren Street. Running down the beach, we passed patches of wild grass to the left and the stinky outhouses of these same respectable homes, while to the right the sea wall kept the Straits away from us and fastened safely to the horizon. At some point the sandy tract met a macadam lane that brought us out to the lower end of Heeren Street, and we trailed home past the crenellated roofs and colonnades of grand *baba* homes.

One afternoon we were wild with excitement. Someone had proposed that we walk along the sea wall and have a picnic out on its furthest point. My mother fried slices of *ubi kayu,* a gray spotted yam-like root, with batter, and we carried these slices with us like trophies. They vanished long before we clambered onto the wall, but the pride I felt at this festive production of family food at a time when hunger was continuous in our lives remains even today. The warm greasy delicious slices symbolized our access still to a condition above that of bare necessity. Malnourished as we were, food for play aroused a joy that food for survival alone never brought.

I balanced on the sea wall constructed of granite boulders; the huge mica-speckled blocks formed an uneven surface at least two feet across. The sun shone on the blue waves to the right, and on the left it burned and caked the mud that would later be reclaimed and built up into housing tracts dividing Heeren Street forever from the shore of the Malacca Straits. The water did not appear very deep to me, although the barrier wall was well above five feet high. My eldest brother gave a triumphant shout; he had dragged up a sea horse in a rusty can that had once contained Players cigarettes. We crowded around his treasure. Barely an inch high, the sea horse flurried its fins and flickered its elegant head in the water that was fast running out of the holes in the tin. I felt the wealth of the world around me—the hard bright sun, my steady feet finding their footing on the hot boulders, the translucent blue water rippling quiescently along an entire half-sphere, and the womanly little creature puffing its chest and ruffling its tail in the little space of water.

The months in Heeren Street mingled plenitude of experience with greater and greater deprivations. I was a minor child in a large house filled with five households (*Tua Peh's* or First Uncle's, *Sah Peh's* or Third Uncle's, *Goh Peh's* or Fifth Uncle's, and Sixth Uncle's or *Luc Chek's* First and Second Wives'). While the women were occupied with laundry, cooking, and childbirth, we children were left on our own. Mother was no more than a figure in the background as I lingered in my cousins' rooms, all of them filled with bedding and presided over by maternal presences. *Tua Ehm* of the spare sharp body and suspicious countenance sent you away, and you were glad she was a stranger rather than your mother. *Sah Ehm's* plump smiling face made you stay and stay, although with four sons and five daughters there was really no space for you in their two rooms.

Besides, I soon found myself unwelcome. *Sah Ehm's* second daughter, Ah Swee, closest to me in age, was a sweet-faced, quiet child, and I looked for her in the afternoons, finding a comfort with her. One afternoon she was holding a doll with blue marble irises and yellow tufted lids that opened and closed when it was laid down. "That's my doll!" I said with immediate conviction. "No, it's mine!" Ah Swee hid the doll behind her. "Let me look," I insisted. "My doll has a red vaccination mark on its arm." So a blemish of paint on one plastic arm had been tenderly worked into a childhood fantasy during those years when I played with my blond doll in our old home. The small smear of red paint confirmed what my fast-beating pulse already knew. But Ah Swee snatched the doll away from me. "She's mine!" she cried, ran into her family rooms, and closed the door. I was not allowed into *Sah Ehm's* rooms again.

Desolate, I visited *Luc Chek's* First Wife. Fair-complexioned and soft-spoken, she was taken up with the care of three children who were much younger than I. But directly behind *Sah Ehm's* chambers, in the very last room on the second floor, with its own winding back staircase for entry, *Luk Chek's* Second Wife and two sons made a space for me. Sixth Uncle's Second Wife was peranakan, like Mother, and the only auntie in the ancestral house besides my mother who could speak English. When my eight-year-old self appeared like an apparition up the winding stairs, she smiled a gentle welcome, as between two equals. "Sit!" she said, motioning to some cushions, and I threw myself down and stayed for the afternoon. Her *nonya* kindness was like a sun-warmed guava to a hungry child. I basked in her attention and helped myself to her copies of magazines and romance novels. She was especially welcoming after Mother left us, although by then I preferred running in the streets to sitting in her dimly-lit, closed-in room.

The rooms downstairs were larger, and we all shared them. Even with the numerous children the front parlor was almost always empty and quiet. Here

the heavy carved front door and decorative fence door—the *pintu pagar*—
swung open onto a room flanked by two interior passageways. Between these
entrances, directly facing the front door, a large altar fronted by a lower table
was draped with a cloth embroidered with colorful fruit, birds, and personages.
Peaches, phoenixes, the high bald forehead of the God of Longevity all called
attention to the desire for long life that haunted the Chinese psyche, a psyche
that had never quite discovered myths of immortality to still the fear of death.

Instead we many children were a testimony to our grandparents' afterlife.
Their sepia-tinged portraits looked gloomily at us as we passed through the altar
chamber to the bright noisy world outdoors or to the clamorous families
secreted in the interior rooms. The altar held a brass urn filled with joss ash in
which we casually stuck a few sticks of burning joss during special ancestral
worship days. Bowls of oranges and tangerines, signifying wealth, offered to our
grandparents' spirits remained untouched for months. In long days of desperate
hunger it never occurred to me to take one of these offerings; except for special
festivals, whatever was placed on the altar was beyond human desire, entering
the boundary of ancestral ghosts.

When we were living on Kampong Pantai we had come to pray before this
altar on *Cheng Beng,* for the Festival of the Hungry Ghosts. Mother stayed up
late the night before, shaping squares of paper with gold or silver centers into
bricks. In the morning she boiled chickens in soy, ginger, and rice wine and
made stews of pork cuts ringed with inches of fat and thick fleshy skin. These
she packed carefully into delicate porcelain bowls. We spent the day at Heeren
Street, arranging the bricks into elaborate pyramids before setting them on fire.
As they burned down into ashy mounds, we placed Mother's fragrant dishes on
the altar together with dishes prepared by the other womenfolk. Later in the
day someone would throw the spirit dice to ask the ancestors if they had
finished their meal. If the two die fell either both closed or both open, we
waited. If they fell with one closed and the other open, then the dishes were
quickly removed from the altar and everyone, adults and children, feasted on the
cold ash-sprinkled remains. Feeding our ancestors every *Cheng Beng* bonded us
as one Lim family, springing from a common root and tied together in ways
that could not be unknotted.

So when Mother disappeared, we suffered no sense of being undone.
Father had been less and less in sight. One night he had come home late, they
had had another screaming quarrel, only this time he had hit her and she wept
for a long time, her eyes and one cheek swollen. In the morning she was gone.
Much later, and with no clear recollection of who told me the tale—perhaps it
was Uncle Ling or Uncle Charlie in Singapore trying to explain why she had
left us—I understood that Father had taken Peng, the young daughter of our

old servant, to the cinema. Fallen as he was, perhaps he had found comfort in the young girl's admiration of his past status. Or had he looked at his younger brother's two wives and longed for a fresh child-woman? Had my mother's frequent tears and sighs about the loss of her house, her furniture, and her gold bangles driven him away? Was he escaping his many-mouthed children and their skinny legs and arms?

Returning to the gloomy crowded bedroom, to an unkempt distraught woman surrounded by hungry children, he must have felt the sentence of his life as an intolerable prison, and struck out. She lost two teeth to his fists. Was this the first time he had hit her? I had never seen him raise his hand against her, and did not see that blow then.

Yet that moment was decisive for her. He had crossed the last boundary in marking her violently and in choosing a younger woman of an inadmissible class, the daughter of our servant. Breaking those taboos, he gave my mother permission to break that final social taboo for women, that of abandoning her children.

Perhaps it was fear for her physical self, the bitterness of broken teeth, to a woman who placed so much importance on appearance. Or was it his bankruptcy, the legal recognition of his inability to provide her with any form of security? Father could never repay those debts. When he died years later, he was still legally bankrupt, and all his possessions were in his children's and second wife's name. Was it the fear that all she could look forward to with him were years of hard labor, sexual betrayal, and violence? Or was it the immediate humiliation of living again in the culturally foreign Hokkien ancestral house, a lowly Fifth Sister-in-Law, after having had her own home? Sometimes I think she abandoned us because she did not want to see our many hungry faces. Or because of our childish neglect of her as we ran wild and wilder every day through the streets and out of her life.

I will never know. She was there and then she was no longer there. Who dressed me the next morning for school? In my royal blue pinafore and white blouse I walked the two miles to the convent. Just before the convent walls came into sight I passed by Mother's Second Aunt's house. Grandaunt was a *nonya* in the grand style, dressed in a meticulously ironed sarong and gleaming starched *kebaya*. The doors and windows of her house were always shut. The front porch was swept clean, its uneven red Mediterranean tiles sober and bare. This morning Mother sat by a window which was opened just a crack. She called to me and pulled me through the door. The front parlor smelled of old joss; the teak furniture was polished as if no one had ever used it. She took me by the arm into the second parlor and I sat at the marble-topped table while she spread a slice of bread with marmalade. I was absorbed by the sandwich;

nothing had ever tasted so good to me. Greedily, she watched me eat, tears spilling from her eyes. I was uncomfortable: Why was she crying? I would be late for school.

I told no one about my mother's treat or about her tears. I met her only in the mornings on my way to school, and each morning I looked forward to that slice of bread and marmalade. Sometimes Second Grandaunt was present, a severe woman with her hair up in a bun, stuck with a filigreed gold pin, who said nothing to me. I carried my mother's tearful face with me all day. In the morning I wasn't certain which I was looking forward to more, the bread and marmalade, my only food for the day until dinner, or her sad eyes fixed obsessively on me.

But in a week she was gone from that window.

Much later I learned that Mother had left for Singapore to join her brothers and sisters, those siblings she had cared for when she was herself a grand *nonya*.

Second Grandaunt never opened the door for me again. Each morning I walked slowly past the shut door, thinking of that slice of bread. I left for school without breakfast, hid through recess till all the girls had finished eating, and waited all afternoon for dinner when Third Aunt would give us each a plate of rice and some vegetables and sauce.

Did Third Aunt feed us out of charity or was Father paying her?

It felt like charity. We waited for her to feed her children first. When our turn came, most of the meat was gone. A few vegetables and some scraps of meat remained as leftovers, and this was what we wolfed down, the five of us, as quickly as we could before the plates were polished empty.

The hunger was a pain in my belly. I was conscious of it all through the day so that it became part of me and I forgot that it was something new and different. Instead I concentrated on the world that had become possible because Mother was no longer with us.

This world was free. Once home from school I was an unshackled animal and followed my brothers and cousins as they ran through the streets. I was always a little behind them; they were faster and impatient with me. But I was persistent. I trailed them and caught up as they stopped to climb a tree, threw stones at a dog, or clambered down from the back of the house to the sandy track and to the sea wall.

Sometimes they got away from me. I turned a corner and they had vanished, into a friend's house, up an alley, or over a drop. I would find myself alone, streets away from Grandfather's house, in the steamy afternoon, no one stirring except me. Every hawker stall, crowded with rubber thongs, plastic braided shopping baskets, goods I didn't ever look at because I knew we were destitute and could buy nothing in the world, was empty of customers. All Malacca except me had fallen to the somnambulant spell of the tropical heat.

Slowly I traced my way back to Heeren Street. How fine it was to be alone and unafraid. I was suddenly proud of myself. Nine years old, I walked confidently through the quiet streets I had just inherited; no bicycle or rickshaw disturbed my vagrancy. I was aggrieved that my brothers had successfully lost me, and I preened myself on being alone. The volatile mixture of sorrowful loneliness and proud independence nags me to this day.

A wild girl who ran around with boys and alone through the streets, I also discovered that crime paid. In a closed room behind the inner parlor *Tua Peh,* who was managing Grandfather's hardware store, had stored boxes and barrels of goods. We found that by breaking open some of these boxes we could grope in the room's darkness and come up with a handful of pipes, copper wires, shiny steel faucets, brass knobs, and iron hooks. These we carried away furtively to a store in the next street over where a barechested man weighed our offerings on his balance and gave us some coins in exchange. We knew we were stealing, although it did not occur to us that it was our own Lim family we were devastating with our thievery.

How rare were those ten-and twenty-cent coins! I held them tightly in my palm and considered everything I could buy with them—dried lemon skins, pickled plums, sugared cuttlefish, preserved fruit. I longed for salty sweet tidbits that I nibbled slowly so that five-cents worth lasted and lasted all day. My thrift was that of the survivor who hoarded against starvation.

Of course, it did not occur to me then to complain that even as my brothers and I went to bed hungry every night, *Tua Peh* and *Sah Peh* were lying together in a middle room smoking their opium pipes. Our raids into the storeroom went undetected because the entire family was disintegrating. *Tua Peh,* the family patriarch, had become addicted to opium. A silent man, thin to the point of emaciation, he neglected the hardware store and instead spent recklessly on opium, which he smoked all day. The trishaw man who brought the opium into the house showed it to us one morning, wrapped in a dried leaf, a ball of tarry substance, smaller than a marble, like a mouse's turd. *"Ahpien sai,"* First Aunt said, wrinkling her nose, "Opium shit."

Sometimes, absolutely silent, I crept up to the middle room where First and Third Uncles lay on the smooth hardwood floors resting on bolsters and sharing a pipe. The pipe was a smooth wooden reed with an aperture in the middle that held a copper clip. The men impaled the opium ball on a long skewer and roasted it over a spirit lamp. When it sizzled and turned oily black it was carefully placed in the clip, and they took turns sucking in its smoke through the water pipe. After the ball had burned away, they fell back on their bolsters and lay dreaming for hours. The only sound during this ritual was the sound of the water pipe as they sucked on it—snorting snores that echoed in the room, repeated as the pipe went around their two pairs of hands. The smell of roasting opium was intense, like a combination of coffee grounds, burned soy sauce, and singed hair. The snores and the dark fumes penetrated every bedroom; the scent clung to my nostrils like a family taint.

This dark scent overlapped with the dark nights when I found myself mysteriously alone. My brothers were asleep in the front open space. I woke up in the bedroom and found Father was gone. Clok-clok-clok. The street below echoed with the bang of wood against wood, the noodle vendor's announcement of his itinerant presence to midnight hungry insomniacs. I stood by the glassless window whose wooden panels had been drawn shut and placed my eye against its crack. A street lamp cast its pale nimbus down the cross street, so dim that it turned the air brown and shadowless. The entire scene was empty, like my body which hummed its hunger in an underkey, and like the room in which I stood for long minutes, without Mother and Father. I was beyond crying, and leaned idly against the window panels, curious about who I was in this world where everything had shut down except me.

Soon even Grandfather's house was lost. We had become attached to Third Uncle's family, and we followed them as they settled into a three-room shack, the first house in a row of four. All four identical shacks shared the same long roof of zinc. Father, Beng, Chien, Jen, Hui, and I squeezed into the tiny back room, about eight by ten feet wide, next to the kitchen of Third Uncle's house, while our cousins, *Sah Peh,* and *Sah Ehm* shared the two larger rooms in the front.

Although the shack was almost five miles away, I loved walking to school each morning, away from the misery of cramped dislocation. The more crowded we were, the more distant I felt from everybody. Walking alone through unfamiliar streets returned an identity to me, and I felt myself as a human in a way that living in my cousins' back room did not allow.

Father gave me ten cents each morning for the bus, but I always walked the five miles to school. I spent the bus fare on food, a lentil cake from the Indian woman who also sold roasted peanuts and boiled chickpeas by the Bandar Hilir Primary School, or a day-old pastry from the Chinese bakery a mile down my route if I could not wait. I saved five cents for the hot walk home at two in the afternoon.

I varied my route so that I walked through different streets, and I peered into Chinese and Indian stores for riches which my five cents could purchase. A Chinese store on a side street near the Indian part of town displayed barrels of clumpy dates, sticky masses in which twigs, dried leaves, pebbles, and bits of insects were visible. These dates were the food with which the poorest Malays broke their fast as the sun set during the month of Ramadan. Five cents bought a fistful of solid sweetness and kept me active all day.

Our first meal of the day came at six in the evening. Eagerly we waited for *Sah Ehm's* family to finish eating; then we sat down to the cold rice and leftover dishes. We left nothing on our plates from *Sah Ehm's* servings—there was simply never enough for us. We never complained or talked about being hungry. A kind of pride had overtaken us, even as our skin pulled tighter and our bodies showed their bones.

Father worried more about me than the boys. I had headaches, and had grown silent and moody. I stared at a wall all evening and cried easily. He asked me to walk after school by the Bata shop on Riverside where he was a salesclerk. He placed me on his bicycle handlebar and biked me through the tedious hot streets home to the shack, then he biked all the way back to the store. I drooped over his bicycle, strangely comforted by the slow pedal of the wheels but unable to revive. He didn't say much as we traveled. Across these years I feel his tenderness and my uneasiness with it.

But Father did not understand my fears. One day I found a rash over my stomach, perhaps formed by heat and my absence of baths. I ran to my aunt and asked her to look at it. Looking glum she said in Hokkien that the rash was called a snake. Nothing could stop this disease once it took hold of you. The snake grew to encircle the waist, squeezing the intestines and stomach until the human host died painfully. "The gold earrings in your ears"—by some strange chance missed by Father's debtors a year ago—"must be removed immediately," she warned. One effect of this horrible disease was that any gold touching the afflicted person's body would become melded into the flesh. "I'll take the earrings out for you," she offered.

I was numbed with the news of my impending death. I imagined the snake twisting around my waist, growing larger every day and the pain that was inevitably approaching. The next morning I headed towards the convent chapel. Kneeling on the pew, I cried wretchedly. I felt the pain of the gold earrings stuck in my soft flesh. That evening I begged Auntie to take the earrings off. I never saw them again.

For the next few weeks I cried easily, withdrew into somber moods, and suffered headaches. Gradually, however, the image of my dying left me. One day the rash was gone and, except for an abiding morbidity, a fascination and belief in my early death, I had almost forgotten the entire incident.

After a few more months, Third Uncle and his family were also gone. In those few months also, Father found his lifelong occupation as a petition writer.

It was 1954; the British had just negotiated with the United Malay National Organization (UMNO) for independence for the Federation of Malaya in 1957. Determined to maintain Malay ascendancy, UMNO had resisted accepting the large Chinese population into the federation as citizens of the new state. Legislation controlling citizenship for Chinese residents was enacted, and suddenly millions of Chinese were legally enmeshed, their loyalties and identities suspended until certain forms, government stamps, notarized certificates, and fees were collected.

Father was trilingual. His Senior Cambridge education and Queen's Scout training had made him comfortable with British regulations and procedures. His Straits-born Malay fluency added social amiability and grace; and his Hokkien descent gave him access to masses of illiterate Amoy kinsmen fearful of British and Malay laws that had been crafted to make illegal immigrants out of them.

Wealthy Chinese had lawyers to do the paperwork for them. English-educated Chinese went through the Civil Service officers and completed the papers themselves. Father's clients were working-class and poor Chinese, illiterate, some with no fixed address, all suspicious of government and fearful of detention and deportation.

Father, a Straits-born British subject, was securely of the place. But without a law degree, he could not practice immigration law, so he could not set a fee for his services. Instead his clients paid him whatever they could afford or thought was appropriate. Sometimes a farmer paid in baskets of fruit. On good days a grateful hawker paid a hundred dollars for a successful petition. Everyone gave something, even if it was only twenty dollars. For a period Father was so successful at writing petitions for citizenship status for China-born Malayans that he came home late each evening with a pocketful of ten- and twenty-dollar notes.

This unexpected and improvised career shift allowed us to move to our own shack next to Third Aunt's house. Father made an attempt to persuade Mother to return from Singapore where she had gone to join her brothers and sisters. He sent an emissary, a mutual friend, who visited us one evening. It was already dark outside and Father went to the verandah in his pajamas to talk to the woman. I could see their two dim figures standing with the night drop behind them.

When Father came back into the house, he had a grim expression on his face. It was one of the few occasions he ever spoke about Mother to us. "Your mother doesn't want to come back. Well, she's not going to see any of you ever again. You will have nothing to do with her. She is out of our lives."

Mother became a huge silence. We never spoke of her to Father, nor to each other. She was forbidden, someone who was not dead and also not alive.

But she tried to stay in touch with us. A few months after she'd rejected Father's overtures, she sent a frock to me through another acquaintance. Furious, Father ripped the frock and returned it. "Tell her she can have nothing to do with her daughter. I will never let my daughter accept anything from that whore." But later when Mother sent me a doll, a huge doll about two feet tall that walked stiffly when you held it by the hand and guided it, Father, by then settled with his second wife, kept it in the house. I was allowed to look at the doll and even to walk it on a few occasions; the rest of the time it was kept for safekeeping in its box on top of the *almeira*. Soon I forgot to ask for it, and, as with my first doll and with Mother, it inexplicably disappeared.

When I was twelve and older, Mother wrote occasional short notes to me, enclosing a five- or ten-dollar bill. She included a return address, but her notes said very little, and the money gave me a tick in my side, like an ache, reminding me of something about my last few mornings with her at Second Grandaunt's house.

The move to our own house was more immediate to me than the few reminders of Mother two hundred miles away in Singapore. At first we were ecstatic with the luxury of the move. Beng, Chien, and Jen slept in the back room, while Hui and I slept with Father in one large bed in the one real bedroom. With our own space, we became a family again, only this time we thought of ourselves as a clubhouse. Casual, untidy, loud with music, card games, and sports, the house attracted my brothers' friends who were always welcomed by Father. The large laterite wasteland in front of the row of houses was commandeered by the boys who measured and chalked with lime the rectangles of a badminton court and set up two poles. Father bought a net, some rackets, and badminton birds, and every afternoon a string of boys rode up on their bicycles and played sets, indulging in flashy smashes and overheads. Father often beat the best of them, chasing after the bird more ardently than anyone. Watching on the sidelines, I was the only girl in these scenes, and, with my brothers, laughed at Father's sweaty antics.

Father bought a radio cum record player, and while we could afford only a few records, we listened all day long to the radio which played British and U.S. pop songs aimed chiefly at the British forces stationed in Penang and Malacca. He found a mail-order catalog for musical instruments and sent for a guitar which arrived with an instructional book. We were stunned by its beauty, this gleaming curved body with its magic hole that hummed each time the tightly wound wires were struck. For weeks we gave up our wild play outdoors and bent together, watching Beng and Chien as they tried the different fingerings that produced those A, C, and D chords called music. In the evenings after our meal and Father's shower, he took possession of the guitar. In his cotton pajamas, the oldest child among us, he embraced the guitar's roundness and strummed melodies that led us through rounds of loud singing. "She'll Be Coming 'Round the Mountain," "On Top of Old Smoky," "Oh Susannah," campfire songs that he had learned in his scouting days drew us in a circle that for a miraculous moment made us complete as a family.

Our weekdays, however, were a shambles. For a while, Third Aunt continued to feed us, and her older daughter, never sent to school and unmarried still, took care of our laundry. Then, *Sah Peh,* a minor civil servant, was transferred to Muar, a small town fifty miles south of Malacca.

Father contracted with a cheap coffee shop situated in the town market for our dinners. Every evening Beng or Chien set out on Father's bicycle to the coffee shop and returned with a *chun* crammed with food. The carrier held three containers set up in tiers. The first smaller container held meat or fish and vegetables; the second of the same size contained soup; and the bottom receptacle which was the tallest was filled with rice.

Father shared the food out among all six of us. Beng and Chien were given more rice for they were the oldest, but I received as much soup and meat and vegetables as they did. Jealously we eyed each other's portions; no one was permitted to have a larger or better helping. If it had happened that one child received a bigger piece of meat, then Father had to take some of that meat away for another child.

The food was always delicious because we were always hungry. If the soup had strips of salted cabbage and pork fat, it called for cries of appreciation. The meat was usually fatty pork, sometimes chicken, and sometimes ray whose fleshy fins were a special favorite since we could eat almost all of its cartilaginous bones. We all had different approaches to eating. Some mixed the small bits of meat and sauce with the rice; others ate the meat first, and lastly the rice flavored with the vegetables and sauce. I kept the best for last; filling up with rice and sauce, I saved my piece of pork by the side and long after everyone had finished I turned to that fragrant morsel as my reward. There were never any leftovers.

When we first moved to Mata Kuching, a Buddhist association, whose temple grounds stood a little way in from the main road, owned much of it. A narrow laterite lane ran past the temple, past other shabby attap-roofed shacks, and about two hundred yards into our row of shacks. The land was half rural; compounds ran into each other without fences and gates to mark private property, and we took shortcuts through gardens and backyards without any remonstrance.

Seeing so much garden fruit, my brothers and I formed a wild pack. A butterfruit tree in a neighbor's yard was a favorite target. The globular fruit was creamy flesh inside, but its skin was covered with numerous small needles like cactus spines that barbed our fingers and lips if we were careless. We ignored the pain of the needles as we picked the ripe purplish fruit and crammed the pulp into our mouths. We scanned the mango trees around and did not wait for the fruit to ripen but picked them as soon as they were of any size. We ate these green, puckerish sour mangoes with relish. A short wayside tree grew right by our front yard. It bore continuously, small berries with a vapid sweet seedy flesh. Unripe, the berries were an inedible hard green. As they ripened they turned pink, then squishy red. We called it a cherry tree, and spent hours climbing its branches, combing them for a handful of pink and red cherries hidden among the fuzzy leaves.

Driven by hunger we clambered higher and higher, moving from one branch to another above it where cherries waved just out of our reach, till one afternoon Chien came crashing down and lay moaning on the ground. Someone must have gone to get his high-school teacher, Mr. Leong, who drove him to the hospital. Tormented by fear for his life, I walked the miles to the hospital and found him in the emergency room where his broken wrist was being bandaged. He never received medical attention again about his wrist. Perhaps no one thought it necessary; there was certainly no money for doctor's fees.

Like everything else about our childhood, that break in Chien's wrist did not set well. For years he wore a bandage around his wrist to hide the ugly angle of the bone. I ached for his private shame, for I understood how he hurt even after the bone had healed.

Despite our deprivations, we were never asked to help with the housework. After our evening meals, we children set our dishes on the floor next to the cement water tank for Father to wash up, and went off to do our homework.

I had never been taught how to clean anything, even myself. Up to the age of nine I had been bathed by one adult or another, first by Ah Chan, then by Mother, and finally Father tried to take over this chore. But he came home so tired and late that he often forgot.

I became grubbier every day. Surreptitiously I would rub one finger along the inner crease of my elbow; shreds of black dirt peeled off. I rubbed behind my ears and flicked off balls of dead skin. Running after my brothers all afternoon I frequently fell and skinned my knees. Small laterite shards stuck to the unwashed raw patches, the wounds turned sulfurous, yellow with pus. Even as a sore healed another formed. My legs and arms were pockmarked with scars and pus-filled sores.

During this period Father tried washing and ironing our laundry himself on weekends. His ironing was excellent; with a modern electric iron our clothes were pressed smooth. But he could not get them clean. Yellow lines showed where dirt and sweat had settled on my white collars, and my white socks had large brown patches at their heels. I had no change of uniforms, so the one blouse and pinafore had to do for the week. Try as I did, by Friday my uniform was rumpled and stained. Every morning I pulled on the same pair of white socks, and set the heels lower into the shoes so that the spreading black soles would not show. I changed underwear infrequently; there wasn't enough to go around until Father's laundry day on Saturday.

One afternoon Auntie May—the nurse whom Father had met in the hospital—visited us. Together they got me into the bathroom, which was merely an unlighted walled and roofed enclosure at the back of the house, equipped with a tap, a large jar beneath it, and a *kong,* a tin scoop. I had a horror of that space, a kind of claustrophobia that included the darkness, the greenish moldy damp air, and the floods of water it took to get myself clean. To take a bath, I usually ran the tap water into the jar. Scooping the cold water with the *kong* I threw it over my body, pausing only to soap myself. A final rinse and I unfastened the zinc door to hurry out of that slippery moldy space with a sense of having escaped one more time from an unhealthy cage.

But that afternoon Father shampooed my hair while Auntie May soaped me thoroughly. I stood still in the middle of their ministering hands, feeling a quiet pleasure in her presence. She was serious where Father was light-hearted, absorbed in whatever she was doing where Father was distracted. I fell asleep early that evening—it was so peaceful to be clean.

During the school holidays that year, Auntie May invited me to stay with her in her quarters in the Malacca General Hospital. The nurses lived in a dormitory building by the entrance to the hospital road. These bare rooms with narrow single beds, uncurtained windows, and institutional chests of drawers were usually empty and quiet. The dining room, serving soft-boiled eggs, toast, black tea and sugar for breakfast, was also stark and antiseptic, with a long table and identical chairs. Most of the nurses preferred to live at home and stayed in these quarters only when they were on night duty and could not get away. But I was awed by the luxury of Auntie May's world—its regularity, its cleanliness, its empty spaces unfilled by people, bedding, and old furniture! Compared to the nurses' silent dormitories, I saw my home filled with brothers and their noises as intolerably irregular, a quarrelsome chaos.

Auntie May took me on her rounds during the few days I stayed with her. She was then on duty in the emergency room where poor Malaccans who could not afford a doctor came with their unexplained coughs and fevers. Perched to the side of the large room, I observed the orderlies and nurses at work. While nurses checked pulses and decided who should be seen by the doctors, the orderlies, all Tamil men, cleaned and bandaged wounds and led the most indisposed to doctors or to their hospital beds. The work was usually not dramatic, the cuts and wounds from various accidents being treated on the spot with iodine and gentian blue.

Bored, I roamed the hospital. I browsed through the varieties of Nestle and Cadbury chocolates and magazines from Hong Kong, Bombay, and London carried in the Indian sweetshop downstairs. Sitting on one of the benches set out among enclosed spaces on the grounds, I studied the small green yards planted with scraggy cannas, unvisited by anyone but bees and midges. The hospital hummed around me: nurses trotted down corridors, ayahs pushed trolleys smelling of steamed rice and cabbage towards the service elevators, and white-clad orderlies disappeared around corners bearing armfuls of bandages and mysterious supplies. The institutional order lulled me. I imagined longingly that the convent orphanage must be very much like this—a safe space with lunch and dinner served regularly at noon and six. This school break spent at the Malacca General Hospital was the closest to a vacation I enjoyed as a child.

But Auntie May dropped out of sight. I never saw her again. Perhaps my moody company that week convinced her that life with my father and his children was impossible. I heard later that she became a head nurse and then achieved the ultimate promotion, to matron, supervising an entire hospital staff of nurses. Something about her briskness already indicated the career path she would take. I only wonder what youthful dreaminess led her to a relationship, no matter how tenuous and sedate, with my father. Perhaps she glimpsed in him the man he could have been under another sky, a gentle, thoughtful, and intelligent man uncrowded by his children, not brought down by the consequences of his body.

Ironically I struggle with the guilt of my father's sexuality in a way I am sure he never did.

Father began to leave us after dinner with instructions to get ourselves to bed by nine. Some nights I kept myself awake waiting for him to come home. In the large queen-size bed, I slept on one side, and Hui, who was about six years old, slept in the middle while Father slept on the other side. Sleep was usually easy and pleasurable for me. My brothers had taken to yelling a chorus of good-nights, competing as to who would have the last word. They interspersed their good-nights with loud farts and rude armpit sounds and Father was sometimes the loudest and rudest of them all. These gales of laughter gradually ceased as one by one we drifted off to sleep. Whenever I roused in the middle of the night, I snuggled my cheek against my bolster and listened for Father's reassuring heavy breathing. Now his late nights meant we scrambled into bed silent and anxious. Lying awake I would hold my breath and watch the dark air before me which I fancied appeared to crawl slowly in a series of dots in front of my eyes. As soon as I heard Father's bicycle clank against the verandah wall, I would release my breath and sink into sleep.

One night I heard a strange voice with Father. He had brought someone home with him who giggled and whispered. Overcome by guilt for being awake, I lay with my eyes shut. I wanted desperately to be not there, to disappear into the bedding the way Hui had disappeared. But fully awake, I felt the motions of people rustling and breathing around me. They did not get into bed but must have sat on the floor. The whispers and giggles continued, then faded into other indistinct sounds. Slowly I lost consciousness, even as an anxious turn in my chest strained to block out every silent sigh that seemed to fill the minutes.

Father brought this woman home on many occasions. I learned to turn over and enter my mind so that those sounds that had so startled me the first night would become unmemorable. They were things of the night so separate from the day's events that I could proceed undisturbed by them, as if they were not true. I did not know who came home with Father although I knew the whisper and giggle well.

One afternoon Father came home from work accompanied by a young woman riding a bicycle. We recognized her immediately: she was our old family servant, Ah Chan's daughter. Ah Peng was only seventeen, seven years older than I. Fresh-faced and happy, she rode up to the house and left her bicycle on our verandah. They had just "drunk tea" together, a Confucianist ritual that conferred on her the customary status of second wife. Ah Chan had not approved of her daughter's relationship with Father. Perhaps she hoped for something better for her daughter than a liaison with a married man burdened with five children at home and bankruptcy; perhaps she felt bound by past ties to Mother and to class taboos. Ah Peng, however, was pregnant. Ah Chan had no choice but to allow Peng to "marry" Father.

Standing by the front door gaping at the sudden presence of Peng in our family, I did not understand how scandalous Father's actions were. "Peng is going to be your stepmother," Father said, beaming with genuine happiness. English-educated, I repeated the word "stepmother" to myself. Snow White and the Seven Dwarfs, Cinderella, Red Rose and White Rose, Hansel and Gretel, all the Western fairy tales in which wicked stepmothers and stepdaughters battled in mortal conflict swam into mind. As Peng swept out the bedroom and moved my clothes out of the almeira into the shelves in the back room, I sat on the doorstep and looked out at the open space that Father and my brothers had limed and netted into a badminton court. I knew Peng would hate me. Finally I acknowledged that Mother was never going to return and nothing was ever going to be the same.

Peng's place in our family was central and total. At the same time, we children proceeded as if she were absent in our midst. Father never intervened in our mutual neglect. I do not remember a conversation with her in all the eight years I continued to live in the same house with her, although we addressed each other occasionally and exchanged remarks. She spoke no English and minimal Malay; I refused to speak Hokkien to her. We barricaded ourselves behind our different languages. We lived together in the closest quarters as linguistic strangers, our mutual hostility remaining unexpressed and seemingly contained.

We always called her "Peng," the name by which we knew her when she was the daughter to our mother's servant. Much later I learned she had resented this callous noncompliance with proper Chinese familial custom. We should have called her "Ma," Mother, for, as Father's second wife, she was also our second mother. Father, however, never requested this of us, perhaps out of his own self-conscious embarrassment. We were Western-educated children; by the time I was six, all five of us spoke English at home and with him. Our home culture was altogether anglophone, including magazines, newspapers, music, games, and sports. Peng was a thoroughly Chinese woman. Barely literate in Mandarin, she had been raised by Ah Chan to do domestic work. She was strong, skilled in needlework, a good cook, thrifty, and already practiced in all the demanding chores of laundry, housecleaning, and child care. The daughter of a servant, she suited our needs as if she had answered a personal ad. We did not refuse to call her "Mother"; it never occurred to us that we should do so.

She was sullen and unsmiling toward me from the very beginning. She lived for when Father came home. Sitting beside him at the kitchen table, she picked the best pieces of meat or fish from a dish with her chopsticks and placed them on his plate. While Father still shared the food out among us, we were less jealously watchful. For the first time in two years, we had as much rice as we could eat, and often even leftovers. Peng and Father washed the dishes together, she giggling and chattering to him in Hokkien. Later when we were in our cots, they continued their conversations in the bedroom. I would hear their murmurs late into the night, pillow-talk that filled me with restlessness and misery.

# PART TWO

# CHAPTER FOUR

# Pomegranates and English Education

A pomegranate tree grew in a pot on the open-air balcony at the back of the second floor. It was a small skinny tree, even to a small skinny child like me. It had many fruits, marble-sized, dark green, shiny like overwaxed coats. Few grew to any size. The branches were sparse and graceful, as were the tear-shaped leaves that fluttered in the slightest breeze. Once a fruit grew round and large, we watched it every day. It grew lighter, then streaked with yellow and red. Finally we ate it, the purple and crimson seeds bursting with a tart liquid as we cracked the dry tough skin into segments to be shared by our many hands and mouths.

We were many. Looking back it seems to me that we had always been many. Beng was the fierce brother, the growly eldest son. Chien was the gentle second brother, born with a squint eye. Seven other children followed after me: Jen, Wun, Wilson, Hui, Lui, Seng, and Marie, the last four my half-siblings. I was third, the only daughter through a succession of eight boys and, as far as real life goes, measured in rice bowls and in the bones of morning, I have remained an only daughter in my memory.

We were as many as the blood-seeds we chewed, sucked, and spat out, the indigestible cores pulped and gray while their juice ran down our chins and stained our mouths with triumphant color. I still hold that crimson in memory, the original color of Chinese prosperity and health, now transformed to the berry shine of wine, the pump of blood in test tubes and smeared on glass plates to prophesy one's future from the wriggles of a virus. My Chinese life in Malaysia up to 1969 was a pomegranate, thickly seeded.

When Beng and Chien began attending the Bandar Hilir Primary School, they brought home textbooks, British readers with thick linen-rag covers, strong slick paper, and lots of short stories and poems accompanied by colorful pictures in the style of Aubrey Beardsley. The story of the three Billy Goats Gruff who killed the Troll under the bridge was stark and compressed, illustrated by golden kids daintily trotting over a rope bridge and a dark squat figure peering from the ravine below. Wee Willie Winkie ran through a starry night wearing only a white night cap and gown. The goats, the troll, and Willie Winkie were equally phantasms to me, for whoever saw anything like a flowing white gown on a boy or a pointy night cap in Malaya?

How to explain the disorienting power of story and picture? Things never seen or thought of in Malayan experience took on a vividness that ordinary life could not possess. These British childhood texts materialized for me, a five- and six-year-old child, the kind of hyper-reality that television images hold for a later generation, a reality, moreover, that was consolidated by colonial education.

At five, I memorized the melody and lyrics to "The Jolly Miller" from my brother's school rendition:

> There lived a jolly miller once
> Along the River Dee.
> He worked and sang from morn till night,
> No lark more blithe than he.
> And this the burden of his song
> As always used to be,
> I care for nobody, no not I,
> And nobody cares for me.

It was my first English poem, my first English song, and my first English lesson. The song ran through my head mutely, obsessively, on hundreds of occasions. What catechism did I learn as I sang the words aloud? I knew nothing of millers or of larks. As a preschool child, I ate bread, that exotic food, only on rare and unwelcome occasions. The miller working alone had no analogue in the Malayan world. In Malacca, everyone was surrounded by everyone else. A hawker needed his regular customers, a storefront the stream of pedestrians who shopped on the move. Caring was not a concept that signified. Necessity, the relations between and among many and diverse people, composed the bonds of Malaccan society. Caring denoted a field of choice, of individual voluntary action, that was foreign to family, the place of compulsory relations. Western ideological subversion, cultural colonialism, whatever we call those forces that have changed societies under forced political domination, for me began with something as simple as an old English folk song.

The pomegranate is a fruit of the East, coming originally from Persia. The language of the West, English, and all its many manifestations in stories, songs, illustrations, films, school, and government, does not teach the lesson of the pomegranate. English taught me the lesson of the individual, the miller who is happy alone, and who affirms the principle of not caring for community. Why was it so easy for me to learn that lesson? Was it because within the pomegranate's hundreds of seeds is also contained the drive for singularity that will finally produce one tree from one seed? Or was it because my grandparents' Hokkien and *nonya* societies had become irremediably damaged by British colonial domination, their cultural confidence never to be recovered intact, so that Western notions of the individual took over collective imaginations, making of us, as V. S. Naipaul has coined it, "mimic" people?

But I resist this reading of colonialist corruption of an original pure culture. Corruption is inherent in every culture, if we think of corruption as a will to break out, to rupture, to break down, to decay, and thus to change. We are all mimic people, born to cultures that push us, shape us, and pummel us; and we are all agents, with the power of the subject, no matter how puny or inarticulate, to push back and to struggle against such shaping. So I have seen myself not so much sucking at the teat of British colonial culture as actively appropriating those aspects of it that I needed to escape that other familial/gender/native culture that violently hammered out only one shape for self. I actively sought corruption to break out of the pomegranate shell of being Chinese and girl.

It was the convent school that gave me the first weapons with which to wreck my familial culture. On the first day, Ah Chan took me, a six-year-old, in a trishaw to the Convent of the Holy Infant Jesus. She waited outside the classroom the entire day with a *chun*, a tiffin carrier, filled with steamed rice, soup, and meat, fed me this lunch at eleven-thirty, then took me home in a trishaw at two. I wore a starched blue pinafore over a white cotton blouse and stared at the words, *See Jane run. Can Jane run? Jane can run.* After the first week, I begged to attend school without Ah Chan present. Baba drove me to school after he dropped my older brothers at their school a mile before the convent; I was now, like my brothers, free of domestic female attachment.

The convent school stood quiet and still behind thick cement walls that hid the buildings and its inhabitants from the road and muffled the sounds of passing traffic. The high walls also served to snuff out the world once you entered the gates, which were always kept shut except at the opening and closing of the school day. Shards of broken bottles embedded in the top of the walls glinted in the hot tropical sunshine, a provocative signal that the convent women were daily conscious of dangers intruding on their seclusion. For the eleven years that I entered through those gates, I seldom met a man on the grounds, except for the Jesuit brought to officiate at the annual retreat. A shared public area was the chapel, a small low dark structure made sacred by stained glass windows, hard wooden benches, and the sacristy oil lamp whose light was never allowed to go out. The community was allowed into the chapel every Sunday to attend the masses held for the nuns and the orphans who lived in the convent.

But if the convent closed its face to the town of men and unbelievers, it lay open at the back to the Malacca Straits. Every recess I joined hundreds of girls milling at the canteen counters for little plates of noodles, curry puffs stuffed with potatoes, peas and traces of meat, and vile orange-colored sugared drinks. The food never held me for long. Instead I spent recess by the sea wall, a stone barrier free of bristling glass. Standing before the sandy ground that separated the field and summer house from the water, I gazed at high tide as the waves threw themselves against the wall with the peculiar repeated whoosh and sigh that I never wearied of hearing. Until I saw the huge pounding surf of the Atlantic Ocean, I believed all the world's water to be dancing, diamond-bright surfaced, a hypnotic meditative space in which shallow and deep seemed one and the same. Once inside the convent gates, one was overtaken by a similar sense of an overwhelming becalmedness, as if one had fallen asleep, out of worldliness, and entered the security of a busy dream.

During recess the little girls sang, "In and out the window, in and out the window, as we have done before," and skipped in and out of arching linked hands, in a mindless pleasure of repeated movement, repeating the desire for safety, for routine, and for the linked circular enclosure of the women's community that would take me in from six to seventeen.

I also learned to write the alphabet. At first, the gray pencil wouldn't obey my fingers. When the little orange nub at the end of the pencil couldn't erase the badly made letter, I wetted a finger with spit, rubbed hard, and then blubbered at the hole I had made in the paper. Writing was fraught with fear. I cried silently as I wrestled with the fragile paper that wouldn't sit still and that crushed and tore under my palm.

My teacher was an elderly nun of uncertain European nationality, perhaps French, who didn't speak English well. She spoke with a lisp, mispronounced my name, calling me "chérie" instead of "Shirley," and, perhaps accordingly, showed more affection to me than to the other children in her class. Sister Josie was the first European I knew. Even in her voluminous black robes and hood, she was an image of powder-white and pink smiles. Bending over my small desk to guide my fingers, and peering into my teary eyes, she spoke my name with a tender concern. She was my first experience of an enveloping, unconditional, and safe physical affection. She smelled sweet, like fresh yeast, and as I grew braver each day and strayed from my desk, she would upbraid me in the most remorseful of tones, "Chérie," which carried with it an approving smile.

In return I applied myself to Jane and Dick and Spot and to copying the alphabet letter by letter repeatedly. Sister Josie couldn't teach anything beyond the alphabet and simple vocabulary. In a few years, she was retired to the position of gatekeeper at the chapel annex. When I visited her six years later, as a child of twelve, at the small annex in which a store of holy pictures, medals, and lace veils were displayed for sale, Sister Josie's smile was still as fond. But to my mature ears, her English speech was halting, her grammar and vocabulary fractured. It was only to a six-year-old new to English that dear Sister Josie could have appeared as a native speaker of the English language.

It was my extreme good fortune to have this early missionary mother. Her gentle, undemanding care remains memorialized as a type of human relation not found in the fierce self-involvements of my family. My narrowly sensory world broadened not only with the magical letters she taught that spelled lives beyond what my single dreaming could imagine, but differently with her gentle greetings, in her palpable affection.

Nurturing is a human act that overleaps categories, but it is not free of history. It is not innocent. For the next eleven years nuns like Sister Josie broke down the domain of my infancy. Leaving the Bata shop and entering the jagged-glass-edged walls of the convent, I entered a society far removed from Baba and Emak.

The nuns wore the heavy wool habit of the missionary, full black blouses with wide sleeves like bat wings, long voluminous black skirts, black stockings, and shoes. Deep white hoods covered their heads and fell over their shoulders, and a white skull cap came down over their brows. Inexplicably they were collectively named "the French Convent," like a French colony or the foreign legion, but they were not chiefly white or European. Even in the early 1950s, some were Chinese and Eurasian "sisters."

Yet, despite their uniform habits and sisterly titles, a ranking regulated by race was obvious, even to the youngest Malayan child. Mother Superior was always white. A few white sisters, Sister Sean, Sister Patricia, and Sister Peter, taught the upper grades; or they performed special duties, like Sister Maria who gave singing lessons, or Sister Bernadette, who taught cooking and controlled the kitchen and the canteen.

Sister Maria was the only woman who was recognizably French. Her accent was itself music to us as she led us through years of Scottish and Irish ballads. No one asked why "Ye Banks and Braes of Bonnie Doon" or "The Minstrel Boy" formed our music curriculum, why Indian, Eurasian, Malay, and Chinese children should be singing, off-key, week after week in a faintly

French-accented manner the melancholic attitudes of Celtic gloom. What was the place of Celt ballads in a Malayan future? What did they instruct of a history of feelings, of British bloodshed and patriotism? Or were the curriculum setters in the Colonial Office in London reproducing in fortissimo an imperial narrative—the tragedy of failed Scottish and Irish nationalism, the first of England's colonies—in the physical pulses of the newly colonized?

Of the nonmissionary teachers from Malacca, many were Eurasian, and a few were Indian, and Chinese. The sole Malay teacher appeared only after the British ceded independence to the Federation of Malaya in 1957. Chik Guru taught us the Malay language in my last two years at the convent, just as now in the United States in many colleges and universities, the only African-American or Latino or Asian-American professor a student may meet teaches African-American or Latino or Asian-American studies. Up to the end of the 1950s, and perhaps right up to the violence of the May 13 race riots in 1969, the educational structure in Malaya was British colonial.

My first inkling of race preference was formed by these earliest teachers. In primary school, my teachers were almost all European expatriates or native-born Eurasian Catholics bearing such Hispanic and Dutch names as De Souza, De Witt, Minjoot, Aerea, and De Costa. They were the descendants of Portuguese soldiers and sailors who had captured Malacca from the Malay Sultanate in 1511, when Portugal was a small, poorly populated state. Expanding into the Spice Islands in the East, the Governor-Generals of the Indies encouraged intermarriage between Portuguese males and native women, thus seeding the loyal settler population with Portuguese mestizos. The Portuguese governed Malacca for 130 years. When the forces of the Dutch East India Company captured the port and its fortress in 1641, they found a garrison there of some 260 Portuguese soldiers, reinforced with a mestizo population of about two to three thousand fighting men. For over four hundred years, the mestizos of Malacca had identified themselves as Portuguese.

The Eurasian teachers were physically distinguished from me. I learned this in Primary Two with Mrs. Damien, a white-haired, very large woman whose fat dimpled arms fascinated me. While she demonstrated how to embroider a daisy stitch as we crowded around her chair, I poked my finger into the dimples and creases that formed in the pale flesh that flowed over her shoulders and sagged in her upper arms. She was a fair Eurasian who dressed as a British matron, in sleeveless flowered print frocks with square-cut collars for coolness. Her exposed arms and chest presented dazzling mounds of white flesh that aroused my ardent admiration. I do not remember learning anything else in her class.

A few Eurasian girls were among my classmates. While they were not as coddled as the white daughters of plantation managers, they had an air of ease and inclusion that I envied. Their hair, which often had a copper sheen to it, was braided, while we Chinese girls had black, pudding-bowl cropped hair. By the time we were twelve and thirteen, and still flatchested, they had budded into bosomy women whose presence in Sunday masses attracted the attention of young Catholic males. The royal blue pleated pinafores that covered our prim skinny bodies like cardboard folded teasingly over their chests and hips. The difference between us and the early maturity of Eurasian girls was a symptom of the difference between our Chinese Malaccan culture and that dangerous Western culture made visible in their lushness. They were overtly religious, controlled by their strict mothers and the Ten Commandments that we had all memorized by pre-adolescence. But their breasts and hips that made swing skirts swing pronounced them ready for that unspoken but pervasive excitement we knew simply as "boys."

The convent held a number of orphans, girls abandoned as babies on the convent doorsteps, or given over to the nuns to raise by relatives too poor to pay for their upkeep. During school hours these "orphaned" girls were indistinguishable from the rest of us. They wore the school uniforms, white short-sleeved blouses under sleeveless blue linen smocks that were fashioned with triple overpleats on both sides so that burgeoning breasts were multiply overlayered with folds of starched fabric. But once school hours were over they changed into pink or blue gingham dresses that buttoned right up to the narrow Peter Pan collars. Those loose shapeless dresses, worn by sullen girls who earned their keep by helping in the kitchen and laundry, formed some of my early images of a class to be shunned.

Instead I longed to be like the privileged boarders, almost all of whom were British, whose parents lived in remote and dangerous plantations or administrative outposts in the interior. These girls wore polished black leather shoes and fashionable skirts and blouses after school. In our classes, they sang unfamiliar songs, showed us how to dance, jerking their necks like hieroglyphic Egyptians. In the convent classroom where silence and stillness were enforced as standard behavior, they giggled and joked, shifting beams of sunshine, and were never reprimanded. To every schoolgirl it was obvious that something about a white child made the good nuns benevolent.

The Chinese nuns and teachers looked like us, yet they had social status and power.

Even as some teachers acted badly, in ways that suggested they were not infallible, we were told that teachers were objects of reverence: they could do no wrong. Many teachers were openly unfair and harsh, yet at the same time we were ceaselessly indoctrinated with their moral superiority.

My lessons in the pedagogy of terror began in Primary Three, when our teacher, Mrs. Voon, asked if any of us had played the Ouija board. Ignorant of the game we all answered in the negative. She chose two of us, her best pupils, to report this to Sister Arthur who was investigating the matter. Pleased at being let out of the classroom even for a short errand, we ran to the Primary Five classroom, where Sister Arthur, a dark-complexioned Chinese nun with pronounced flat cheekbones and owlish glasses, was teaching. When I announced that no one in *our* class had ever played with a Ouija board, Sister Arthur's gaze bore down on me. *"No, no,"* she exclaimed, "your teacher sent you here because you-oo are the one who has played the game!" I protested that it was not so; she only had to ask Mrs. Voon herself. "No, no, I know how wicked you are, I can see it for myself. *You-oo* are the one who has been playing this devil's board." I burst into tears, but Sister Arthur held firm. "You are not getting out of my class. You are a liar and you'll stay here until I decide what to do with you." She sent my companion to report to Mrs. Voon that I was detained, and I stood sobbing in front of the older children for the rest of the school day. It was only later in the afternoon that Sister Arthur sent me away. "I hope you have learned your lesson now," she said, and I worried for weeks about what that lesson could be.

Mrs. Voon never explained what had happened, and it seemed to me that only I knew that a horrible injustice had occurred. I hated Sister Arthur from then on, and remember hardening myself for years as her pupil. She taught art for all classes from Primary Four upwards, and there was no way convent girls could have avoided being in Sister Arthur's class at least once a week until they left the school.

Sister Arthur was vigilant against any form of talk during her class hours, and irrepressible child that I was, I could not help occasionally whispering words to the girls around me. Turning around quick as a gecko from the blackboard where she was writing directions, she would command me to stand up on the desk chair. Then, selecting a stick of chalk, she strolled up to me and asked me to place the chalk upright in my mouth. While the jaws ached from the forced open position, my saliva flowed copiously. To avoid the humiliation of slobbering over my pinafore, I worked my throat and kept swallowing my own bodily fluid. As the minutes changed into hours, the chalk disintegrated with the saliva and I kept choking down this foul combination of spit and gritty chalk, until such time as she allowed me down from my public perch.

My first meeting with Sister Arthur coincided with the year that my father lost his shop on Kampong Pantai, we lost our home, moved back to Grandfather's house on Heeren Street, and my mother left us for Singapore. In a year of such misery, I turned Sister Arthur into a joke, Old Battle-ax. Her penetrating voice was to be immediately exorcised with ridicule. Her myopic gaze allegedly unearthing evil thoughts in our faces taught me that the convent, like my own disintegrated family, held no certainty of trust or goodness.

In one sense Sister Arthur was correct. Though I had not used a Ouija board, I was full of questions that no known spirits in my family or in the convent could answer. I talked back to my teachers not because I was defiant but because my thoughts in response to their actions and statements appeared irresistibly logical. It always surprised me when teachers were offended by my answers and remarks, though they were frequently, it is true, unsolicited. I did not understand why they were angry, even inflamed, when I said something that appeared to me obviously correct. This pattern of punishment in the convent school for speaking what appeared transparently true continued for years.

The first time I understood fully that, unlike other children, I lacked the self-protective skill of silence, I had just turned fourteen. Until then I believed what the good nuns had repeated often, that I was a "naughty" child. The many disciplinary occasions that saw me standing for hours outside a classroom door or writing hundreds of lines of what I should or should not do, I believed, were directly related to my "stubborn" spirit. Although Sister Arthur was wrong to punish me for something I hadn't done, her act did not signify that I had not deserved punishment, since I was in any case a "naughty" child.

But at fourteen, one could become a "bad" girl. Mrs. Ladd, who was held in greater awe as one of the few British teachers in the secondary school, was upset because none of us had completed the class assignment. She was especially provoked by Millie, a timid Chinese orphan boarder, whom she accused of talking, and therefore not paying attention in her English-language class. Mrs. Ladd became so incensed that she left the classroom to call Mother Superior Paul to speak to us, a terrifying prospect.

In Mrs. Ladd's absence, a hubbub ensued. She had never assigned us the exercise she was now accusing us of not completing. Also, poor Millie, who was crying furiously, had not been talking. Too timid ever to break rules, she had been hushing us just as Mrs. Ladd had stalked through the door. We decided that we had to tell Mrs. Ladd the truth: she had made a mistake, and we all knew it. I asked for a show of hands of those who would stand up with me to offer this information to Mrs. Ladd when she returned with the Mother Superior, and every hand went up.

When Mother Superior walked in with Mrs. Ladd, whose square Irish jaw was set hard, I sprang to my feet and brightly made my little speech. Mrs. Ladd glared at the class and asked how many of the girls agreed with me. I was amazed when no one stood up.

"How dare you call your teacher a liar!" Mother Superior said, her face ruddy with rage. "What shall we do with her?"

The two white women talked above my head as if I were no longer present. I was banished from Form Two A to Form Two B, the second-rank class for weaker performing students.

I knew no one in Form Two B. For a whole month I kept my silence before the new teacher who treated me with disdain, and with my new and former classmates for whom my disgrace had made me an untouchable. I was certain I would stay in the B class the rest of my life, but one day without any explanation I was asked to gather my books and to return to Form Two A where I picked up my position as class leader and scholar as if the entire episode had never happened.

This incident with its month-long banishment taught me again what I was learning at every stage of my life, that speaking what is evident to my senses as plain common sense can bring swift punishment. I was confused by the difference between what appeared manifestly correct to me and what adults with power—my parents and teachers—insisted on asserting or denying, and I was infused with outrage by this difference. As my teachers punished me daily for my brashness, what they called my talking back, the burn of defiance in my chest became a familiar sensation. My defiance made me an outcast and a social leader at the same time, and my clashes with authority became a source of amusement for my classmates.

These conflicts with teachers and reverend sisters continued throughout my years at the convent. With Sister Sean, Sister Patricia, and Sister Peter, my Form One, Form Four, and Form Five teachers, I enjoyed the most intense relationships and at the same time suffered the most abject treatment. All three responded to me with an affection, pride, and tenderness that I assumed I deserved because I was the funny student, the quick and bright one. All teachers loved bright students; that was a law of nature. Everything about my life testified to the fact that my value to the world lay in my demonstrated intelligence, and I took their keen interest as natural.

As with Sister Josie, I was Sister Sean and Sister Patricia's pet. "Shirley!" they would call out confidently each time a student answered a question incorrectly or floundered for a date. And so, when the sisters secretly punished me, I believed that they were simply participating in my secret life of the imagination.

I believed my mind held depths of associations, feelings, and understanding that effortlessly distinguished me from my peers. The one subject I could not or would not master was math. Because my math scores were a dismal D or C at best, I needed to compensate for its drag on the annual averaging of grade points that ranked us from first to last girl in the class. Thus I endeavored to score perfect hundreds on every other subject. History, geography, and scripture were study subjects in which my mathematically talented competitors could also achieve. But it was with English, a subject every Malayan student believed was mystically beyond mere study but was achieved as innate talent, that I hoped to overcome my self-imposed handicap. I marked myself as different from the brilliant math students whose scores I scorned with my contemptuous Cs and Ds: what I lacked in math I would make up for in imagination, the gift which is endowed neither by race, class, or religion.

One afternoon, Sister Sean, exasperated with something I had said, asked me to stay behind in the room after the rest of the girls had left for physical education class. There, her face contorted with passion, she slapped me hard across my face. I was astonished and dry-eyed. She was doing this for my own good, she said, blinking hard behind her thick glasses. I was never, never to talk back to her like that again.

So when Sister Patricia asked me two years later to follow her to an empty classroom and shut the door behind me, I knew what to expect. Sister Patricia had been called to a meeting just before our English period with her. I said "Hooray!" in what I thought was an imitation of British comic book characters. I only meant that her absence would relieve us of tedious English parsing, but her angry glance in response to my remark prepared me for the worst. Once in the classroom she spun around, her face a scowl of pain. I was rude, I didn't care for her feelings, how dare I suggest that we didn't care to have her as our teacher. She struck me hard on my right cheek, then told me to wait till the physical education period was over before joining my classmates.

After she'd hurried out, I wondered what it was about my mouth that always got me into trouble.

My badness, evident at every turn, seemed to be produced by my intelligence, which I also believed would have to save me from myself.

The next year with Sister Peter I was determined not to give her cause for grief. I would watch my mouth and concentrate on preparing for the O levels, the Overseas Senior Cambridge Examinations. The results of the exams would determine whether I would be accepted for the pre-university classes.

By then I was reading T. S. Eliot's *After Strange Gods*, D. H. Lawrence's *Sons and Lovers* and *Lady Chatterley's Lover*, Erskine Caldwell's *Tobacco Road*, even Henry Miller's *Tropic of Cancer*, banned volumes that my older brothers smuggled home, but which they discarded once they found their reputation as pornographic literature overrated. One hot afternoon while Sister Peter read us Henry V's stirring address, "Once more unto the breach, dear friends, once more," I pondered the vast gap between Shakespeare's language and that in the clandestine publications with their chatter of private organs, illicit sensations, and hidden and dangerous thoughts. Idly I wrote at the back of an exercise book all the dangerous words I had learned just that year: "cock," "fuck," "penis," "cunt." They formed a neat list of about seventeen words: then I forgot about them.

Two days later, Sister Peter asked me to remain behind after class: I had handed in an English essay in the same exercise book. Her long face paler than usual, she berated me for my wicked ways. Her disappointment was horrible to me. Among all the sisters who'd taught me, she was the one I wanted most to please. She was graceful, grave, reserved; the simple twinkle in her green-blue eyes was large reward for any witticism or eloquence, and I had striven to please her by flaying my mind to a high pitch in completing every writing assignment. Now she withdrew any warmth of approval, and for the rest of the year, her anger laid a cold glance on me. I would rather she had slapped me and forgiven me, like Sisters Sean and Patricia.

My sense of possessing a reservoir of feelings and associations had everything to do with the misery of my everyday life and my withdrawal from it into books. At ten I learned to ride my father's discarded bicycle. Since its bar was too high to straddle, I rode it sideways by placing one foot under the bar, as if it were a pedicab. I must have looked a comic and awkward figure, but the bicycle permitted me an expansion of physical mobility that spelled greater freedom.

With my second brother I bicycled to the Malacca Library about five miles from our home. Within the thick red-colored walls built by the Dutch in the 1640s, a room lined with shelves of children's books welcomed me. Behind this front room was a larger chamber filled with shelves that narrowly divided the old red clay floor. This adult section was filled with hard-cover romances, detective thrillers, and books simply categorized "fiction." The librarian, perhaps out of boredom, for we never met more than another occasional visitor to the library, allowed us to sign up for a children's card, good for a book each time, and for an adult's card, which extended borrowing privileges to three books. Imagine the immediate riches that fell into our hands! Four books a day, no questions asked, and another four the next day when we returned the first four. The world around me vanished into the voices, the colors, and the dance of language. I gazed, dazzled, into interiors that Malacca never held.

Even the external world became bathed in the language of imagination. Books in arms, I took to climbing a mango tree that grew a little ways up the lane to get away from my father's wife, Peng, and from the trapped sticky afternoon heat in our three-roomed shack. Leaning against the trunk with my feet securely hooked around a branch, I studied the resin oozing from a cut as tiny black ants trailed evenly up and down the grainy bark. The dark green leaves waved a cooling presence around and above me. In the distance, through the dust of the red laterite that separated me from my home, I could hear my brothers' shouts. This world, I understood dimly, was somehow connected to that world which I clutched in my hands. It had little taste of adventure, unlike the wars, princes, murders, and balls that took place regularly in books. But it was my world, red soil, green leaves, hot sun, cool shade, sturdy body, distant noises. What connected the two was myself, and I knew I would someday write this world down, finding a language that would do justice to it.

Discovering in books how large the world was outside of Malacca, I also began to see how large my own world was. As reader, I never surrendered my freedom to an author but always asked how what I was reading related to my observations, the people around me, and my surroundings. Knowing that children elsewhere read these books, I assumed that they would also want to know about someone like me. It was in this way that I took up pen-pal writing. The children's comics that Father bought as treats for us carried personals from children in Scotland or Wales or Exeter, who wished to correspond with children from other countries of the Commonwealth. I could not afford the stamps to take up these offers, but for a time I wrote letters to imaginary pen pals, writing details of my life and stories of school plays and exhibitions, and expressing a desire to hear from them.

In these letters, like children all over the world tracing home as the center of all arrivals, I sent the following address: Mata Kuching, Malacca, The Straits Settlements, Malaya, Asia, The Earth, The Milky Way, The Universe. Malacca was at the center of everything. It was what made the universe imaginable, the address which brought all the letters home.

Pumping my Schaeffer pen full of ink from an inkwell that winked a copper-green eye, I also considered writing a history of the world. It was convenient for me that Malacca was at the center of that crooked hunchbacked peninsula that filled an entire page, just as Australia or North America each filled a page. Malaya was in the middle of the earth, and everybody else fell out over the edges—China, cramped like a squeezed orange half, India, an inverted pyramid, leaking Ceylon as a teardrop.

This geography, placing me at the hub of the universe, was more than childish egocentrism. I felt the depth of my existence, and accepted that it was full of meaning. Meaning radiated from me, the subject on whom experience fell and the potential author on whom experience was dependent for sense. At the center of the world, of color, sound, sensation, touch, taste, movement, feeling, the shapes and forces of people and actions around me, I knew myself to be the agent of my world, my life, and the meanings that infuse both.

I was a child who never saw the universe as outside myself, but when I read Blake's line, "to see the universe in a grain of sand," I understood myself to be both that marvelous grain of sand and the speaker who made that image visible. Life's miseries dissipated into the sharp fertility of sense through my fixed idea that all I saw and felt would become words one day. The ambition for poetry, a belief in the vital connection between language and my specific local existence, was clearly irrational, even perhaps a symptom of small madness. By eleven I knew I wanted to be a poet, and nothing has changed that desire for me since.

My convent teachers had little directly to do with my emergent sense of self as a poet. After Sister Josie, every teacher-nun bore down on me with an attention as painful as the stinging red ants that overran Malacca. Their crushing devotion to my behavior, my misdeeds, and my psychology, as well as their occasional malevolence provided a counteruniverse for the diminishment of my family. Still, it was their domineering secretive discipline, together with the unspoken disintegration of my family, that brought me to rebellion and to literature.

# CHAPTER FIVE

# Dancing Girl Scholar

M y brothers and Daryl, their schoolmate, were chasing each other on the second-floor balcony. A small but tough five-year-old, I chased them even as they ignored me. Suddenly Daryl ran after me. Delighted with fear, I ran into the room where he caught me. We tumbled onto the floor. For a moment his muscular body squirmed on top of my back as he pinned me down. A new sensation tickled between my legs; I didn't push him away. He was up and out on the balcony in a minute, but I never forgot that sharp pang of physical pleasure associated with a male body.

Some hot afternoons I lay on the cool wood floor of the bedroom and stroked my legs, enjoying the feel of fingers on my skin, enjoying the feel of skin on my fingers. This autoeroticism was bound up with the long boredom of being alone after my brothers had successfully shaken me off to maraud through the streets. But Feng, Mother's cousin who had just come to stay with us, was too old to play in the streets. As I lay vaguely discontented and concentrating on the tactile zones of my senses, a warm body pressed on mine.

Disgust and revulsion stir my memories now. I see the child safe and alone in an autoerotic half-sleep, then a sudden weight of an older body, a wet kiss on the lips. I did not open my eyes or cry out. As quickly as that physical intrusion had made itself felt, I understood that I should continue to lie still, eyes closed, that pretended sleep was necessary to ward off a dangerous knowledge I was not supposed to have. An unfamiliar mixture of sensations swarmed within me. As long as I was asleep, I did not know what was happening. As long as I did not know what was happening, it was not happening. But of course I felt that body as it shifted and rubbed against me. I willed myself not to feel, for then I would have to wake up. But I felt I don't know what. It was secret, not to be shared even with the person who was doing this to me. I could not say it, think it. The kiss was unpleasant, but as that weight moved on me, an odd surge went through my body that was not unpleasurable. Later I saw Feng looking at me secretly, but I did not look back. It was important he receive no sign that I knew what he had done.

Another hot afternoon. I lay again on the cool floor, half-fearful of what would happen. I wished for that new physical sensation, and at the same time I was steeling myself to endure those horrible lips. I kept my eyes shut tight. This time I felt his breath on my face, the insistent flesh. But he must have heard somebody coming up the stairs, and the weight was removed hurriedly. I never attempted sleeping in the afternoons again. Even today, whenever I meet this cousin, I feel a looming void of contempt for him and for that little girl who could feel pleasure in his abuse.

I was afraid of the male body in a way that I wasn't afraid of mine. My body was not a secret to me, but my childhood sexual confusion led for a long time to resistance and shame about what it might become with a male. Father's and Peng's late-night murmurs, audible through their thin bedroom walls, became part of this shame.

During the weekends I sat listlessly by the doorstep, unwilling to play badminton or hide-and-seek outdoors with my brothers and unwilling to enter the house where Peng was cooking, washing, sewing, or talking with Father in their bedroom. Gloomily I suffered the tropical heat and retold the story of Snow White to myself. I was determined to cast Peng as the wicked stepmother with the poison apple and myself as the much hated stepdaughter. All her pillow-talk, I was convinced, were complaints to Father about my behavior, and explained Father's increasing aloofness and coldness.

One Saturday, steeped in self-pity, I saw Bak Lye walk down the lane with a bundle in his arms. Bak Lye was a vegetable trader, traveling by lorry to bring in fresh *bok choi,* long beans, cabbages, chilies, lady's fingers, and *brinjals* from the farms to the Malacca Central Market. A large, strong man with a missing eye lost in a fight, he was also gentle and sincerely attached to Father for saving him from deportation to China during the citizenship legalization movement. Years after his papers had been successfully filed, he continued to visit our home with gifts of cabbages and *bok choi.* That morning he brought a puppy he'd found wandering in the market.

Gone were my brooding fantasies of wicked stepmothers. I immediately claimed the puppy as mine. She was a dirty white mongrel, a no-breed, what Malaysians called a *pariah,* with small brown patches like muddy stains on her head and sides. She was smaller and skinnier than myself. I loved Pongo because she was so weak. She could hardly stand on her wobbly legs and she whimpered through the night. As soon as I believed Father and Peng were asleep, I sneaked out of my cot and carried her from the open-air interior yard into my bed. Each afternoon, instead of wandering through the Malacca streets, I hurried home to release her from a rope tied to a post in the front verandah. She was soft, warm, a trembling tiny body which I hugged to me the rest of the day. Unhousebroken, she left wet messes throughout the house, and I cheerfully mopped up after her.

A month or so later, arriving home from school, I did not see Pongo wagging her tail by the verandah. Second Brother came out of the house to say, "Pongo's lost." I burst into tears. Together we searched the wasteland behind our row of houses, dank and overgrown with bamboo and secondary vegetation, buzzing with mosquitoes. Right by the outhouses giant bluebottle flies carommed. We paced up and down the lane, calling and peering into the thick clumps of *lallang*. As the afternoon drew on I borrowed Peng's bicycle and rode with Second Brother Chien to the Central Market, the stalls all shut after the day's sales. Calling her name over and over again, we poked through the empty reed baskets and mounds of garbage before mournfully returning home.

Father was already home, and he and Peng were shouting at each other, so I took refuge in Mrs. Lee's house, two doors from ours. "Your mother threw the puppy into the Malacca River," she said. Unbelieving, I sat listening to Father and Peng quarrel. Through my silence I understood Peng loudly declaring in Hokkien that Father's attachment to me was unnatural. What does "unnatural" mean? As I cried, I watched plump good-natured Mrs. Lee look at me sympathetically. "This is what a wicked stepmother is," I thought, filling up with satisfied self-pity at the same time that the image of Pongo floating dead on the river ran through my mind. Loud crashes came from our home: Father was throwing dishes on the floor in his fury. I never wanted to go home.

A half-hour after the house grew quiet I did go home; I could not sit in Mrs. Lee's front room all night. Sullen, tears rising involuntarily, I sat wordlessly by myself in our front room. Father and Peng were in their bedroom. Through the walls I could hear them whispering in Hokkien. He had forgiven her.

Nothing was ever said about the incident. No one, not even Second Brother, talked about Pongo again. I wept at home for weeks, it seemed, almost continuously. I had not cried so much when Mother left. Years later, I could not recall the puppy without tears springing up. The unassuaged grief perhaps had as much to do with Father's betrayal as with the actual loss of a pup. After Peng's accusation I never felt the same way about Father. I was afraid of touching him. I could not bear to be near him. His body which I had loved as a child seemed possessed with a power of revulsion instead. He became a fully recognized sexual creature to me, and I abhorred his sexuality. The father I had trusted to bathe my young body was as lost to me as poor sick Pongo, who may have been tied in a sack and drowned in the Malacca River, or who may have been abandoned in the Central Market. Every time I passed by the market I looked for dirty white pariahs with brown spots.

Father's relationship with me grew more strained. When I needed money for school books or school trips, he asked me not to tell Peng about it. At home, he seldom spoke to me except on those occasions when he was driven to fury by some horrible thing I'd done. Then, as he beat me with the rattan or slapped me, he would complain that I was a bad girl, and more trouble than all my brothers put together.

Through this turmoil I persisted in believing that Father loved me. When I was thirteen he bought me a Raleigh bicycle which opened Malacca to me even more. Now I could bike miles up to Klebang or all the way to St. John's Fort and the far reaches of Bandar Hilir, places I had visited as a child when Father had his Morris Minor but which had remained inaccessible to a mere walker. Some afternoons after school, instead of returning home for lunch, I biked to the coffee shop where Father consulted with his clients. He worked on his Royal typewriter in the back room, and his clients bought drinks and food from the coffee shop, an ideal arrangement for everyone. The noodle-stall cook liked me, and each time I came by, Father bought a bowl of fat noodle soup for me which the cook lavished with slivers of chicken and roast pork and fishballs. Eating this delicious lunch in the coffee shop, I felt almost as if Father and I were alone in the world. He gave me his large happy-go-lucky grin and slipped me some coins, which we both knew I was not to tell Peng about. I could count on Father's affection, but only in secret.

During that year between twelve and thirteen, I found something else to make me happy. At a school concert I had been fired by a ballet performance, by the transformation of sloppy mass into lightness. Ethereal girls in tutus and delicate slippers glided effortlessly on stage. The droop of a neck and its long line with the trunk, arms arching like tender branches, and feet that jettison shapes: as I viewed these arabesques for the first time, I wanted to dance ballet more than anything in my life. Visiting Father in his coffee shop, I begged for ballet lessons, classes of one-hour weekly sessions that cost five dollars a month. "All right," he said, "just don't tell Peng about the money."

I borrowed the tunic—a sleeveless, square-cut white linen frock with a short gathered skirt—from a classmate, and asked Peng to make me a copy. It was for school, I lied. I wrote to Mother for a pair of ballet slippers, the first thing I had asked of her from Singapore. For almost two years these weekly classes were the center of my life. At night, while my brothers played Monopoly, I set out a kitchen chair and using its back as a barre did my pliés, jetés, and exercises.

Something about the discipline of the body enmeshed my imagination. The barre enacted an exercise of will over body which served as a physical meditation. I approached every class as if holding my breath to discover how much more I could will my legs and arms to pain and grace. The slightest fraction of an inch, the mere shift of the head, signified the difference between awkwardness and beauty. I was gripped by that difference and commanding my body to perform it.

My first ballet teacher was the wife of a planter. Mrs. Stead, it was rumored, had danced at the Sadler Wells. Her classes were held at the convent hall after regular school. Plainly dressed, stern, and reserved, she commanded our full attention at every meeting. She was a classicist who concentrated meticulously on barre work and a few exercises in improvisational dance movements. Each hour was a marvel of total control on her part. The hall held no mirrors to allow us to observe and correct our postures and movements; her eyes were the mirrors for the twenty girls in the Grade One class, catching our mistakes and reflecting an ideal of physical form. It seemed as if no degree of an out-turned ankle, half-inch push into a plié, or a slight diversion of a shoulder escaped her reproval. A newcomer, I did my barre exercises behind the best students, using their bodies and stretches as models.

When Mrs. Stead's husband was transferred, another teacher took her place, a redhead who was more interested in jazz dance. It was said that she had been a chorus girl in a cabaret somewhere in the West. Although determined to continue, I lost my pure pleasure in the discipline of the barre, for she paid little attention to our form. Without those authorizing mirrors of discipline, I could flop my knees and sit down into a plié, and it didn't matter. She set us skipping and swirling in gay gypsy dances. We were supposed to invent different combinations of jettés and pas-de-deux. When she left a few months later, Malacca was without a ballet teacher for a couple of years and that ended my ballet passion.

After Peng came to live with us, Father was pleased with me only when my report card indicated that I had come out first in the class. Like all English-language schools in Malaya, the convent ranked its pupils by exam performance. Of two hundred girls in Standard Five, the top fifty were grouped in Five A and had the best teachers, the second tier in Five B, and so forth. In this hierarchy, the lowest achieving girls in the A class were already judged as weak. At the end of the school year, an A class girl could be demoted to B class, or a B class girl could move up. Generally, however, pupils remained tracked at the same level. Father's joy came in my achieving first in class. Even if I had received seven out of eight possible A's, coming in second brought a frown, and it was unthinkable I should rank lower than second. When my report card showed me as first in class, the smile he gave was rare and uniquely mine. I longed desperately to make him happy with me, and I dreaded his disapproval.

Gradually, even as I began to find classes dreary, examinations became more and more important. In Mrs. Tan's Standard Five geography exam, I stared at the question, What is the name for large sand hills? I knew the answer, it was at the edge of my consciousness, but a sudden freeze had stalled all my resources. In my desk, however, I had a novel about a shipwreck in Tunisia, where the young heroine was kidnapped by her Tuareg knight. In that novel, I knew, the word for those sand hills had appeared. But I could not recall the word, although I knew the plot so well. Cautiously, I pulled the novel from the desk and turned its pages. But Mrs. Tan, with the peculiar alertness of the convent teachers to any form of cheating, reached for the novel from behind me.

Sleepless weeks followed when I worried about how to explain to Father the zero I had received for cheating in geography. I envisioned the mad red flash in his eye, the cane's swish, and particularly my grief at his disappointment. Worrying, I plotted a way to deceive Father. Going without food during recess, I saved enough money to buy another report card, as the grade books that tracked our triannual academic results were called. When Mrs. Tan gave me the little red booklet with its shameful zero, I carefully traced into the new report card every subject and numerical date in the old one. Then, copying Mrs. Tan's inscriptions, I added a four before the zero, giving myself a forty out of fifty. Fortunately, even with the zero for geography I was ranked second in the class, and did not have to lie about that.

Father signed my counterfeit with a frown because I had not been ranked first. Later that night I carefully traced his signature into the real report card and returned it to Mrs. Tan. I trusted my instincts that when Father signed the report card the next year, he would not recheck the past grades. Father, after all, lived only in the present. Regrets were unknown to him, and such a man would never turn back a page to read what was past. As for me, I kept the counterfeit tablet concealed among my books and papers, and it has followed me to the United States, a concrete sign of my precocious and desperate cunning in trading for my father's love.

Those anxious weeks showed me that cheating was not a successful way to achieve the results that would win me Father's love. Yet I could not study the way that my classmates did. The daily schoolwork was too dreadful, the store of library books too enticing, the noisy play of my brothers and their friends too distracting, and my misery with Peng too insistent. Instead, I developed a method of preparing for exams that saw me into the university.

While I did the minimum homework to avoid my teachers' ire, I took the time to collect diverse, curious materials on the class topics. Because there was no money for supplementary texts, study resources, exam guides, and other aids which my classmates depended on, I borrowed these books. Proudly I rationalized that no one would mind loaning her book for a short time; thus, it became a fixed point with me to borrow each book for just one night. Whenever I was permitted to borrow a text, I stayed up all night transcribing it into note form, and returned it promptly the next morning, confident that I had extracted from it every idea that was useful. I went through the shelves of libraries looking for sources on the Ottoman Empire, for example, or the Great Continental Rift Valley. Pieces of information surfaced everywhere, in newspapers, magazines, encyclopedias, and heavy tomes with titles like *The Decline and Fall of the Roman Empire, The Wonder That Was India,* and *Chinese Civilization.* At the end of the school year, I had gathered stacks of notes on each exam subject. By the time I was taking the O and A level exams, I had perfected this system of solitary study, which later threatened to harden into autodidacticism.

All this knowledge-gathering was interspersed through the years with the drift of pleasurable reading, late weekend dances, the delirium of motorbikes, and continuous poverty, the last of which gave particular practical urgency to my studies. By the time I was eleven, a dreadful sense of disaster would come over me a week before every examination period. I saw the cheapness of my home most keenly then: the vulgar linoleum that covered the living-room floor with square patterns and embossed floral swirls in each center, already ugly when new, now pitted and shredded so that its black tarry underside tracked across the gold and silver squares; the scuffed walls that hadn't been painted in years; the splintered unmatched chairs and stools wedged against the dining table, and the old kitchen cupboard blotched with peeling stain, stolid stuff that one had to squeeze through in order to get to the bathroom or the outhouse. I never saw these scruffs and scars except during the week before examinations. Then, as if the only thing between this poverty and myself was that A grade, I set myself to work to escape from my home with an intensity I have seldom felt later in life.

In the week before exams, each evening, after everyone had left the cramped kitchen, I spread my papers and books on the linoleum that covered the splintered wooden table. Beginning with the very first topic and reviewing all the lessons for the year, I organized the information I had gathered into patterns and arguments. Sometimes, if there was a lot of material, I worked right through the night to five or six in the morning, and then washed up for school.

A week's worth of all-night study was usually sufficient to earn me A's.

The truly brilliant students, it was rumored, were bad exam takers. Children of wealthy or professional parents, they were chauffeured to piano classes, sheltered, and so painfully shy that they could only peep from the fringes at our manic games and sparring. Teachers boasted of these students' sensitivity, but faced with the pressure of regurgitating information in the form of five essay responses per three hours to an unexpected battery of questions, they froze like mousedeer in the headlights of killing cars.

I could not understand their failure. My own necessity—to move out of the range of the grinding millstone of poverty—was like a miniaturized engine implanted in my body, that I was fearless in the face of exams. What I feared was poverty. Exams were a challenge I enjoyed, and that this challenge could lead me out of hunger, shame, ugliness, and deprivation was a wonderful mystery to me.

The national standard examinations were set by British teachers and professors and administered from Cambridge University. Even the University of Malaya exams, which were graded by local lecturers, were scrutinized by famous Oxford or Cambridge dons. The state apparatus that administered these examinations globally operated through the threat and process of mass extinction of subjects. With so many thousands seeking "distinctions," the British term for A grades, only a few could be admitted into the elite circle of the distinctive. Beginning with the Standard Six exam at age eleven, continuing with the Lower Certificate Exam at fourteen, proceeding to the Senior Cambridge Exam at age sixteen, and concluding with the Higher Senior Cambridge exam at eighteen, masses of schoolchildren in the British empire faced a uniform life story composed of acronyms—LCE, SCE, HSC—that would be comic in a Swiftian satire if it hadn't been so violently oppressive to our childhood.

One could easily read the damage of colonial education in the children, for failures dropped out of school at each gated moat. At eleven, some girls returned to the rubber estates to help their parents. Others left at fourteen to train as nurses' aides or to work as salesclerks. At sixteen and seventeen, many went to teachers' training colleges to staff the elementary schools. Many more married or stayed home waiting for marriage. From all the state schools, from the cohort of thousands living in Malacca who were six going on seven or already seven in the year 1951, only about sixty students remained from the years of exam slaughter to enter the Arts and Science Lower Sixth Form. And from that sixty, perhaps only fifteen entered the University of Malaya in 1964.

Unlike my classmates, I never thought of exams as mere regurgitation of information. I imagined a long table of examiners, neither men nor women, but all English, reading these hundreds of thousands of essays pouring in from the British Empire. It wouldn't matter to them which essay was written by a headmaster's son in Ireland, a washerwoman's daughter in Hong Kong, a goatherder's child from the Kenyan mountains, or a bankrupt petition writer's daughter in Malacca. These readers formed a formidable audience, for, reading as fast and tediously as they had to, only a different voice could reach them through those fortress walls of exam booklets.

I thought of that voice as the voice of the mind, but a distinct mind, one at ease with information but not burdened by it, a mind that worked with rules and patterns but that manipulated them playfully or deviously or adroitly rather than repeating them. It was a mind that collected and arranged. Sometimes the collection was impressive enough; sometimes the arrangement was surprising or fresh. Because the mind was full and confident, it could suggest that what it said was inadequate, that something else eluded it. The memorization of information was never mere data collection, as many of my classmates believed. The selection of "facts" to memorize was itself a painstaking, necessary, and formative preparation for the final task of analysis and presentation.

Entering the exam hall, my mind overflowed with dates, names, maps, diagrams, statistics, titles, quotations, citations, all those unarguable details, discreet pieces of knowledge that together construct academic facticity. Students had been known to copy these information tags onto their shirt cuffs or their palms, on tiny torn pieces of paper slipped into their socks. The hundreds of memorized items that zipped about in my head as the proctor placed the exam question sheet on my desk could not be put down on such imperfect receivers. From one or more nights of cramming I was confident that I held as much data as I would need for three hours of essay writing. What preoccupied me instead was how to shape my answers so that the long table of bored cynical superior readers would sit up a little straighter and say with a sigh, "Well, here's someone who's interesting."

Being interesting was the difficult part. These readers were not to be condescended to, like my neighbors who loved an easy laugh. I hoped that if I could write my essay as a singular subject, then my faceless nameless paper would rise to claim that it—I—signified. At the same time, every one of my classmates also wanted desperately to claim a subject status; and read individually, with care, their essays could be seen to speak eloquently. The misspellings, ungrammatical syntax, labored sentences, and dull prose testified not to a lack of schooling but to lives and experiences mismatched to the well-oiled machinery of the English-language essay. The irony was not that my companions were uninteresting or unlearned, but that what they learned was so far removed from their senses that the learning remained separate, unvivified, and undigested: many of them did regurgitate class notes, lectures, and globs of memorized passages for the exams, an undifferentiated vomit of words, dates, ideas, and scrambled facts.

As I grew older, the exams became more onerous, requiring more and more all-night study sessions. When I was fourteen, a classmate boasted of pills that her older brother took to keep him awake for cramming sessions and agreed to get me a supply. The bottle held a warning that the pills shouldn't be taken if one suffered from heart palpitations, goiter, and a host of other ailments. The medical name of the drug made no impression on me; only the claims that the drug led to alertness and energy. Later I knew that these were amphetamines that kept me buzzing from 10 P.M. to seven in the morning. I took these pills only for all-night study sessions for the major exams, and the one bottle lasted me until I entered the university. Then, in Kuala Lumpur, I entered a Chinese pharmacy with the mystery bottle in hand, and discovered that the pills, imported from a busy pharmaceutical trade with Thailand, were inexpensively available without a doctor's prescription.

Through these exam-haunted years, we frequently heard rumors of students dying of heart failure or "brain fever," but it did not occur to me that the amphetamines I swallowed were related to these fatalities. I finally understood how physically damaging my study habits were when, in my final year, in my push to be the first student to achieve a First Class in English in the university, I set out to study a full five weeks before the exams. Staying up with friends in the English seminar room from 8 P.M. to 7 A.M., like them, I took an amphetamine pill each night. After one grueling night of studying the Augustans and attempting to figure out how Jane Austen was and was not an Augustan, on my way back to the residence hall for breakfast, I fainted in the corridor. Summoned by my friends, Second Brother, then a tutor in history and no longer subjected to punitive exams, took me back to the hall on his Honda motorbike, lectured me on my health, forbade any more pills, and later brought bottles of essence of chicken to build up my strength. During those five weeks I had lost almost twenty pounds. I was never tempted to take amphetamines again, perhaps because that was the last British-style exam I had to sit for, perhaps because, coming to the United States two years later, I moved to an elite selection system that would never approach the colonial system for monstrous repressiveness.

Finals week itself was a blur of repetition: I wrote in cramped handwriting arguments that I had held with myself through those long sleepless nights—arguments on the nature of alienation for Malaysian writers; why Yeats revised certain poems and what the revisions signified for his opus;

what Pope's *Dunciad* had learned from Dryden; why Jane Austen should not be read as an Augustan.

What did all these arguments prove beyond getting me a First Class Honors? Thinking back through the cultural imperialism of British colonial education, I regret the loss of the potential Malaysian intellectual in that precocious child and young adult. Of all the essays I wrote through my years as a child and student in Malaysia, only that one question on the alienation of the Malaysian writer remains resonant, communally embedded, and historically useful. Everything else had been desiderata, lavishly, excessively non sequiturs.

My classmates were perhaps even more ground down than I. For ten or eleven months of the year, I wandered, strayed, malingered, daydreamed, read novels, danced, ran around, got into trouble, climbed trees, biked, followed boys furtively with my eyes, gossiped and screamed with my girlfriends. Others, the studious students—pale girls with watery spirits who stood helplessly on the sidelines while the game was played—stayed home after school. In a dim although overpowering way, we all understood our families' and communities' hopes. Thus those wretched grinds whose childhoods were lost to school texts; thus the amphetamines that my classmates and I surreptitiously took during the exam cramming period; thus the parents' unquestioning silence as their children studied all night, grew wan, lost weight, threw up, died of "brain fever," or hanged themselves. In my years maneuvering through the maze of exam requirements, despite the frequent incidents of mental breakdowns, heart failures, suicides, and other calamities due to exam stress, I never heard a complaint uttered against the educational system itself. The lost children and their bereaved parents entered a dimension of nonimagination. The hegemony of British colonial education was so total that even those who questioned it as advocates of Chinese-language and Malay-Islam-centered education were not heard by the general population.

The Malaysian Chinese adapted to colonial education with a ferocious ease that speaks for its historical affinity with the Imperial Examinations in China and for the community's ambition to self-rule. Rather than being money-grubbing sojourners with no attachment to the country to which they had immigrated, a stereotype that British administrators fostered about the Malaysian Chinese, these Malaysians invested their desire for country affiliation in their children's English education. From these cohorts were to come the teachers, nurses, doctors, dentists, court clerks, and officials who would assume the underlying governance of the country. Exam success was therefore not merely a matter of material and professional mobility. In a colonized setting it was one of the few routes to civic power that the British permitted. While one might not necessarily become rich through garnering

A's, one would be admitted higher and higher up the ascending spiral of elite training, into the outer reception room of administrative servitude. At the same time, the inevitable grind of the process usually resulted in obedient administrators, dogmatists of the objective and impersonal through whom the Colonial Office would speak transparently. Colonial education set out to produce not leaders but intermediaries, those strange people who are both good order-takers and good order-givers. It set out to teach assent, not dissidence. It would work well were everyone to agree on what laws and orders to submit to.

But Malaysia was never a homogenous society, and colonial education failed in preparing Malay Muslim royalty and peasants—the *rakyat*—Chinese miners and Confucianist urban tradespeople, Tamil Hindu plantation workers, Pakistani merchants, Eurasian Catholic fishermen and lower-level functionaries, and diverse people and occupations in between, for democratic self-governance. Or rather, the elite it trained was irrelevant to the new and contingent circumstances of independence, in which race, religion, language, and gender—four glaring sites totally ignored in British colonial education—shaped the emergence of the Malaysian nation-state.

Most of the time I was not a scholar but a willful child for whom rock-and-roll was an introduction to teenage sexuality. After the solipsistic body that ballet affirmed, I found a small pleasure in the church socials to which my Catholic neighbors brought me. There, on Saturday evenings, in the public room attached to Saint Peter's Church, boys and girls fox-trotted and quick-stepped to such lugubrious American music as "A Summer Place" and "Red Sails in the Sunset." Rosie, three years older than I, took me with her to these socials. I was a naive chaperone who, admiring the circle of her boyfriends, hardly understood the nuances of her flirtations. Sometimes, a beau waiting in line for Rosie would take pity on me and swing me onto the dance floor. But later that year, after I had seen Elvis Presley in the movie *Jailhouse Rock,* the fox trot was no longer a pleasure. I practiced jitter-bugging to my brothers' amusement, and was overcome with gratitude when Byron, a Eurasian acquaintance, taught me the simple two-step hip-swaying swing that is still popular today.

Rock-and-roll made public and almost respectable a kind of abandon forbidden to good Malaysian daughters. Westerners who cannot understand why rock-and-roll would have been banned in Maoist China have not lived in a non-Western body. While sex as intercourse may or may not be repressed in many Asian societies, the body itself, especially the female body, is socialized to be nonexpressive of its sexuality. In Malacca in the 1950s, this deliberate non-expressiveness, valued as "modesty" and inculcated through humiliation and familial and public shame, was so naturalized that minor transgressions like a short skirt or a glimpse of breasts could damage a girl's reputation. Even today, especially in Muslim-dominated Malaysia, the muscular male body may be revealed shirtless on the beach or on a construction site; tawny male legs may stride everywhere, clad in khaki school-shorts. But the woman covers herself and moves demurely, so that her body will not speak before the male voyeur.

At fourteen and fifteen, I moved easily from wearing my brothers' shorts and shirts—chiefly because I had so few clothes (Peng sewed about three skirt and blouse sets for me for Chinese New Year to last the year)—to the open physicality of rock-and-roll. For other Malaysians too, Elvis in a black-and-white striped prison uniform snaking down the jailhouse stairs was an instant icon, not to independence but to freedom. Independence, we British colonized subjects knew, meant responsibility; you had to be taught to be independent. Freedom, our bodies discovered, signified pleasure, a forgetting of social responsibility in the irruption of the sensuous to the surface. Of course there is something ludicrous about nice well-behaved Asian children suddenly twitching skinny hips and jiggling absent breasts. The percussive drums and orgasmic rocking and rolling, the suggestive lyrics and gestures of Bill Haley and His Comets, Chubby Checker, and similar American pop singers effected a visceral Westernization of Asia that years of reading Shakespeare's plays had not achieved.

Every cultural change is signified through and on the body. Involuntarily the body displays, like a multidimensional, multisensorial screen, the effects of complicated movements across the social keyboard. And, conversely, bodies are players, passionate amateurs, mobile, and nubile, and culture is the scene in which their continuous, promiscuous, nervous performances unfold. My Westernization took place in my body. As a young woman I wanted movement: the freedom of the traveler, the solipsism of the engine, the frenzy of speed, that single intensity inseparable from danger. I was drawn to motorbikes the way I was drawn to fast music. For a few months I went around with some young men, necessary accessories to those gleaming black and silver machines whose giant beetle-bodies lured me like pheromones.

Victor's Suzuki 250 was the leanest and newest. Settling into the passenger seat, I felt the engine kick off between my thighs. Its steady throb changed to a scream as Victor pumped the gas pedal. The air streamed past and, as Victor, the Suzuki, and I leaned into a turn, I whispered into Victor's ear, "Faster, faster!" The dark night rushed past, howling, and we were perfectly still, perfectly quiet, before the power of an enormous world speeding through space, with something very dark just below us, tracking us. Then we burst into noise, and

Victor throttled the engine, and we slowed down, stunned by the force of the wind and that sickening darkness that was just beginning to dissipate.

Night after night, I visited the street where the boys and their motorbikes congregated. Robert's Norton 500 was my favorite machine. Built like a patriarch, it was twice as fast as Victor's Japanese motorbike. It rode like a house, steady, heavy, and stable, its engine pounding in a low bass. In my memory, it sounds nothing so much as Sarastro invoking Isis and Osiris, rumbling, deep, wholly male and priestly. Mounted behind Robert, who was years older than Victor and not given to steep corner maneuvers, my teenage feet dangling many inches off the ground, I knew the Norton was the undisputed prince among the Hondas, Suzukis, and Vespas. But safe mature Robert would never race. I caressed the Norton's curved belly, admired its high handles, and laughed at Robert's caution.

Soon, even the Suzuki boys found me too wild. After a while they refused to race their motorbikes faster. Bored, I returned to rock-and-roll. At least there I could tell my body how fast to move.

# CHAPTER SIX

# Turning Woman

I learned how to be a woman from watching other girls. One afternoon, dark-skinned Rosie took me on a bus ride to visit her Malay friend, Ismail, in his bungalow at Klebang. A radio broadcaster, Ismail was a lean brown man with a smile that made his good looks even more seductive. They encouraged me to cross the road to where the warm placid water of the Straits of Malacca lapped gently over a shell-encrusted beach. Immersed in the wash of waves that lifted strands of palm fronds and sea-almond nuts to my feet, I picked handfuls of salt-bleached cowries until Rosie fetched me back to the house where Ismail was knotting a fresh sarong around his waist. "Aiii! My sarong got wet," he said to me, his eyes twinkling, and I was pleased I had managed to keep my shoes dry even as I treaded between the waves' rhythms.

As a child I had no clear models of womanhood. My stepmother was repugnant, while my missionary teachers represented themselves as unsexed humans: the very notion of a nun using a bathroom reduced schoolgirls to convulsive laughter. I outgrew Rosie and the boring dances organized by the Catholic parish in the airless anteroom. My Indian and Malay classmates matured early, and I anxiously, unavailingly compared their burgeoning breasts with my own flat chest. At thirteen, I picked up a rumor that older girls bled monthly, and that that blood was secretive, shameful, but also a matter of pride. Although no one explained why girls took pride in first menstruation, I took it to signal entry into a different society, out of ignorant childhood and into the world of powerful adults. I checked my body for these signs of passage—breasts and blood. Within my body I was a fully sexual human; my dreams and fantasies were often about or gave rise to erotic pleasure. But my body was late in maturing. I didn't menstruate until I was past fifteen and didn't receive my first kiss till my sixteenth birthday.

Together with most of my friends, I was convinced that becoming a woman signified losing my virginity. No one ever talked about this experience, and yet so much of what we said circled obsessively around it. Through the walls of our convent school and our homes, we absorbed the unspoken yet ubiquitous lesson that we should be virgins when we married. Virginity was the secure barrier between ourselves and prostitutes. Unmarried women lost their reputations when they lost their virginity, as if reputation and virginity meant the same thing. Or they received a reputation. It seemed that sexual notoriety was the only means by which a woman could become noteworthy in Malaccan society. Of course, without her reputation, or with such a reputation, a woman would never find a man to marry.

Despite the everyday presence of the nuns in our lives, I did not question that women should want boyfriends and marriage. Nor did I question the contradictions between my romantic fantasies and the ground-down realities of life in Malacca. The marriages my thirteen-year-old eye observed appeared sad, loveless, sordid, demeaning, or empty. My friends' parents were distant fathers and distracted or dull mothers. Susan's parents, despite four children, were publicly mocked as sexless: the mother was rail-thin and sharp-tongued, and the father with a bad heart was pallid, permanently bedridden, and terrified of his wife. Anna's Catholic parents lived apart most of the year: the father worked in a different town, and the mother was bent on getting her five daughters well married. My only paternal aunt, childless, kept house for her bullying mother-in-law in a moldering ancestral shop-home, while her husband lived with his second wife in a comfortable semi-detached bungalow in a new housing estate outside of town. My friend Biddy's mother, a second wife, waited for her husband to drive up from Singapore to spend the weekends in the neat airy home she maintained for him.

Married women were almost always home when I visited their daughters. I saw them cleaning the kitchens, reading magazines under the living-room ceiling fans, or waking up from naps. Even at an early age, despite my raggedy clothes and the constant hunger that dogged me then, I had felt no shred of envy for their comfortable furniture or their positions. Their reality was a glue into which they were stuck. Perversely I began to value my absence of social respectability, my home which was not a home, my family which was not a family. My parents' outrageous marital behavior left me unprotected and without social standing. As an outsider, I was not confined to an interior of domestic regulation. No mother lectured me on female morality. No aunts warned me of unfeminine ways.

Surrounded by my four brothers and their chums and my stepmother's three sons, I learned something about being a girl from boys. My brothers sneered whenever I cried. A girl was a crybaby. I learned to swallow hard and to blink off tears before they could well up and fall. Through the years I swallowed hundreds of large hot lumps composed of rage, hate, self-pity, or plain physical hurt, while my chest constricted with something withheld, pushed in, that I associated with being a girl. When I came home with A's on my report card, my brothers mocked me, "Boys can see better than they can think!"

A serious thirteen-year-old, I stood before the small discolored mirror and worried about their meaning. I looked at the inflamed acne on my unwashed face. Angry at I didn't know what, I seized the postules and squeezed them. The pain satisfied me for that brief moment, but I felt worse when the acne appeared even more swollen.

The next day I begged Father for some money. With my head buzzing, I walked toward the Central Market, down the busy side street that smelled of fresh roasted Javanese coffee. Cheap clothes hung from poles in the stalls that crammed the five-foot way. Thin made-in-China towels flapped in the afternoon breeze beside flowered cotton and nylon panties, and blossoms of brassieres sprouted beside them, rubber cups dangling like swollen fruit. I bought the smallest, the size 32A.

Once home, I took the precious bra out of its newspaper wrapping and tried it on. The cups rose volcano-shaped from my chest. My nipples took hardly any space in the seeming cavernous vacuums. I tore up the newspaper and wadded the pieces in the cups. The rubber surfaces pushed in firmly like responsive flesh.

I wore the bra all week to school, but no one noticed I was different. When I finally washed it and hung it to dry in the open-air bath area, my brothers found it and fingered it, laughing and hooting. I never wore it again. My brothers' contempt crawled on my chest each time I considered padding my body to look like a woman.

At fifteen I met a pair of sisters whose reputations as run-around girls were so notorious that my oldest brother, usually taciturn, called me aside: "I don't want you to run around with Mandy and her sister," Beng glowered at me. "They're bad girls and you'll get into trouble with them."

But that was exactly what I wanted. Aside from the daily grind of school and the annual pressure of examinations, Malaccan life was a stagnant round of sweaty afternoons and lingering steamy evenings followed by long dull nights. I looked at each sunset with disappointment. The sulfurous orange and purple fires that burned the tropical days away were like death by drowning in *gula malacca*, that brown coconut syrup that enterprising Chinese neighbors down the lane stirred in four-foot wide vats and poured into recycled condensed milk cans for sale in the local market. Every day biking home from school I passed the steaming vats and the pallets of cooling cans.

"Sleepy Hollow," Miss Lee, the Fourth Form English teacher, called the town scornfully. She was newly graduated from the University of Malaya and noted for her shades of lipstick and the ruffled petticoats that kept her skirts permanently afloat around her skinny legs. Her dissatisfaction with finding herself in Malacca was audible as she rustled by the school corridors. But Miss Lee was not available to me as a model.

Instead, Kim, a year older than I, and her younger sister, Mandy, became my co-harridans. They were singing sisters who imitated the Everly Brothers in the talent contests organized by the radio station, and their American-style behavior attracted a host of teenage boys, chiefly Eurasian. They were fast in a slow town: they stayed out late, danced close, dressed in tight clothes, and didn't mind what people said. Kim was the sister I had always wanted. She laughed easily and shared her clothes and make-up with me. Mandy was the sister I would never want. She did figure-shaping exercises every morning, and her knitted jerseys and jeans fitted her burgeoning breasts and hips like an advertisement. She kept her hair silken-shampooed and Nancy Kwan-long and tossed the mane freely as she talked. She had a habit of opening her lips as she listened and sticking the tip of her tongue out mischievously. Kim and I suspected that all the boys desired Mandy, not us, but that didn't prevent us from having a good time. Mere excitement was what I craved, for I would not have known then what to do with a "boyfriend."

A few months after we met, the boys we knew drove me in a borrowed car on Chinese New Year's Day to the sisters' home, a series of small rooms next to a commercial garage. I climbed out of the car, happy in my Chinese New Year finery, and ran towards the door hung with traditional red cloth, when Mandy rushed out.

"How dare you steal my boyfriends!" she flamed at me.

Kim came out with apologies, but with Mandy pouting indoors, the boys drove me back home. I spent the rest of the day alone, cracking melon seeds, acutely conscious that somewhere in Malacca, Mandy and Kim were partying with Angus, Junior, Jimmy, Larry, and Donald.

Mandy was usually occupied with one boyfriend or another. I learned to stay out of her way, and spent most of my time with Kim. Unmoored to men, Kim and I shared a different sense of adventure. Often in the company of boys, we went biking to Muar and camping by the Tanjong Bidarah beach. We were both crazy about rock-and-roll and found different groups of boys to go dancing with, none of whom we considered "boyfriends" in the way the word was used in Malacca with its particularly salacious association.

Father insisted I come home before midnight; I fancied myself Cinderella sneaking home before the carriage changed into a rotten pumpkin. When he limited me to Saturday night dances, I told him that I had debating-team practice on Friday nights. At Kim's home I changed into a borrowed dress, then went off with the boys to dance all evening in the one Malacca nightclub by the beach. Before midnight, I retreated to the ladies' room, fished my school uniform from the shopping bag, and changed out of Kim's dress. The boys drove me home and dropped me a few houses before my door, in case Father was up. But he never questioned me about the debating team nights. The blue convent uniform was sufficient proof of innocence.

The Christmas before I turned sixteen, Jimmy, one of the sisters' admirers, invited us to his home, a small concrete house in a housing tract a little out of town, to meet his cousin Dan who was visiting from Singapore. Dan bought beer, and as I drank my second glass, he kissed me behind the bathroom door. In the fuzzy lightheaded whirl of my first taste of alcohol, Jimmy's cramped living room lost its seedy working-class sadness. And while Dan's acne-cratered face didn't transform itself into the smooth complexion of an irresistible prince, I could and did close my eyes and give myself up to the new queasy sensation of a large fleshy tongue probing my teeth and mouth.

It was my first kiss, and that was all I could think of when Larry, whose relatives were away for the holiday, invited us the next day to his home, an impressive bungalow set within its own garden. Larry brought out bottles of whiskey, vodka, and gin. I would turn sixteen after midnight, and Dan sang "Sixteen Candles" although there were no cake and candles. Kim went with Donald into the outer dark of the garden, Mandy vanished into a bedroom with Junior, and I sat out by the dry drain at the back of the house, slapping at large mosquitoes as they settled on my sweaty arms and legs and exchanging long kisses with Dan. It was thoroughly boring and after an hour or so we returned to the living room where Angus, Jimmy, and Larry were listening to records. Tall skinny Angus with his long thin face was drooping over Mandy's rejection. He held my hand as I listened sympathetically. "You're a good girl," he sighed. "I wished it was you I was crazy over."

Somehow I believed him. Dan was a child of a longshoreman of the Singapore Keppel Harbor; his ungrammatical Americanisms appeared gross against Angus's sensitive St. Joseph-educated confidences. My lips and tongue felt assaulted, blistered, after being with Dan. Angus's arm around my shoulder was reassuringly gentle, and I began my sixteenth year thinking of Angus as my very first "boyfriend."

Despite his declaration of affection, Angus met me only twice, briefly, after my sixteenth birthday. On the last occasion, he waited for me to get out of school, and over a glass of ice-cold coffee achingly sweetened with Milk Maid condensed milk, warned solemnly, "You shouldn't spend time with Kim and Mandy. They're bad girls, and you'll lose your reputation with them." I sipped the caramel-colored coffee and stared at his handsome head, dazed that he wanted me. Under the whir of the fly-specked ceiling fan in the tiny coffee shop, the air between us felt as thick as the liquid I was sucking in. I couldn't speak, and as he walked away, I was aware only of a sense of elasticity that seemed to stretch in the distance between our bodies.

Back home I wrote pages in a journal rhapsodizing his finely etched jawbone and thick eyelashes, the curious Adam's apple that bobbed up and down his skinny neck each time he spoke. My first sexual love was experienced alone, in the lush descriptions of his body I scribbled each afternoon at home after school.

But barely two weeks later, Mandy dropped Junior. Mysteriously, with nothing said to me, she and Angus became a serious couple. The Friday night I saw them disappear into the dark Malacca streets together I felt my chest close up as with the phlegm of a high fever. The next morning, I stayed home re-reading my pitiful love journal and tearing the pages into shreds. Then ritualistically I took the thick fragments outdoors and put a match to them. Mandy dropped out of sight, ensconced in Angus's home. Artistic and dreamy, Kim did not continue after Fifth Form but went to Kuala Lumpur to look for a job. For months I stayed home close to tears. Ironically, when Father noticed my sadness, he suggested that he had been wrong and that I could stay out late more often if I wished.

As a senior student at the Convent of the Holy Infant Jesus, I had been elected a prefect, an honorary position derived from British public school traditions, which entailed helping to maintain discipline in the school. It was rumored that I had received the most votes, which should have resulted in my election as Head Prefect, but that the nuns were divided on whether I should even be appointed a prefect. It would be easy for me to keep up the expected good behavior, I thought; that year, grieving over Angus's unexplained rejection and preparing for the important Senior Cambridge Exams, I planned to avoid boys and to stay home reading.

I was extraordinarily proud of the school honor, conscious as I was of my many past misdemeanors which included untidiness, truancy, smoking cigarettes, rock-and-rolling, motorbike racing, and other evils hidden from the nuns. The yellow tie that prefects wore came to symbolize for me my new social respectability. It was the only item of clothing I kept clean and ironed at all times, and I took numerous lessons from my brothers in tying it properly. Wearing it, I felt distinguished from my female classmates, as if I were putting on the power of a boy.

Toward the end of the year, my cousin, Heng Soon, invited me to join a group of his friends for a party at the nightclub on the beach to celebrate his departure for Australia. He was a serious science student two years my senior, and he had received a Colombo Plan scholarship to study at the University of Adelaide. A convert to the Bahá'í faith, he had never been to a dance, and had invited me as a safe partner.

The Saturday night was a usual dark sultry evening, and the open-air nightclub, an ugly concrete floor in daylight, was suffused with vague colors from a few strings of fairy lights. The soft woosh of waves curling up by the sea wall played in syncopation with the local band's plodding versions of the Hawaiian Wedding Song and Pat Boone's "April Love" as couples jogged in clumsy two-step together. We drank Coca-Cola and orange squash and danced all evening. As Heng Soon talked excitedly about his departure, I felt a stab of regret that I might never see him again and planted a good-bye kiss on his cheek. The evening was more sedate than even those church socials held in the small shadow of St. Peter's steeple.

But next Monday afternoon, I was told that Mother Superior wanted to see me. Wondering what I could possibly have done wrong, I went up to her as she waited by an isolated spot on the stairs.

Fair and short, seeming to shine in her creamy robes and clean glinting glasses, she stood very straight and said, "You were seen kissing a boy at a nightclub on Saturday."

A current of fear went through me.

Sister Peter, who had accompanied me, was silent.

"The question is whether to expel you from the school."

Suddenly I understood the seriousness of her statement. It was only a month to the final examinations. Expelled, I would not be able to sit for the exams; my life as a student would effectively be over. "But that was my cousin I was with. We were celebrating his leaving for Australia, and I only kissed him on the cheek!"

Mother Superior ignored my explanation. Instead she listened to Sister Peter who spoke with finality, her face sad rather than stern, "Shirley has many gifts, but she is emotionally immature." It did not occur to me to speak again. I felt only a crushing pressure, as if a pattern were being repeated from which there was no escaping. I felt the inevitability of Mother Superior and Sister Peter's judgments. They never seemed more white to me than at that moment, in their starched cream gowns and bright metallic glasses, and I was deeply conscious of my own brown-edged socks, my dark sallow skin, and flyaway black hair. There was no one to appeal to above them, and they were already gazing at each other in perfect understanding, like two avenging angels with arms locked above my head.

"We've decided not to expel you. But you are stripped of your prefectship, and you will have to stay behind every afternoon in the classroom till five, until the year is over." Mother Superior reached over and unknotted the yellow tie that identified me as a prefect.

A tide of nausea rose from my stomach. I left them standing there, as I rushed off to the toilets and stood heaving over the soiled tin sink. The toilets, always wet, cluttered with litter and smelling of urine, were not a place for refuge.

Reluctantly I returned to face Mother Superior and Sister Peter, my head seeming to balloon with the unreality of the scene. I knew they were wrong, as they had always been wrong about me, and I knew I could do nothing to persuade them otherwise. I felt myself move inwards, as when my father beat me for the first time. As the inner room thickened, inside it I watched the melodrama Mother Superior and Sister Peter performed as they waited on the stairs: I saw that they were foolish, but also that they were frighteningly out of scale.

I hung my head as they spoke words I didn't hear. Instead, I wondered what to tell Father, how to face my classmates, and what shame my brothers would feel because of me.

I felt shame at the thought that I would be riding my bicycle each morning and afternoon shorn of the yellow tie, its absence a notorious statement of my disgrace made visible to the judgment of the small town community. At the same time I felt anger—again!—at the nuns' injustice. I would never become like them or like my petty, finger-pointing, gossiping Malacca acquaintances. My loyalty would be to the small, the lowly, the bullied, the rebellious, the poor. But my anger was mixed with despair: it would take years before I could begin to shake off this overpowering passivity before the experience of injustice, to believe that one could struggle for a countersociety where justice might overrule the tyranny of judges.

For weeks, every afternoon from 2 to 5 P.M., I stayed behind alone in the sun-baked concrete classroom on the second floor. The building stood across the road from the refectory, and no one ever came by to check on my penance; still, I was too afraid of expulsion to leave. I read my schoolbooks, but they were straw to the mind. Chiefly I looked out of the door to the cloudless blazing sky outside and checked my solitude as if it were a temperature. Most afternoons were quiet and still; sometimes, from the playing field below I heard girls at extramural sports. By the time I walked down the stairs to the bicycle rack, no one was in sight. Yet I was not unhappy, for I knew I had only to endure until the exams at the end of the year, after which I would be sprung from the stone and blue confinements of the classroom and glaring sky outside the doorway.

I never knew who told Father about Mother Superior's punishment. By then, my eldest brother had left Malacca for a two-year agricultural college where he trained as a laboratory technician for the Government Fisheries Institute. Perhaps another of my brothers reported it, or more probably a neighbor was glad to bring him the bad news.

He did not ask me what had happened but as he came through the door late one evening he began to shout, "You've disgraced me!" His rage was terrifying, but I did not shrink as he slapped me repeatedly. I believed I deserved his beating. As he yelled at me, bubbles of spit frothed from his mouth. "Get out of my house!" he screamed. "Don't ever come back. I don't want you here." My brothers looked desperately at me; they dared not intervene.

I was glad it was dark outside so the neighbors peering from their windows could not see me as I walked down the red laterite lane: I would not stand where anyone could see me, but there was nowhere to go. As I walked, the night around me felt as huge as my pride. There was no one to turn to, for I could not look for Mother nor for any other relative. Yet I would not cry, although I allowed myself to feel the desolation of my situation.

I went up the adjacent lane, towards a row of respectable bungalows in which one of Father's mah-jongg companions lived, and stood in the shadow of his garden, plucking at the sharp leaves of the ixora bush. I stood so long that my legs ached. Stubbornly I turned over the possibility that Father had thrown me out of the house for good. I was not afraid, only lonely. But the loneliness was not new; it was strong, brooding, embracing. I felt like a ruminative animal, emptied of fear or sorrow or pain, and conscious only of the increasingly cold air and the silent darkness.

Second Brother found me later. "Baba says you can come home now."

Silently I walked behind him. Everyone was already in bed by the time I slipped into the house, including Father.

No one in the family ever asked me why I had been stripped of the prefectship. As for Father, it was as if this last disgrace had beaten him, and he never raised his hand against me again.

When the Fifth Form examinations were over and I was admitted to the coeducational Malacca High School at seventeen, my exhilaration, which has remained with me over the years, was akin to a prisoner's incredulous relief at escaping with her life. The morning I returned to the convent school to pick up my grades, Mother Superior came up to me, dazzling in her unspotted cream robes. Her glasses glinting nastily, she said, "You don't deserve those grades," to which I murmured, "No, Mother Superior." I never visited the school again.

My brothers and their friends had attended Malacca High School, an elite British-style all-boys' school that took on girls at the Sixth Form level. Beginning Sixth Form in the Malacca High School, I gradually picked up earlier friendships formed at the convent school. Classes became hugely enjoyable for all of us, for the first time in the company of the other sex. Released from the nuns' good-girls' regulations, I was comfortable with the masculine behavior that pervaded the high school, drawn from notions of the good sport, the jape, and the wit that were current in British popular literature. Second Brother had resigned himself to my reputation as a madcap which preceded my entrance to the high school, but certain moments revealed the fractures unspoken in my usual comic surface.

I was openly contemptuous of classmates who dressed up and flirted with the boys. Ostentatiously feminine, Nan was a favorite opponent. We argued incessantly. Unthreatened and with good humor, she would rebut my untidy personage with a swing of her hips. Mandy had also entered Sixth Form with me, but we hardly spoke to each other. Although she had long ago dropped Angus for another man, our earlier intimacies had vanished.

One Friday afternoon, returning papers for Mr. Moe, our history teacher, I made a comic comment on Nan's make-up.

"Don't you dare say that about Nan!" Mandy flashed from her seat by the windows. "I dare you to repeat that!"

Everyone looked up as surprised as myself, Mandy not being Nan's particular friend. Her hot challenge frightened me, but a stubbornness against humiliation asserted itself. As I repeated whatever unmemorable remark I had made, she hurled herself at me.

Mr. Moe, a small mild man, danced up and down the front of the class. "Babies, babies," he cried out, "don't fight!"

I would not give Mandy the satisfaction of a fight. With the entire class watching, I packed my books, left the class, and went home in a fury, wondering what it was now that had set her off against me.

That Saturday she came to the house with a bunch of yellow chrysanthemums. "I'm sorry," she said, giving me a hug. "I was angry because you had won the *Herald Tribune* essay contest. You know I have always wanted to go to the United States. And you told everybody you entered the contest just so you could get to Kuala Lumpur. I would have paid for you to go to Kuala Lumpur. Why should you have stopped me from winning if you didn't want to go to America anyway?"

I was too surprised to tell her that her essay might not have been the state prize-winner, even if I hadn't submitted an essay for the competition. Nor was it certain that I would be selected as the United Nations youth representative. In fact, when the state essay winners were interviewed in Kuala Lumpur, I was placed as the alternate, the judges declaring that a male should represent the country in the United Nations youth gathering in New York.

It is too easy to cast Kim and Mandy in the good sister/bad sister dichotomy; jealousy between women is a dynamic for which there is not yet an iconic representation, in the way that the figures of Oedipus, Lear, or Othello clarify specific complexes. While some sisters admit to rivalry, female competition is usually ignored or evaded. Mandy's adolescent slaps that set my ears buzzing were not as dangerous as knives and guns but no less violent in intention. Indeed, its rancor, coming from a woman, appeared to me more sharply deviant and terrifying.

For years I continued to believe that there was a kind of woman I wanted to be. But not my absent mother or silent stepmother, not the punitive nuns or my friends' sad mothers, nor the rubber woman my brothers laughed hysterically at, not jealous Mandy or acquiescent Kim. The problem that confused me for years, until the years themselves shaped their own ironic answer, was what to do with my life as a woman: not simply, what kind of work I wanted, but how to grow up as a woman. That problem kept bringing together what are usually mandated as separate—sexuality and career, emotion and intellect, the personal and the professional.

Father had been so harsh about Mother that I had stopped thinking of her as someone I could ever possibly meet, even though I had never stopped longing for her. One hot miserable evening, after Father had scolded me for something Peng had complained about, I stood in the dark behind the door of the back room, holding back the furious tears. "Mother," I said aloud, for the first time since she had left, "Mother." If Mother were with me, I thought, I would not be so angry and sad. The darkness hid my hatred for Peng, and it promised solace and love from my missing mother.

When I was seventeen, after the Fifth Form examinations, Father inexplicably said that I could visit her in Singapore for a week. On this first visit, I took the bus with Kim. Although I wasn't sure what Mother looked like or even that she would welcome me, I was certain that she was better than Peng. I sat through the eight hours on the bus with a mixture of intense longing for what I had promised myself Mother would bring to my life, and fear that she would not want me. Bringing Kim along was my defense against disappointment.

Mother met us at the bus station at Bras Basah, appearing anxious, proud, happy, and very pleased that I was there. We stayed only four days, all of us sleeping in a room she was sharing with Auntie Amy and Amy's little girl, Elizabeth. The room was in an apartment building of single-room residences, with all the tenants sharing a common kitchen and bathroom on each floor, but the crowded conditions were alleviated by tidiness and polite distance. We slept on mats that we rolled off the floor each morning, and our visit had the air of a cheerful camp-out. Mother took us out each morning and evening to eat some delicacy at the roadside stands that lined the open-air market behind the building—barbecued duck, fried *mee hoon,* Indian curry, and all kinds of sweetened and chilled concoctions.

Three-year-old Elizabeth was a fair, pretty child, whose father was a mysterious figure—a sailor or salesman, some indeterminate traveler who came by to stay with them whenever his business brought him to Singapore. Only his race and ethnicity were fixed: he was a Scotsman. Auntie Amy called him Mac, so I was to think of him as Uncle Mac. In the cluttered room that Mother shared with them he had left behind Raymond Chandler paperbacks and Penguin copies of Bloomsbury writers. Imagining Uncle Mac as a disgraced colonialist still savoring the rarefied delights of his intellectual heritage in the tropical slums of Singapore, I didn't ask why he wasn't there with them and why Elizabeth and Auntie Amy were living in poverty.

Mother did not go to work on the first day of my visit. Instead, she took me to meet her fellow salesclerks in Robinson's and to her sisters' and brothers' homes. I was shown off to Auntie Goh, Uncle Charlie, Uncles Ling and Mun, all grown, married, with children of various ages, aunts and uncles whom I remembered as bedraggled unhappy children from my own childhood. Mother beamed as if I were a prized reference to her character. Affable, with the reflexive acceptance of family displayed by most Asians, my long-missing relatives poured orange crush, looked me up and down, and talked as superior city folk about what I could look forward to in Singapore: the department stores, the night markets, the car park food stalls, Marine Parade, Elizabeth Walk, and the many new delights that awaited an *ulu,* a rustic like me.

Mother was determined to make me over into a city sophisticate. She gave me an expensive gold-inlaid compact, lipstick, perfume, and a Swiss wristwatch with changeable straps. At night, after she came home from work she took us to People's Park, city blocks of closely packed stalls selling cheap shoes, blouses, fabrics, pajamas, brassieres, panties, dried packaged fruit, Chinese pastries and barbecued meats, and heaps of *durians,* litchis, *rambutans,* and *dukus* which were then in season. As we trotted on dizzily winding narrow paths between the stalls and their goods, draped and hanging from bamboo poles, garishly lit by giant fluorescent rods and kerosene lamps, she gave me dollar notes to buy strapless push-up bras, five-inch high heels, see-through blouses, thick brass-studded belts, and skintight ski pants. I was giddy among the noisy pushing crowds, the scents of fried dough and murky perfumes, and the city excitement. Everything I bought transformed me, no longer that wretched thirteen-year-old with torn newspapers in her brassiere. So equipped, I felt certain my sexual inadequacy would be banished. On our last day in Singapore, Kim and I visited Dan at his cramped home in the Keppel shipyard compound. From my newly bedecked position, he appeared awkward, merely an acned teenager with no money. We didn't stay long and spent the last evening by ourselves shopping at Change Alley.

This first introduction to Mother and her world made me long to visit her again. Returning to Malacca with more clothes than were in the *almeira*, I would take out the high heels, the belts, the compact, and recall the happy evenings shopping with Mother.

During the next long school holidays early in 1963, a year older and with such good exam results that I was confident I would win a scholarship to the university, I took the hot tedious bus trip to Singapore alone. Father gave me twenty dollars, barely enough to pay for the return ticket. I hoped to stay with Mother for a month, but when she met me late that evening at the shabby bus terminal, she said I could stay with her for only a few days. She had permed her hair short, she wore thick pancake make-up with bright lipstick, and she was living in a different part of the city.

"I'm going to introduce you to my friend. He doesn't know I have any children, especially such grown children, so I want you to call me Auntie."

The man she was living with was a tall lean Chinese of middle age, with an angular face and menacing smile. He spoke no English and barely glanced at me when we met. A businessman of some kind, he was gone all day, and his acquaintances, other rough-looking Chinese men, came and went to and from the apartment during the evenings.

Unlike my first visit, Mother and I stayed inside the apartment all day and night, for he did not like her leaving the apartment unattended. As the apartment was a distance from the city center, I stayed in the darkened rooms with her, not daring to talk, even if I had wanted to, for fear of letting slip our relationship. Instead I watched her as unobtrusively as possible. The gay flirtatious laugh with which she greeted his return to the apartment sickened me. She cleaned, washed, cooked special dishes for him, massaged his back, chatted with his visitors, and was subdued only when she was alone with me, as if she feared being caught in our mutual deception. As she sat beside his reclining body, gently fanning the air above him with the palm-leaf fan, I silently repeated her request, "You must call me Auntie." The hope I had held against my stepmother all those years, that I would find my mother some day, slipped away that January. I had found a stranger instead, a woman called "Auntie."

One Saturday a year later, having won a federal scholarship to the university that covered tuition and living expenses, I visited my classmate, Biddy, in even higher spirits than usual. Biddy's father, a stern man old enough to have been her grandfather, was up from Singapore to spend the weekend with his second wife and family. He glowered at us as we chatted over the glossy pages of *Seventeen, Vogue,* and *Her World,* expensive women's magazines that Biddy, with more pocket money than most, subscribed to. I envied Biddy her glamour, copied straight from the advertisements, which a tomboy like me could barely comprehend.

"Let's take the car for a ride!" Biddy impulsively offered. She had just passed her driving test, and her father had given her a lumbering black Hudson. It was already past six and completely dark. As we sang our favorite pop songs, she drove around for a little before coming to a secluded area outside the town where the road wound past quiet fields dark with tall rice stalks. A short way in, she stopped the car and we sat talking about our plans for the university.

I leaned idly against the car door when unexpectedly Biddy shrieked, and I saw two masked faces by her window. Her door was wrenched open. Her mouth muffled by large hands, she was dragged out of the car. As she struggled I pushed the lock button on my door. Another masked figure dragged at my feet from the other side of the car, but leaning hard against my door, I jammed a foot against the car horn which blasted violently. I was more frightened for Biddy than for myself.

From my frantic position, I saw the bicycle headlight of a cyclist passing by. "Help, help!" I screamed. He didn't stop. Ringing his bicycle bell furiously, he passed in a flash. Then as if by miracle Biddy appeared at the door. The men had been scared away by the horn and the passing cyclist and had let her go. Terrified we locked the car doors and she drove home. As soon as she saw her father, she broke into hysterical sobs.

He glared even more fiercely at me. "Why did you bring her to the paddy fields?" he demanded.

"We wanted to talk and sing," I explained weakly.

"You could have talked and sung in the house." He spoke more gently to Biddy. "Where did this happen? I want you to take me there."

I was horrified at the thought of returning to those dark rice fields, and sat silent with fear and shame in the back seat as he drove quickly back to the paddy fields.

"Is this where it happened?" he wanted to know, and stopped the car by the same road. As he got out and walked about, peering around him at the dim lights of houses just off the road, I knew I would never possess his physical courage. I cowered as he lectured me on the way back. "I don't want you being a bad influence on my daughter." Biddy continued to cry hysterically as he scolded. "I'm taking you to a doctor to check if they have raped you."

"But they didn't have time, Apah!" she pleaded. "They ran away when they heard the bicycle bell and horn!"

Trembling, I got on my bicycle to ride the four miles from Biddy's house to mine. It was a tropical pitch dark. I biked as fast as I could, my heart pounding at the approach of every shadow. Then on the lane toward home, I slowed down and pretended calm. Unlike Biddy, I could not tell my father about what had happened. As soon as everyone was in bed I wept, shaking with terror. I covered my face with the pillow as I cried: I was afraid someone would hear me in the crowded house.

Believing that her parents would refuse me entry into their house, I did not visit Biddy again. Months later, at the university, she told me her father had taken her to a doctor the next morning to check that she was still a virgin. By then she was occupied with a steady boyfriend, and we spoke only in most casual terms.

The assault left me timid in a new irreversible way. The pleasure I felt in the world became haunted by uneasiness, and I could no longer hike on a quiet trail or consider attending an evening concert without fearing the isolation and the approaching dark. Confused I began to doubt my ability to live alone in the world.

At the same time, I couldn't wait to say good-bye to everything my life had held—my father, stepmother, brothers and stepbrothers, the shabby house more crowded each year, the teachers with their arbitrary tyranny, the town whose streets I knew by heart and which yielded only boredom, the small circle of friends whose same-same jokes wearied me. My weeks of cramming had resulted in Distinction in all parts of the Higher Certificate Examination, a rare achievement in the Arts stream, and I received sufficient awards and scholarships so that I would be financially independent of Father.

He was full of glee and smiles. "Well," he said, "I have to wait a few more years for you and Chien to begin earning any money." Second Brother Chien had received a scholarship the year before and was already in his first year at the university. "But don't forget, as soon as you get your first salary, you give me 50 percent of it."

"Fifty percent is a lot! How about one-third?" I thought about the cost of rent, clothes, and food. Fifty percent of seven hundred Malaysian dollars would barely cover it.

"But you know I have to wait for you to begin earning. You could start working now and I could have the money sooner."

"She isn't out of the house yet and already she is arguing with you about how much to give," Peng whispered that night, loud enough for me to hear.

I didn't care because I knew Father would have to accept my offer—I was no longer dependent on them. Still, I knew that Father had been counting on Chien and me to begin contributing to the family, and guilt nagged at me that night: Jen and Wun had a few more years of school ahead, and even after three boys it was clear that Peng would continue to have babies.

Years ago, when she was pregnant with her third, I asked Father, "Why don't you stop having children?"

They were sleeping with two babies in their bed, and with only one other small bedroom which I, as the only girl, occupied, my brothers were crammed in cots and on mats in the living room at night. Convent-restricted as I was, even I knew that there were ways not to have babies.

Embarrassed, Father laughed. "I'm trying to get a sister for you," he replied.

I felt infinitely older and wiser than he.

Sex was not forbidden, but it greatly complicated what we young women could plan of our lives. We were snared in the uncertainty of male desire on which our social status depended, and in the unexplored territory of our own sexuality. By seventeen we were joking nervously about losing our virginity. Those of us who went on to pre-university classes, with years of university education ahead of us, understood that, despite what our mothers and the convent teachers repeated, we would not remain virgins till our wedding night. Our repeated joshing over at least seven to eight years as to who would take away our virginity signaled our fears not so much about illicit sex as about what was to become of us. The older we grew, unmarried and career-bound, the clearer it became that sex was not forbidden. Too many people were doing it and getting caught, like Gina who became pregnant in her final year at the university and was married just before the final exams. Or doing it and not getting caught, like Tsing-Tsing whose faithful naval officer waited six years for her to complete university studies, only for her to run off with a visiting student from the United States.

Whatever the reason, until I was twenty-one I did not take men seriously, even though I knew enough to take sex seriously. I did not wish for marriage with anyone I met. Each man seemed desirable only for a limited time—an evening at the movies, a night of dancing, a drive to the beach. In those long nights of slow sticky fox trots and sweat-pouring rock-and-roll frenzies, my partners were simply bodies to dance with, and their sometimes unmistaken hardness as we pressed together to the oompah-pah of the local bands was a mere nuisance. We never went beyond a wet-lipped kiss—there never seemed enough private space for anything else in Malacca—and the most intense of my crushes for moony-eyed visiting university men never lasted more than a couple of weeks, by which time fantasy had changed to even more intense revulsion.

For a few months before I left Malacca for the university in Kuala Lumpur in May 1964, Ian took me to the movies on Saturday and for drives to the beach. A tall handsome Eurasian from Johore, Ian was older and more polished than Angus, Dan, or any of the other Eurasians I had met. He spoke wistfully about the university, but worked in the immigration office, filing forms and interviewing petitioners. Although Father was acquainted with him, Ian never came into the house to meet my family; he honked and waited in his car for me.

Ian kissed violently. I came home from an evening in his car at the Bidarah Beach with neck blisters I was careful to hide from my brothers and father. But his passion was a curiosity to me, for I felt no impulse to move beyond kisses, which seemed like the mere pressure of alien lips against each other. I thought my problem was fear of sex and that perhaps once no longer a virgin, I would be done with the awkward frigidity of adolescence.

One evening Ian took me home to his apartment and introduced me to his roommates, young Chinese men who examined me oddly as we were introduced, and left soon afterwards for dinner. We went to his bedroom. As he kissed me, I was neither afraid nor excited, but passively dissociated, as if I were sitting by the bed watching him, while my body felt like a bag of straw. Polite as ever, Ian stopped, rose from the bed, and we went to a movie for the rest of the evening. He didn't call again until the week I was leaving, and then it was to say good-bye. Excited as I was about leaving home and living in the university dormitories, I didn't miss him.

Once in Third College, the all-women dormitory of the university, I began to regret how badly I had treated him. A gathering of a few hundred women, most sharing rooms with strangers they disliked, Third College was no place for any kind of serious thought on a woman's life. The popular topic at lunch and dinner, which we ate en masse in the barracks-style dining hall, was men. Many already had steady boyfriends, and their days were divided between lectures, library study, and time with their boyfriends. After dinners of rice, beef liver curry, and wet spinach, women went off to their rooms to wait for their phones to ring, announcing their boyfriends' presence in the public lounge downstairs. Those without steady boyfriends were teased about contenders or went about shyly glancing at the male undergraduates who usually herded together for fraternal support. Trained to note-copying, memorization, and test-taking, they saw the university as a repetition of what had succeeded for them in the past, the last hurdle before admission into prized professions and marriage. The university years were to produce a husband as well as a degree, and either failure was supposed to be devastating.

I was amazed at how bored I was when I finally arrived at what I had worked so hard for: the interminable lectures outlined what the textbooks more efficiently and eloquently detailed, and the university lecturers stood more remote and alien from their students than even the convent nuns. The silly giggles and gossip of hundreds of women, focused on men, their self-consciousness about clothes, hair, and face, their calculated behavior, positioned between innocence and signals of availability: these had been features of my social world from when I turned thirteen. It was inconceivably deflating that these same features controlled university life seven years later. Although we attended hours of lectures and tutorials weekly, and daily studied the library reserve books, we never discussed ideas among ourselves—ideas were saved for papers and exams.

In contrast to the boredom of academic life, the vividness of the present pressed in from the university's pastoral isolation. With two guarded entries, the sprawling campus represented a protected playground. The entire country looked towards its only university as the hallowed site for training its elite. Every student was conscious of her envied place in a hierarchy, a hierarchy that, so recently achieved after Malaysia's independence from Britain just seven years earlier, was more fragile than we or our professors suspected.

A few older undergraduates, active in the Student Union, were rumored to have placed their futures at risk. As a loud-talking and noted debater, I had been invited to stand for elections in the Union, but Second Brother warned me against such distractions. "You be careful!" he said darkly. "So many smart students come to the university and get in the Union. They don't have time to study and flunk out or get a Third Class—the lowest pass possible for a degree!" I had a vision of these student leaders arguing among themselves late into the night at the Student Center and the meeting being broken up by the Internal Security Officers with arrest warrants, but I had no vision of the substance of their meetings.

Tied to the residence hall by the exigencies of my limited scholarship funds, I had simply moved to a larger confinement. Malacca, with all it offered of the familiar, suddenly appeared appealing, and when June, a Malacca student driving home for a weekend, offered me a ride, I went along. Alone in town, I called Ian who took me out for dinner and a movie. Back once more at the university, the conversation was all about the Freshie Ball, the annual dance to welcome the freshmen. The women who already had partners lined up were smugly victorious. Many kept silent, for they had no hope of attending, while a flurry of anxious flirtations netted partners for others. I saw it was ludicrous to assume Second Brother Chien would accompany me to the ball; he would be attending it with five of his friends to check out the women.

I began to see Ian through a sentimental haze and invited him up to the university. Noticeably handsome, more graceful than the undergraduates, he wheeled me around the open-air concourse, transformed with fairy lights, buntings, and balloons into a juvenile fantasy ballroom. I wore an expensive tight *cheongsam* that Mother had had tailored for me on my now-annual visit to Singapore, and I gathered numerous envious glances as so many bouquets.

Under the strings of dim twinkling lights, embraced by a tall attentive man who waltzed me among other beautifully dressed young people, I was going through the motions of a fantasy; but my delight, like everything else about university life it seemed, was shallow.

I hated the dining-hall teasing about rich boyfriends with sports cars, the lounge evenings when pale men, newly showered, avoiding the avaricious stares of other College women, waited for the women they were calling on. Residence life was a marriage market, more respectable than prostitution, and the only alternative to this society was the mockery of the ugly unwanted woman. Ian with his gentlemanly pursuit of my body appeared from that distance refreshingly different from the voyeuristic boys who stood in the shadows of the library building each night watching the Third College women walk back to the dormitories.

In the middle of the second semester, I decided I would give up my virginity to Ian. Again I got a ride to Malacca from June. As her sporty car careened past rubber plantations, flashing past sunny village compounds bright with crimson hibiscus and slower Mercedes taxis loaded with passengers and goods, we giggled and gossiped. My excitement was nervous rather than sexual, but I was determined that the weekend would see the end of my fears and the beginning of a new maturity.

Ian sounded pleased when I called him, and again we ended up in his bedroom. Timidly, feeling curious and curiously removed from the scene, I allowed his hands to move over my body. Again he rose from the bed with a baffled and patient look. "Look," he said, "let's just go out for drinks."

He drove to a friend's house outside of Malacca and we sat on rattan couches drinking beer. For once appearing grim and angry, he drank two beers in quick succession, then decided to drive to town for food. The narrow country road was unlighted and winding. A car honked behind us, its headlights flashing as it screeched past. Ian pressed down on the accelerator, chased it briefly, and passed it. The two men laughed; it was a triumph for Ian.

But the headlights continued to flare behind us, and in a few minutes the car cut us on screeching wheels. Uneasily I watched Ian's hands wrench the wheel as he pressed on the gas. The Renault jumped forward, there was a squeal, and I lost consciousness.

It was freezing cold. I heard voices, then lost consciousness again. Later there were men and women, then much later I found myself in bed unable to move. I had been in a coma, no one told me for how long. I was aware that my left foot was bandaged and raised, and vaguely I heard the nurses talk about blood poisoning and gangrene. My head was swathed in bandages and a large plaster was taped to one cheek where apparently I had received a number of stitches. The car had spun out of control and wrapped itself around a telephone pole. Ian and his friend were unhurt, but I had been thrown out of the door, my body had scraped across the tarmac, and my back was lacerated with what the doctors said were the equivalent of third-degree burns.

Because of the concern about gangrene and the loss of my leg, I had to lie on my back with the leg raised, although this meant that the lacerations on my back could not heal. Every morning the nurses came by, peeled the bandages off my back, applied more antibiotic ointment, and pasted more bandages so I could lie on the bed. Each time I screamed throughout the hour it took them to delicately rip the cloth off the raw flesh to which it had melded. I screamed for Mother because I couldn't think of anyone else.

The first evening I regained conscious, my father and brothers hovered wordlessly by my bedside. When they left, Eldest Brother Beng lingered at the door. Scowling he said, "I told you never to go out with Eurasians!" He never came back to visit during the month I remained in the hospital. Nor did Father.

Peng rode on her bicycle every evening with a *chun* of food—liver for cleaning the blood, watercress soup for cooling the body, egg custard for easy digestion. She brought the same dinner every night, till I was hopelessly sickened by the meals and large salty tears slid into my mouth as I tried to eat.

Father got Mother's telephone number from Grandaunt and called her. During the second week after I had come out of the coma, Mother came in the afternoon with a transistor radio. We cried together as she sat on my bed.

"I asked a fortuneteller about you," she said. "The fortuneteller wanted to know the time of your birth. You will cross water, and your life will be better after this."

I was glad Mother had come all the way from Singapore to see me in the hospital; despite everything, I knew she loved me. She left after the second day, but I kept the small radio by my side day and night, its continuous murmuring music like a mechanical reproduction of her presence.

Later, however, I am not sure precisely when, the pleasure in her solitary visit became entangled with discomfort. I grew to resent not so much her absence as the gifts she gave me—the pearl ring which was stolen when I was unconscious, the jade pendants which I never wore, the platinum cross and chain that I eventually pawned and didn't reclaim, the gold-inlaid compact I gave away to Kim. I saw these presents as guilt-tainted, cold objects reminding me of her abandonment. Eventually I forgot that the transistor radio was her gift and have no memory of what happened to that once consoling object.

Ian came to visit me the first week. "You know you can sue my insurance for the accident," he had said with no particular emphasis. Father reminded me of this after the month in the hospital when I returned home to recuperate, but I believed a suit would mean criminal charges against Ian and refused to do so.

I moped around the house, unable to face returning to the university, and rejecting Ian's invitations to dinner and movies. The hair was gradually growing back in funny frizzy curls at the back of my head where the concussion had occurred. The scar on my cheek was beginning to fade, and gradually the large gash on my left foot began to heal. But the lacerations on my back itched and formed ugly red keloids which I checked every morning, weeping at the irrevocable damage to my body. I thought of suicide, and resolved to save the tranquilizers which I was sure the university doctor would prescribe for me. During that period I hardly spoke to anyone. Father and Peng left me to brood, and all my friends were at the university in Kuala Lumpur.

After two months, I received a letter from the university registrar assuring me that for medical reasons I was permitted to sit for the final first-year exams midway through the long vacation—the additional months would give me time to catch up with the missed lectures. I returned reluctantly to Third College for the last few weeks of the term. Against the averted stares of the residential women and the buzz of the men as I walked past them, I looked forward to the two months alone in Kuala Lumpur before the make-up exams. I found a room with a quiet Eurasian-Chinese couple from Malacca, made friends with Joseph who was also taking the make-up exams because colitis had prevented him from sitting for the regular exams, and slowly climbed out of my depression.

A devout Catholic, Joseph ferried me on his Honda moped to and from my rented room to the library, spoke admiringly of my intelligence—for my exam results had made me famous locally—and was more comfortable than my brothers. We were usually the only students in the university library, and when the library was closed we studied together in a classroom. His companionship was a wonderful tonic, but I recognized for the first time that I would never be able to feel sexual with a Chinese male because of the strong incest inhibitions that I had formed in my family. With eight brothers and troubled memories of Father, I could only feel familial about Chinese men: they drew me as strong companions and brothers or repelled me as tyrants or weaklings, but a bar was raised between my body and theirs beyond which I could not imagine. Joseph was charming but without sexual danger.

Instead I plotted to avenge myself on Ian. After the long tedious exams, I returned to Malacca and called Rajan, an officemate of Ian, to whom he had introduced me a few months ago. Ian had joked about Rajan's marital status; he had married young, to a Chinese girl whom he'd gotten pregnant, and was pining for the kind of license he fancied Ian enjoyed with free university women like me. Rajan had looked at me with lascivious envy and respect. I knew he would tell Ian everything about me.

Rajan was surprised when I called. "I'll be in Singapore this week visiting my mother," I told him. "Do you ever come to Singapore?"

"I can get there."

"Can you get a room there?"

"Are you sure?" he asked.

"It'll be my first time. You'll have to be careful."

"I'll take care of everything. I promise you, you will be fine with me."

I imagined the glisten in his eyes. He had stared at me all evening when we first met.

"Give me your mother's telephone number. I'll call you on Saturday."

Mother had separated from the mysterious Chinese lover and had moved in with Uncle Charlie and his family who had made the down payment on an apartment with a loan from her. She had the best room in the apartment which appeared newly middle-class after Auntie Amy's tenement room. In the evenings during my week's stay I waited on the tiny balcony, watching for her plump figure to get out of a taxi.

She never talked about her job the way she had talked about being a saleswoman at Robinson's. Each night she came home with her black handbag full of small change, and she kept two or three Horlick jars full of ten- and twenty-cent coins in her *almeira*. Exhausted she asked me to pound her shoulders and back. With her face washed and smoothed with cold cream she sat cross-legged by the balcony, dreamily fanning herself with the same straw fan she had waved at her lover just two years ago. She was no longer a nervous chatty woman. Instead she seemed to have aged in a sullen manner. Her lips pouting unconsciously, she stared for long minutes at me, as if I held a secret to her life. She was respectable in her brother's house even if whatever she did outside was unmentionable.

Like Mother, I kept my secret. On Saturday evening, I bathed carefully. Mother boiled hot water for my bath, but when the hot water ran out, I continued throwing the tap water over myself, dumbly lost in the cold fluid flow over my body. Alert to the texture and shape of my limbs and breasts and the smoothness of my skin, I was keenly ashamed of the ridged keloid roughness on my back. I sprinkled Mother's eau de cologne under my armpits and behind my ears, put on the Janzten shirt and dark green ski pants that Mother had just bought for me, and a pair of five-inch stiletto heels, and waited for Rajan. Mother peered over the balcony to spy on him as he parked his car below. In crisp white shirt and a tie, he shook Uncle's hand, and we left for the movies.

At a quiet residential lane away from the city center, we took the elevator up an apartment building, to where an old woman in a black *samfoo* was sitting outside a door. Silently she handed him a key. The apartment was clean, sparsely furnished, with no sign of domesticity, and in the bedroom the air conditioning was already humming. Using an elaborate system of pillows, Rajan tried not to crush me. Still, in the dim light, glimpsing his tense dark countenance, I was aware only of pain. His tenderness was almost clinical, my acquiescence sacrificial. I was grateful that he was helping me overcome the taboo of sex; finally, I thought, I could get on with finding a relationship with a man without the begrudgingness of the fearful virgin.

We didn't linger in the apartment. Rajan brought me back to Uncle's apartment well before the movies could have ended. "We decided to have a drink instead," I said in response to Mother's surprised inquiry. The pain of penetration remained with me for the next few days, but even in the skintight ski pants no one could tell that my body was no longer intact.

Shirley Lim, circa 1950.

The certificate Shirley received from the Royal Academy of Dancing upon passing her examination, 1957.

THE ROYAL ACADEMY
OF DANCING

BALLET IN EDUCATION
CHILDREN'S EXAMINATIONS

Family portrait, circa 1951. Shirley is seated in front at far right.

Shirley in Malacca, 1958.

Shirley and friends, Malacca Beach, 1959.

Class picture, Convent of the Holy Infant Jesus, 1959. Shirley is seated at bottom right.

Emak in Singapore, 1982.

Shirley with her husband, Charles, and son, Gershom, visiting her mother's grave in Singapore, 1985.

Shirley in her study in Katonah, New York, 1988.

Shirley with Gershom in Bangkok, 1995.

# PART THREE

# CHAPTER SEVEN

# Outside the Empire

For almost two decades, politicians had argued first for home rule, then for nationhood, and finally Tunku Abdul Rahman, a Malay prince, presided over the separation of the Federation of Malaya from the British empire. In 1957, when I was twelve, the Federation of Malaya received its independence—Merdeka—and joined the Commonwealth of Nations as its eleventh sovereign member-state. Throughout the peninsula thousands of people cheered, had dark thoughts, prepared their passports for departure, sighed, felt relief that they were finally able to protect their rights from alien newcomers, checked their identity cards and citizenship papers. Thousands others never knew it was happening, made love to someone of a different race, brought a pagan to mass, washed their feet at the water tank before entering the mosque for prayers of thanks, held meetings to secure financial holdings, checked their identity cards and citizenship papers, talked about multiracialism, wondered about the status of the English language, ate *chapatis* and mutton curry for lunch and *rendang* for dinner, proclaimed the Chinese would own the country, worried about the departure of the British Army, checked their identity cards and citizenship papers. Thousands argued about the rights of the sultans, and assumed everything would remain the same, only better. The terms of the debate for those in English education were rhetorically reassuring—a constitution, national identity, citizenship rights, a parliament, a judiciary, free elections. The British Empire was dead. The British Commonwealth was alive. The new university graduates, setting the course for a multiracial, multicultural, pluralistic democracy, set bold topics for our English papers and our debating teams— What is a democracy? Who should run the country, the army or the civilians?

Which should we value more, the individual or society? Is free speech ever wrong?

A young student, I was not so much apathetic as complacent. British education had trained me for the privileged ranks of the Civil Service. Hungry and ragged or socially disgraced, I never doubted that my talents placed me in a meritocracy. The empire promised impartial evaluation under the socialist standards of the civil bureaucracy that the British prime minister, Harold Wilson, had established in defense against communist criticism of capitalism and entrenched class interests. With high grades validated from Britain, earning me respect where none else existed, I believed that scholarly excellence alone would decide my professional life.

I was a resident in that sheltered elite village, the University of Malaya, from 1964 to 1969. But the changes taking place in the political and social fabric of the new nation were causing rifts even inside the campus gates. Little was expected of the undergraduate except folly, frolic, and academic obedience. Lecturers were lofty men, chiefly white, to whom we were uninteresting children of the Asian masses. I signed up for history, geography, and English in the first year, but all that remains vivid are the weekly English tutorials, composed of five randomly selected freshmen, to whom were assigned a young lecturer newly arrived from Cambridge.

Tall, gangly, and awkward, as if his arms and legs had grown too remote from a center of command, Mr. Preston was shy about women but voluble concerning Shelley, Byron, Keats, Yeats, and other assorted English poets. At our first meeting, he handed us a mimeographed booklet for the Practical Criticism course and asked us to analyze an anonymous poem, "Ode to Limestone." I recognized the style as Auden's. Unriddling the poem's structure and intertwined themes was the kind of thing I did when I had turned to poetry for consolation during my years in the cramped Malacca house. At the end of the third meeting Mr. Preston returned my essay without a grade. "You are supposed to write this without any help," he admonished me. "Which reference did you use in the library?"

"I wrote this myself," I protested, alarmed and flattered that he thought I had cribbed my essay. But he ushered me out of his office disapprovingly.

The rest of the tutorials, however, went by without a fuss. He never questioned the originality of my essays again. They were returned with comments and grades, and I looked forward eagerly to the weekly meetings when, for the first time, it seemed to me, I was able to talk freely about language and ideas with someone who understood and shared my pleasure in both.

Academic standards for the bachelor's degree in English literature were ensured by a form of quality control, with the English department operating under the anxiety of Britain's shadow. Back issues of *Scrutiny* were required reading; external examiners from Cambridge and Oxford scrutinized our exam papers for softening of intellectual rigor in the department's offerings. The English department was notorious for its emphasis on standards, a term which seemed synonymous with British upper-class culture, and the university, which had separated from Singapore University in 1965, had never awarded a First Class in English.

During the mandatory Chaucer, Shakespeare, Augustan, Romantics, and other traditional survey courses, listening hard but not hearing, students diligently copied every word the lecturer uttered. In my three years as an undergraduate, I had only one woman lecturer, a British medievalist who taught the great mysteries of Middle English. All my tutors were male. Mr. Lark crammed his hands in his pockets and jingled the coins throughout his hour-long peroration. Mr. Hughes prowled from microphone to blackboard to locked door before taking off his shoes and sitting on the desk. Dr. Wismal stood very straight and lectured from note cards which he turned over meticulously after each point. Their presence really didn't matter; afraid to miss a syllable, every student's head was down. Above the air conditioning's hum and the lecturer's drone, usually only the slur of note paper turning and the skittering of ball-points were audible.

But even within the anglophile offices of the English department the world was changing. In my final year, an eccentric visiting French professor offered electives on the Continental novel. He held late-night showings of avant-garde films by Alain Resnais and Francois Truffaut, during which the students tittered politely. He gave parties in his apartment in Kuala Lumpur where he grumbled as we gulped down expensive French wine as if it were sugar cane juice. "Sip slowly!" he urged as he ogled us.

Mr. Farley, the first visiting Fulbright professor in the department, introduced us to Mark Twain, Ralph Waldo Emerson, Walt Whitman, and Henry James. The United States appeared in my imagination for the first time, from a literature more mysterious than that of Victorian England. A New Englander, very tall, gray, and stooped, Mr. Farley was also the first professor to encourage me unstintingly. His formal kindness offered me a glimpse of teaching as a nurturing relationship that the years of British education had disavowed. After I received a tutorship with admission to the master's program at the university, he urged me to apply for a Fulbright fellowship to complete a doctorate in the United States. Whereas the British lecturers had questioned my legitimacy in their subject, he serenely assured me that my future lay in American literature.

In contrast to Mr. Farley, when Mr. Hughes called me after the final exams results to tell me that I had achieved a First Class Honors, he did not congratulate me. Instead, he added, "Of course, you know you were fooling us in some of your papers. But remember, you can't fool all of the people all of the time." The British lecturers consistently warned me against studies in English literature. Even as I fervently memorized "Tintern Abbey" and long passages from *The Prelude,* they shook their heads and advised, "You cannot hope to understand Wordsworth unless you've been to the Lake District."

This British superiority had always grated on me. I wondered why they were teaching us what they believed we who were not English could never possibly appreciate. Besides, I didn't believe them. The physical sensation of expansion in the chest, even in the head, as I read a profoundly beautiful or mindful poem was conclusively and possessively subjective. The literature may have been of Britain, but my love of literature was outside the empire.

A Malayan professor, a dark Eurasian of Sri Lankan descent, offered us as countercurriculum a course on "Commonwealth Literature." Undergraduates were intimidated by Dr. Wismal's air of stern reserve, perhaps a mask for his struggles against both British and Asian racism. From Singapore University Dr. Wismal had gone on to receive a Ph.D. from Leeds University. His ascendancy to head of the English department appeared as a triumph of local merit against British expatriate snobbery, for it was generally agreed that his publications in Victorian literature had gained him the position. But we knew also that the new government had determined to replace Britons in positions of power with local professors. His appointment, therefore, mirrored the shift in Malayan society, from colonized to national culture.

Together with Amos Tutuola's and Chinua Achebe's novels from Africa and the works of West Indian writers, including V. S. Naipaul and George Lamming, we finally read a few Malayan writers in Dr. Wismal's course. Studying the poems of Ee Tiang Hong and Wong Phui Nam, many of which lamented an alienation from Malayan society, I saw the contrast between their concerns and those in Wordsworth's poetry. From my position of undergraduate superiority, I was pitiless in my criticism of these poets' separation from their national landscape. While their simple act of writing against colonial disparagement was to be admired, I puzzled over their images of displacement. Truly I loved the hibiscus bushes that bloomed all over the campus; I never tired of the delicious foods sold in the night food stalls all over Petaling Jaya, the suburb that had sprouted around the university, and even the steamy afternoons brought their own keen sensations of tropical languor and heightened sensuality. In contrast, in the poems of these pioneer English-language writers, Malayan identity was of something absent. I wanted to write a literature like Wordsworth's *Prelude,* but overflowing with native presence: writing should be an act of dis-alienation, of sensory claims. If we were not Malayans, who could we be?

As a concluding paper, Dr. Wismal asked that we each write a short story. The night before it was due, I wrote my first short story, a brooding imagining of an abortion witnessed and abetted by the young unknowing daughter. The pleasure in writing the story, which flowed unforced, confirmed my belief in the vital connection between the English language and the breathing emotions that ran through my body. Dr. Wismal later included it in the first published collection of English-language Malayan short stories, many of which had been written as assignments for him.

Dr. Wismal's readings directly contradicted the exclusive claims on English that British lecturers like Preston and Hughes had repeated. His course was part of a struggle to extricate a valuable sense of self-in-language from the colonialist's etymological grip. We had grown up in a compulsory language system, but, as if to strip us of all language, we were constantly reminded that this language did not belong to us. Depriving us of Chinese or Malay or Hindi, British teachers reminded us nonetheless that English was only on loan, a borrowed tongue which we could only garble.

Closeted within my love of the English language, I did not hear the increasingly hostile language debates breaking out all over Malaya till it was too late. In 1967 my joy at being admitted into the circle of English literature was pure, naive, and tainted at the source, for, of course, there could be no easy future for "Englit"—Britain's canon of great English works—in the context of postcolonial politics.

In 1964, in my first year as an undergraduate, many university students were heady with optimism toward a new kind of human, the Malaysian. Meeting on the common ground of multiracialism and multiculturalism, politicians of all races had seemed to agree to the formation of a new political unit, composed of island pieces colonized by Britain in Southeast Asia: the Federation of Malaya, Sarawak, and Singapore. One evening I followed the crowds in Malacca to Coronation Park, now renamed Merdeka Park. A lean Chinese man dressed simply in a short-sleeved white shirt and khaki pants addressed the milling audience from a plain unadorned platform. "We have to make sure everyone has something," he shouted into a microphone. "When people own things, they don't riot. When they see a riot forming, they run home and they take their motorcycles inside their houses and lock the doors." He was Lee Kuan Yew.

But Lee, prime minister of Singapore, offered an economist's vision of Malaysia, the view of a pragmatic Chinese immigrant generation. It did not succeed in assuring the Malays who feared their claim to indigenous ownership eroded by precisely the kind of materialist striving that he urged. By 1965, the racial divisions in the region had become clearer in the polarities that finally led to the dissolution of the Malayan-Singapore union.

That weekend in Singapore when I was embarked on my mission to rid myself of my virginity, Uncle Charlie called me excitedly to watch Mr. Lee's address on television. Tearfully, pleading for calm, the distraught statesman spoke of finding a separate destiny for Singapore. The Malaysian prime minister, Tengku Abdul Rahman, perhaps acutely accepting the increasing electoral tensions between Chinese-dominant Singapore and Malay-dominant Malaya, had summarily expelled Singapore from the union. Jostling the lines at Customs as I crossed the border at the Johore Causeway, I felt fearfully sad. The meaninglessness of my sexual encounter—the physical rupture in my body—with Rajan, the stranger I had chosen to initiate me in bed, appeared enlarged by the violent meaningfulness of the political split between Singapore, the city I was just beginning to know through my mother's residence, and Malaysia, the country I implicitly loved.

My second year at the university was filled with continuous debates on the cultural future of the country. More and more, the term "Malay" appeared where "British" once stood. The "Malaysian," that new promise of citizenship composed of the best traditions from among Malays, Chinese, Tamils, Eurasians, Dayaks, and so forth, seemed more and more to be a vacuous political fiction, a public relations performance like those put on for Western tourists at state-run cultural centers: a little Wayang—traditional theater and puppetry—some Malay candle dances, a Chinese ribbon dance, Tamil dramatizations of the Ramayana, and the national anthem concluding the evening. One group's empowerment appeared to lead to another's oppression. As a thoroughly English-educated mind, emptied of Chinese racialized sentiments, I was a mold into which the idealism of a progressive multiracial identity could be poured. Chinese chauvinism offended me as much as other racisms, for, although of Chinese descent, I was usually treated by Malayan Chinese speakers as foreign, alien, and worse, decadent, an unspeakable because unspeaking, degenerate descendent of pathetic forebears. But Malay chauvinism was no better.

In the face of competition for dominance between Chinese and Malay elites, I was attracted contrarily to Eurasians and Indians, a romance of minoritism, as a way out of the fixedness of race identity. Tentative about my social position, I was most comfortable with those who were on the outside. Frequently mocked as different, they did not suggest there was something wrong with you simply because you were different. To many xenophobic Malays and Chinese, Eurasians and Indians were always the wrong race. Eurasians were jibbed at as "half-breeds," "mongrels," white-lovers, loose, unambitious, the disintegrating fragments of a dying race. Indians were mocked as the wrong color, communalistic, quarrelsome: they smelled, used coconut oil, and worshipped strange gods. Chinese and Malays were equally dogged by negative stereotypes, but, larger in numbers, many of them also asserted a palpably contemptuous superiority from which I cringed.

In my second year, I refused to return to Third College. Its regime of gossip, regulated hours, and enforced women's company was, after all, only an adult version of what I had thought I had escaped in leaving the convent school— the pettiness of schoolgirls. I bought a Honda motorbike, rented a room in Petaling Jaya with another defiant undergraduate woman, and became engaged to Ben, a Eurasian student a year my senior.

"Going steady" had seemed the only alternative to risky independence, and Ben's devotion was balm to my sense of physical damage. He was more than devoted; he was sentinel and guard, for I was in his company every evening. I was always a little bored and a little flattered in his company: half-asleep by eleven or midnight, I would beg him to leave, then watch his slow retreating back with confused emotions, not quite able to figure whether the slight depression I felt was remorse at my relief that I was finally alone or regret at his leaving me alone. Nagged by a sense that there was something more important than simply walking or making love, I had no idea what this more important thing could be.

Being without him was grievously lonely. In my small sad room my roommate, whose boyfriend had just broken up with her, sulked because I wouldn't stay still. Attending lectures, going to the library, and returning to the room was an intolerable routine which I could only escape with Ben's help. With Ben I could stay out late; I could avoid the endless small talk of university women. With Ben, I needed never to return to Malacca; instead I stayed in his parents' home in Penang at every university break. There I shared a room with his sister, and his mother politely ignored me.

I was always braver with him, even at night, even riding without a license, even when a sudden police block stopped us on the Federal Highway. Tall, brown, and gentle-spoken, Ben repelled unwanted male attention either with a twenty-dollar bribe to the police or with an aggressive stare at jostling strangers. I was secure with him, and he played on that, calling me his lamb, his little one.

Although he was a geography student, Ben wanted to paint. In his home, his doting mother had set aside a room for his studio. Through the university breaks I sat in the airless room reading aloud from the *Encyclopedia of World Art* while he painted. In between passages on the pointillists, Duchamp, Matisse, and Chagall, we discussed my supporting him. As we stretched his canvases together, I thought I would be muse to his talent. His canvases showed a facility with figures and landscapes, a restlessness with colors, and growing obsession with abstraction. He was sure he had talent and could become a famous painter, given money for canvas and oils and time. He spent his money on expensive magazines like *Artforum* and introduced me to Penang artists whose batik-style paintings that sold well to tourists he excoriated. It was true that he could produce paintings just like those but chose not to. Yet he was conflicted between his love of painting and his desire for security. I was proud of his intransigence, his apparent contempt for money, and his belief in art, but after twelve hours in his studio, he wanted only a good time.

Also, it seemed to me that Ben's love for me usually led to his comfort rather than mine. He insisted I come up to Penang, but I stayed indoors all day beside him while he painted. For my twenty-first birthday he brought me a rose and a basket of tinned Western delicacies—mandarin oranges in syrup, deviled ham, soft-centered chocolates, smoked almonds. I was pleased by his thoughtfulness, but he ate the delicacies. When I returned to Third College to concentrate on the examinations that would decide my degree in my final year, Ben, who was teaching in Penang, called me every night. The calls were a loving reassurance, but it was impossible to stay out late without having to account for my absence. I had to be back in the College and waiting by the dormitory public telephone every night by nine.

I couldn't understand my restlessness and grew more passive with him, as if I were deliberately disinheriting that bad and dangerous child within me who kept wanting to run away. After I took on the position as tutor in the English department, Ben moved down from Penang, found a job teaching at a Malay college in Petaling Jaya, and brought lunch to me at the university every day. When I began having tea with the other tutors, he came by each afternoon and sat glumly through our giddy conversations.

I was flushed with success. The boring hoop-jumping of exams had given way to the disorienting freedom of independent studies. Tutors read alone in their library carrels to produce a master's thesis at the end of two years. Any famous writer was fair study: Gerard Manley Hopkins, Eugene O'Neill, Anthony Burgess. Out of the unyielding structure of the exam system, I found myself in the unsupervised zone of graduate studies. You could die in a carrel and it might be two weeks before your body was discovered. Certainly you could work on a master's degree, and it would be two years before anyone discovered your thesis was missing. I alternated between happiness at the unaccustomed absence of surveillance and despair at the anomie of graduate work.

Similarly, I zig-zagged between valuing the claustrophobic security of Ben's possessiveness and acting on a growing confused discontent. Moving to Petaling Jaya, Ben had given up painting. His life seemed to be devoted to waiting for me, for he didn't enjoy teaching. While I read in the carrel, he played billiards for hours. I was sometimes particularly tender. He reminded me of Father in the way his life drifted along shallow currents of desire and pleasure. More often I quarreled with him in order to feel an emotion sharper than pity or boredom.

Each master's student was assigned an adviser. I was intimidated to have Mr.

Hughes, he of the prowling peregrinations during the lecture hour. He had just returned from sabbatical in England, wore black turtlenecks, and smoked a pipe which entailed a great deal of fussing—unscrewing a tin of tobacco, knocking off the ash and cleaning the bowl, stuffing it with a careful measure of the brown shredded leaves, striking a match and holding it to the bowl while clamping strong white teeth on the stem, sucking on it attentively, and finally succeeding in blowing clouds of smoke over the head of the person before him. I was attracted to such little-known women poets as Edna St. Vincent Millay, Elizabeth Jennings, and Laura Riding, and wanted to write my thesis on selected women poets. Mr. Hughes frowned on the proposal. "You have a problem with being scattered," he said, "and should work on fiction which will provide you with external structure." I had just read *The Lord of the Flies* and was drawn to its gloomy Christian aesthetics, so much like my own experience with colonial Catholicism; it was simpler to acquiesce and to turn to William Golding's novels for my master's thesis.

We met a couple of times to discuss my progress. Materials had to be specially ordered by the library or requested through international interlibrary loan. Everything took at least three months to arrive. Researching the history of allegories and Augustinian theological treatises on free will and determinism, I was pleased to be learning curious things, the way a hermitic scholar hidden away in a cell was supposed to do.

During the same period, as I teetered between an idea of adulthood that appeared ever more removed from myself and the passive sexualized adolescence that I was locked into with Ben, a group of fellow tutors began gathering in the Senior Common Room in the afternoons, smoking furiously and drinking beer. Mr. Hughes came to sit with us for hours, smoking his pipe, his long legs pulled in along the low rattan chair. No longer a remote lecturer, he reveled in our excessive drinking and frivolous talk.

A few months later, he asked me to his office to discuss my work. The English lecturers' offices on the fifth floor were little visited except during tutorial sessions. "Come in," he said when I knocked, his voice calm and professional. The usual cloud of pipe smoke filled the small room. Through the windows tinted for privacy, one saw only empty sky. As I shut the door, he put down his pipe and came up to me. Putting his arms around me, he muttered, "I love you, I love you." He was trembling and very warm in the air-conditioned chill. His words ricocheted in my mind, shocking because of their seeming finality. He had always appeared so much older and superior. An English man, married with two children, he had never entered my imagination as a sexual person. In that brief moment, he had moved, flatteringly, from teacher to lover.

Speaking with lowered voice, he said, "I have to see you alone. Will you come? I'll get a room at the Station Hotel for Saturday. Please come at eight. I'll be waiting for you." Through his thick turtleneck sweater I could feel his heart pounding. His face was distraught, and he clutched at me almost impersonally, as if with despair.

What should I have done on this occasion? Sometimes, reminded by debates on sexual harassment in the universities, I ask this question. I did not think of him then as a harasser, although his actions then and later clearly had the effect of harassing me. I should have refused his request and discreetly asked for a different adviser, so ending the matter right there. But in the dim tobacco-scented room crowded with books and papers, I was intrigued by his passionate clumsiness and the dangerous secrecy of the encounter. Above all, I felt a sense of power, that unwittingly I had been able to reduce this superior man to frantic begging.

Telling Ben I was ill and had to stay in bed, I rode on my Honda to the Station Hotel. The hotel was a Victorian fantasy of Indian Islamic architecture that the British had constructed early in the twentieth century to mask the bleak functionality of the railroad tracks that carried them, imperial transients, up and down the peninsula. It was not a place I had ever visited. I was grateful for the tropical dark. The Moorish-style towers and arabesque porticos deepened my mood of fatal romance. James, for that was how I was beginning to think of Mr. Hughes, had placed a note with simply the room number written on it in my mailbox. Avoiding the front desk, I kept to the far walls of the cavernous reception room, took the elevator, and rode to the fourth floor.

James had brought a bottle of red wine. Light from a street lamp below the window steeped the room in shade and shadow. He was jubilant, moody, depressed, and talkative. I reminded him of his first love, another high-strung graduate woman who had died in an accident after an argument. He was in pain in my presence. As he made love to me on the stark white hotel bed, I wasn't sure he was aware of me or of that long-lost spirit. Even his endearments sounded like a soundtrack from a British film. I left the hotel room as dumbly as I had entered.

James was dazzled by my personality and completely uninterested in me as a person. I had no history for him before the moment he fell in love with me. Immediately I regretted the affair. When we met at the Senior Common Room, which was almost daily, he threw quick significant glances at me, and paused extravagantly as he uttered philosophical abstractions that the other tutors listened to with awe. Enmeshed in his melodrama, however, I was conscious only of paranoia. I was afraid Ben would suspect James's feelings and that James's wife would discover our night at the hotel. Fleetingly, I imagined marrying James and running off to England, but I dreaded a future in the company of his academicism, in a cold country I didn't wish to live in, saddled with his history, the dead woman, the abandoned middle-aged wife and sweet children. After a few more clammy embraces in his office, I warned him of Ben's suspicions and asked that we stop meeting before Ben confronted his wife.

It was true that, as I grew more unhappy, Ben became more jealous. When I house-sat for a German professor and would not tell him where I was, he went to James's home to find me. Later, he followed me to the house. Finding it locked, he broke in through the bathroom louvers. He refused to accept my need to be alone. Since I didn't have another boyfriend, he argued, I was merely confused. That Christmas break, acceding to his demands, I accompanied him to Penang, where I slept for more than fifteen hours each day. Groggy and depressed, I woke up in the afternoons, took slow subdued walks with him, then fell into bed exhausted.

Back in Petaling Jaya, living in a spartan room intended for servants which I rented from a wealthy Malay family, I received no visitors except Ben. His overpowering daily presence constricted me. I felt I could not live without him and yet I did not want to live with him. In a poem I described the position of Daphne as she attempted to escape Apollo: dreading him and yet unable to win the race, she metamorphoses into an olive tree, a bitter ruckle, whose leaves the god ironically takes as the symbol of victory. One night, I took out the bottles of tranquilizers prescribed after my accident which I had saved for just such a moment. I closed the door and swallowed all the little white pills, then fell asleep.

I slept for more than twenty-four hours; but when Ben finally succeeded in rousing me, I had suffered no more than a bad headache. Remorseful, he promised that he would accept my wish for more privacy and my desire to be with other people. We would remain engaged, but he would stop hounding me. Feeling I could breathe again, I moved to a married tutor's house, where I spent evenings washing my hair and discussing literature with her. Ben stopped by only on some evenings.

One afternoon, while I was buying cigarettes at the Senior Common Room, Iqbal, my brother's colleague in the history department, came up from behind and commented on my taste for mentholated cigarettes. Iqbal had just returned from a five-year fellowship at the University of California in Berkeley, bringing with him a veneer of American sophistication. He was casual where Ben was pretentious. Dressed simply himself, he seemed to like my usual costume of blue jeans and print shirts. One afternoon, early in our relationship, he took me in a taxi to the university apartment he had just moved his things into to give me a well-washed work shirt that he had brought back from

Berkeley. We both knew the gift was a symbolic act of cultural and sexual claiming. The next month I moved into the apartment. At the same time, Iqbal asked that I keep a room in Petaling Jaya, warning that if his traditional Punjabi mother should ever visit him, I would have to move out for the duration of her stay.

Later, when Ben found out that I had been seeing Iqbal, he wondered at my terrible taste. Iqbal was the ugliest man I could have picked, he said. Not much taller than I, inclined toward fat, with a mass of unruly black hair that looked greasy even when clean, and wearing thick glasses that gave him the myopic popped-up glaze of a goldfish in a small bowl, Iqbal charmed by more tenacious routes than the body. Fresh from the Berkeley Free Speech Movement, he brought to the decaying British tradition of the university an irreverent intelligence and institutional skepticism that caught me completely.

For a month, over afternoon tea, he listened to me talk about my confusion over Ben. When he first asked me to leave Ben, I refused. Then he invited me to a party. I was intrigued as the taxi drove through an expensive Kuala Lumpur suburb that I had never visited. Patting my hand confidently, Iqbal said, "Just stick around, baby!" The evening was full of older professional people whose interests I didn't share; someone remarked snidely that Iqbal was cradle-snatching. As the taxi took us back to my rented room, Iqbal's flippant Americanism echoed in my head. "Just stick around, baby!" I was tired of scenes, tensions, the heavy inertia of my relationship with Ben, like living in a sack with its neck slowly drawn closed. Iqbal's patience, his American past, even his older Malaysian professional circle, seemed desirable, an alternative to Ben's emotional dead-end.

Ben was waiting in my room when I came upstairs. "You were with another man, weren't you?" His anger was blazing even as I was unable to feel anything except weariness. I could no longer ignore the contrast between Iqbal's intimate liveliness and Ben's stultifying rage. "I won't let you leave me, I'll kill myself first!"

The threat usually brought on a rush of guilt and pity. I would find myself anxiously smoothing his hair, consoling him, with tears of frustration in my eyes. Tonight, Iqbal's casual offer, "Just stick around, baby!" played jazzily against Ben's words. "I don't care," I murmured, amazed I was actually saying it. Suddenly it was clear to me that I really didn't care. I wouldn't miss Ben if I never saw him again.

"I'll kill you before I let you leave me!"

I felt strangely calm, immutable: I couldn't bear to be with him, my unhappiness was intolerable. "I'd rather be dead than be with you."

"All right," he said. His voice was stricken. "I want you to keep the ring. Tomorrow, we go to Chee's house and tell all our friends our engagement's off."

That last afternoon with Ben was also my last afternoon with the friends we had made together as undergraduates. None of our mutual friends, who usually gathered at Chee's home for dinner, appeared surprised at the news, although I knew they blamed me for the break. Leaving Ben was leaving the community I had known for the last three years. I went home to Malacca to gather my thoughts and called Iqbal from the Arts Concourse public telephone as soon as I returned to Kuala Lumpur. "Wait there," he said, and came in a taxi to fetch me to his unfurnished, waiting apartment.

What I loved first about Iqbal was the openness of movement he offered.

For the first few months he spoke continuously of Berkeley and the United States: the Indian student naked under her wrapped sari; the hundred-dollar steak dinner his adviser had bought him; driving over the Golden Gate Bridge and seeing San Francisco from the hills; the secondhand bookstores and the good cold beer. Chain-smoking, with my long unkempt hair, faded dungarees, motorcycle, and obsession with literature, I was like a fragment of Berkeley he had dislodged from the backwaters of Kuala Lumpur.

However, except for the straight-arrow American literature course a year ago, I had no interest in the United States. I was ambitious about my writing; I wanted to be a Malayan writer, and walked around somewhat askew, looking for materials. I began a novel, wrote poems, completed a few more short stories, and worked on my thesis on Golding.

I thought Iqbal's simplicity ravishing. He refused to have a telephone or a television in the apartment, and would not learn to drive. Living with him held a lightness of being, an improvisational spontaneity that made each day fresh and mobile.

After a month of eating muesli and milk, Iqbal bought me a copy of *The Joy of Cooking*. We shopped together for a roast beef, and with extreme anxiety I found myself alone among the gleaming untouched kitchen counters. I had never cooked in my life. I had never faced such a large mass of beef. The roast had shrunk to a dark brown butt by the time I served it. Sitting in solitary grandeur at the dining table, Iqbal cut into it. "You will have to learn to cook if you want to live with me," he said as I stood, crushed, by the kitchen door. Resentfully I returned to the kitchen to wash the dishes. Why was he smiling and why wasn't I, I wondered. The kitchen door between us seemed to me an ominous sign of something already wrong with our relationship.

But I applied myself to learning to cook. It was a new challenge. Besides, Iqbal began throwing elaborate dinner parties. On my Honda I carried home bunches of orchids, fresh plucked chickens, yogurt, anchovies, pineapples, spinach, *garam masala*, bottles of red wine. I worked all Saturday arranging a bountiful display, then slipped in and out of the kitchen door serving the lecturers, the visiting fellows, the U.S. embassy people he favored. Occasionally I followed a fascinating conversation; more often I glowed in Iqbal's social success. After weeks of such parties, I began to resent the work, the unsatisfactory uncompleted sentences as I served the salad and the dessert, removed the dirty dishes, and brought out more wine bottles.

One afternoon, Iqbal saw me at the university. "I've invited two more for dinner tonight," he added casually. "You'd better make sure there will be enough food."

I rushed to the market and shopped furiously for another chicken, then stood in line at the supermarket for a frozen Sara Lee cheesecake.

"Did you buy wine?" Iqbal asked when he returned to the apartment later that afternoon. "We can't have only beer!"

It was raining as I set out once again on my motorbike for the six-mile round trip to the supermarket. As the rain pelted my hair and soaked through my clothes, I cried at my own submissiveness.

That night there was just enough cheesecake for everyone except me. The American woman Iqbal had invited with her handsome husband was a green-eyed blond whom he seated beside him. Gulping glasses of wine, she laughed drunkenly at his jokes. I was sullen and silent, and Iqbal fell asleep without noticing my anger. But I did not speak to him of my resentment: I could no longer imagine a life without him.

One morning I woke up to hear someone crying in the living room. When I went out in my pajamas, I saw an elderly woman in a sari crouched on the rattan sofa weeping. Knotting his sarong around his waist, Iqbal came up behind me and whispered, "That's my mother. You have to leave."

Numbly I took some clothes out of the closet and rode off to the room I had rented and that I had never slept in. The Chinese family who took my check monthly stared to see me in the house. I sat on the bed, gazing through the window at the other small working-class houses with their tattered front yards and bare concrete driveways. It struck me that I was homeless. Iqbal's apartment was not my home. I was like the live-in Malay maid whose place in the apartment was functional and without rights.

Iqbal told me I could return two days later, after his mother left, still weeping over his taking up with a non-Punjabi woman. "My mother will never change," he said. "She will never be able to accept a Chinese daughter-in-law."

The next time I heard her crying in the morning I didn't wait for him to tell me to leave but dressed immediately and left him still sleeping while she moaned in the living room.

I was desperately jealous of Iqbal's mind.

Our first week together, he gave me Kahlil Gibran's *The Prophet* and asked me to read it. I was amused by its pretentious profundity. It wasn't as good as Fitzgerald's translation of the *Rubb'iyat,* and I told him so. His vast look of approval signaled that I had passed some kind of test. On weekends he read Wallace Stevens and William Carlos Williams aloud to me. He had a caressing deep voice which made "Sunday Morning" sound gorgeously musical.

He was the first person to convince me he was intellectually superior. He publicly corrected my pronunciation. Visiting the father of his ex-girlfriend, he was angry that I had mispronounced "pediatrician." Together we had unpacked his boxes of books from Berkeley. In the yellow highlighted pages of Theodore Dreiser's *Sister Carrie,* Henry James's *The Golden Bowl,* and dozens of other college paperbacks, I glimpsed a different kind of mind from the *Scrutiny* essays that I had so scrupulously copied.

He took me to an expensive French boutique in a new shopping mall full of Western stores. Choosing a white pleated skirt and emerald green knitted top, he told me I had to stop dressing like a shop girl when he took me to social events like play openings and embassy parties. At these gatherings everyone had just come from Europe or the United States. They talked about how difficult it was to find graham crackers in Kuala Lumpur, how hot Washington D.C. got in August, and how cheap wine was in California. I was Iqbal's girlfriend, and they talked to him around me as if I were only a penumbra of his body.

Before Professor Farley returned to New England, he asked me to apply for a Fulbright scholarship. "The university needs someone permanent to teach American literature," he told the head of the department. He had met both Ben and Iqbal and had been attentive and kind equally to both, but unlike the other Americans Iqbal and I knew, he was chiefly concerned about my future. "Be sure to take the GREs," he had told me. "Massachusetts is a lovely state with a wealth of resources. You will be able to visit Harvard." Each time he met me on the campus, he would lean down with twinkling eyes toward me and say, "I hope you are considering going ahead with your Ph.D."

Iqbal didn't like Professor Farley, but he said nothing as I sat for the Graduate Record Examinations (GREs), then was interviewed for the Fulbright fellowship, dressed in the sedate white and green outfit from Paris that he had chosen for me. Of course, my first choice of graduate school was the University of California at Berkeley. Then, checking the college guides at the United States Information Service Library, I read about Irving Howe at Brandeis University and put Brandeis down as my second choice.

I was perversely persuaded in this choice by the first open disagreement I had with Iqbal. In June, soon after we began living together, we argued about the significance of the Seven Days' War. I was convinced that the efforts to destroy the Jewish state were anti-Semitic and historically related to the

Holocaust. Iqbal, arguing that Israel was a territorial aggressor, rebuked me for my position. For once I refused to back down. The hostility I felt at his criticism of Israel was strangely personal, as if it threatened my own being. The prospect of studying with Irving Howe at Brandeis appealed to me as a strenuous counter-Americanism to Iqbal's Berkeley laissez faire.

The GREs were amazingly easy. They were my first multiple-choice exams, and I was surprised to find that the answers were provided on the question sheets. You merely had to identify the correct answers. Compared to the onerous strategies of arranging masses of memorized information to shape comprehensive yet original thought, these pencil-dot responses were nonintellectual exercises.

The interview for the fellowship seemed similarly undemanding. With the local Fulbright director, a visiting neurosurgeon, and Professor Farley, on hand, I assured them that besides reading I enjoyed cooking and long walks, and that if there were no publication resources in Malaysia after I returned from the United States, I would begin my own journal. The Fulbright director was very excited at my GRE results which had impressed even Iqbal.

Soon after I was offered both a Fulbright and a Wien International fellowship at Brandeis.

Iqbal said nothing as I went through the application processes. Since he had said nothing about marriage, we were both silent about my future.

At university parties, acquaintances began to have conversations with me. In winning these fellowships I had become visible, a person separate from Iqbal. But my public excitement about leaving for Massachusetts was forced. I had not yet accepted the fellowships because I was wretched at the prospect of leaving Iqbal.

As unhappy as I was, my attachment to him was total. In the apartment I sat quietly beside him while he smoked, read, and listened to music, observing the fine black hairs on the backs of his hands or his small fingers tapping with the hypnotic tabala accompaniment to Ravi Shankar's sitar. He had put on weight. I loved the little brown roll of fat around his waist. When we walked together, I felt an emotion of completion akin to bliss. Alone, I suffered keenly from a sense of emptiness. With him, the present was vivid.

When the English department placed an advertisement for a local lecturer, my relief was enormous. With the best academic record among the tutors, I was certain I would get the position, and then Iqbal and I would manage together as we had been doing for over a year. But the university administrator was cold and contemptuous as he interviewed me, and Dr. Wismal was quiet. The position was offered to Karmal, a Muslim male colleague.

The official rumor alleged that the selection committee believed I would accept the fellowships and leave the country. Months later a visiting professor at a party said that the university administrator had described me as an opinionated woman. I believed that the university preferred a male and a Muslim over a Chinese woman. For the first time I saw that the prejudices I had believed the product of small-town religious bigotry were systemic in Malaysian society. Worse, it became clear to me that merit was not the main criterion for professional status. In Malaysia, I would always be of the wrong gender and the wrong race.

Still pressing was the unavoidable moment of choice between accepting the fellowships or staying with Iqbal and leaving the academic world forever. Professor Farley was leaving Kuala Lumpur in February. Seeing me with Iqbal in the Senior Common Room, he spoke with concern about my delay in accepting the fellowships. "You'll have to decide soon," he warned. "Brandeis has to hear from you before March. Otherwise, the university will give the fellowship to someone else."

Iqbal and I were both silent as we walked back to the apartment. The late afternoon was warm. With the academic year over, the road was empty. Plodding along the dull road, I felt the heavy tropical foliage recede, as if I were already hovering over the scene, looking back on it as past.

Glancing at my pensive expression, Iqbal said, "Let's get married! I don't want you to leave." Whimsically, he added, "I'll buy you a washing machine!"

I knew I should have been glad; I did not want to leave him. But I also knew I wanted to continue with graduate studies. I wanted to teach at the university.

Married to Iqbal I would be a faculty wife, one of those women on the outer circle of every university party I had attended, who sat with folded hands, like low fires banked for the night. Their demeanor was, in fact, even less open than the convent nuns who had tried to train me, as if I were a vine to be contained by wire and clipped. I could not bear the prospect of sitting in that domestic outer circle, excluded from the interesting talk, the arguments and jokes and important information.

At faculty parties, men abandoned their wives to cluster with each other, forming inner circles, tight groups sharing beers and Tom Collinses. Their company was charged; explosive laughter ripped through them, and low exchanges, loud interruptions.

I wanted to circulate in this talk, not circle outside it. I wanted not only Iqbal, but also myself.

When we arrived at the apartment, I sat on the bed and said miserably, "I can't marry you. I need to grow." More than my present misery, I saw that I would be infinitely more unhappy sitting in Iqbal's shadow. Giving up the fellowships, I would be giving up my hopes to write, to learn more, to spend my life with books. I would be only Iqbal's wife. I passionately wanted to be both, but felt offered only one or the other.

Ironically I was more devastated than Iqbal by my decision. For weeks, hating to have him out of my sight, I intensely and tensely negotiated each moment. Counting the days till the flight to Boston, I begged him to spend more time with me, but he subtly withdrew. In the apartment he became morosely preoccupied. When he found me close to tears, he was impatient. "I can't live at this level of intensity that you want me to," he said, and turned to his books. He accompanied me to farewell parties and glumly denounced my friends as immature or as windbags and bores.

I was frantic as he pulled further and further away from me. He began to play mah-jongg all weekend and stayed out till late at night with different groups of people. At first I went with him, and sat beside him as he played. One evening, after he had been playing at a friend's house for hours, I walked out of the pleasant suburban home into the cool walled garden. The sun was close to setting. Impulsively I climbed a low branching tree. Perched on a fork I looked out at the green watered lawns and red tiled roofs of the exclusive housing estate. I was twenty-four, but finding myself in a stranger's home, waiting for Iqbal as he gambled with his friends, I remembered the Malacca childhood hours hidden in the mango tree branches. I was still waiting, still dreaming, still unhappy.

Once the decision was made to leave, events rushed onward as if without my volition. To pay for warm clothes, I taught evening courses at a private school which offered tutorials to students preparing for the A-level exams. I hated teaching the class. We were reading Shakespeare, and the students sat dazed through the hour, understanding nothing in the text and very little of my explication. *Macbeth* meant nothing to them, and their blank gazes forcefully conveyed to me the truth that English literature was meaningless in Malaysia except to anglophile freaks like myself.

On Friday May 13, we read the witches' scene, which in demon-haunted Malaysian society reads like a child's caricature of evil. "Tail of newt" and "eye of toad" were comic trivia beside what Malaysians whisper of blood-sucking *pontianak* and entrails-flying *hantu*. Doubly disturbed by this vision of my future career in English literature in Malaysia and by my confusion about leaving Iqbal, I stopped at the corner gas station. As I was pumping gas into the Honda tank, the attendant came up to me. "You better hurry home," he said.

All the street lamps were going out. I sped up the hill, wondering about the uncanny darkness that had fallen over Petaling Jaya. Iqbal hugged me as I came through the door. "I was so worried about you," he said. "Didn't you hear? There's a curfew on."

All we had was the radio; without a telephone, we were cut off from news for the five days of the curfew. Over the radio, we heard that Malay counter-demonstrators, brought in from the *kampongs*—their rural villages—to protest against a Chinese postelection victory march, and armed with *parangs* and knives, the report said, to defend themselves, had turned violent. Much later, first through rumors and then through foreign news reports, we learned that streets of Chinese shophouses in Kuala Lumpur had been burned down and hundreds of Chinese killed. Later estimates placed the number at about two thousand massacred. The army was called in, but the Malay soldiers had been slow to stop the race riots and had allegedly shot at Chinese instead.

During the next few volatile days, to offer us some protection should the murderous attacks ten miles away move closer, a Malay professor and his white wife in the apartment below invited us to stay with them. She spoke passable Malay with a broad Irish accent, and among his small-boned mother and sisters shyly hanging back in the kitchen, she carried her fair babies like a Nordic giant. No one discussed the curfew. "Aish, the soldiers! They'll take care of things," she said carelessly as she brought out the domino set. I wondered at her concentration on the game and her lack of self-consciousness among her nervous sisters-in-law.

Two days later, the curfew was lifted for a few hours. Iqbal refused to leave the apartment building, but I was worried about Second Brother and insisted on riding to Chien's rented bungalow. He was safe with his wife and baby girl and scolded me for taking risks. Speeding back through the deserted streets, however, I knew that hiding out was not security. No place in Malaysia was a refuge as long as racial extremists were free to massacre and burn.

A palpable tension hung over the university community. The Chinese students and lecturers who usually did not mix with the Malays were even more visibly segregated. Miriam, the daughter of a Scots mother and Malay aristocrat, who was also completing her master's degree in the English department, said exultantly in one of those moments I carried with me for years like a scriptural passage, "We Malays would rather return Malaysia to the jungle than live with Chinese domination." She was simply expressing the strong racial antipathy to the economic success of Chinese Malaysians that was suddenly orthodox among Malays. To the question, how will Malaysia succeed without Chinese industry and labor, she replied, "We don't need the Chinese. We will be happy to sit on the floor if that's what it means to do without the Chinese!"

I looked at her angular features, surely inherited from her Celtic ancestors, and marveled at the ironies in her position. A tough, hard-working woman who was outspoken about her social snobbery and wealthy background, she appeared an unlikely voice for those protesting Malay poverty and dispossession; indeed, in an earlier age her aristocratic connections would have separated her from a parvenu like me. However, even after achieving independence, Malaysian society had remained structured on the meritocratic policies that Harold Wilson had implemented for Britain then, and on capitalist competition. Miriam, already poised high among the elite, had more directly to gain than less well-situated Malays in the change from democratic multiracial competition to Malay or Bumiputra privilege, presented as a kind of affirmative action carried out through strict quota systems and governmental preferential treatment.

In the process of the formation of a Malaysian elite, the May 13 riots provided the bloody revolution that changed Malaysia from the ideal of a multicultural egalitarian future—an ideal already tested by hostilities over power-sharing—to the Malay-dominant race-preferential practice in place today. Listening to Miriam's unrestrained words, even as I swallowed the humiliation of my position—to be informed that I was not an equal citizen, that my community was a "problem," and that race massacres were an appropriate way of dealing with that problem—I rebelled against the notion that I would have to submit to such attitudes. Sitting dumbly before Miriam, I thought that I might never return to Malaysia.

Almost twenty-five years later, I am still not certain that I made the right decision. Miriam was speaking from the blood victory of May 13; I was suffering the cowed paranoia of the defeated. It seemed easy then to walk away from a violated dream of a national future which included people like me—people not tied to race-based ideology, who were looking to form a brave new nation. Hundreds of thousands of Malaysians have also emigrated to Australia, Hong Kong, Singapore, Britain, Canada, and the United States. A young Malaysian, young enough to be my son, living in Oxnard, California, recently asked me to write of the pain of this aborted community, of the anger of people who unwillingly leave their country because of laws that discriminate against them. Yet now I understand that this story is only one part of the political narrative. The other story to which Miriam was speaking is of people who perceive the justness of their claim for special rights in an original homeland.

As I was struggling to make sense of the May 13 riots and of my ambivalence about leaving Iqbal, I was also trying to complete my thesis. With five chapters on Golding's novels written and only a few footnotes to write up, I handed the thesis to James. He had followed my break-up with Ben and attachment to Iqbal from a sardonic distance, permitting himself heavy-lidded glances and an occasional unsympathetic comment. At the same time, he remained friendly, if removed. The structure of the master's program did not encourage interaction between adviser and student, and, aside from reminders that I should be writing, he maintained little contact with me.

A few weeks before my departure, he sat across from me in the Senior Common Room. Tamping tobacco into his pipe, he said, "Your thesis is very good!" A grateful relief washed over me. The anxiety of writing the master's thesis together with the messiness of leaving Iqbal had been dreadful.

"It's really quite brilliant," he continued. "In fact, it is publishable." I did not process this statement; all I could think was that he would approve the thesis and I would leave for the United States with the degree completed.

"Of course," he added, "it should be published in both our names, as I gave you most of the ideas and you merely followed up on them." Stricken, rising from my seat, I fled the room and ran into Iqbal who wondered why I was so upset. Later, I refused his advice to complain to Dr. Wismal about James.

It is easy now to see James's behavior as harassment from which I should have been protected. More difficult to explain is my refusal to ask for that protection and my silence since then. What is it that shapes women like me to forbearance in the face of bullies and oppressors, to flight and silence rather than justice in struggle and speech? Perhaps my parents' physical and emotional abandonment had led to my despair, to my profound distrust of any available protection. My childhood education, illuminating powerful adults as unloving, unjust, and violent, had driven me underground to avoid further damage, exchanging the hurts of trust for the hurts of futility.

I never finished those footnotes for the thesis. I carried the five chapters to the United States, and they lie unread in a file cabinet, a material sign of my abandoned academic future in Malaysia.

In 1969 I saw myself as a passive and innocent victim of the conflict between elites and races. After May 13, most events in Malaysia, whether public or domestic, were, and possibly still are, inevitably charged with a racialized dimension, whether in civil service or private business, whether professional or personal, economic or literary. However, even after this violent rupture, I held on to the necessity of art as aesthetics; the notion of living in a society where every aspect of one's life was unavoidably cathected in the political horrified me. I wanted social justice without having to struggle for it, a position I see now as available only to those already privileged.

After May 13, thousands of Malaysians like myself withdrew into mass depression. The censorship of news accounts, the compulsory black-out of commentaries and analyses, and the consequent governmental revisions of parliamentary rule to enact Malay domination only confirmed our paranoia. Twenty-five years after this trauma, however, millions of Malaysians of Chinese descent still resident in the country, and thousands more in a global diaspora, continue to bear witness to the ideal of an equitable homeland for all Malaysians.

Weeks before my departure for Boston, Iqbal had asked me to leave the apartment. Withdrawn and moody, he did not want to deal with either my fears or his feelings. The national anguish after May 13 echoed inside our own domestic division. I was leaving him voluntarily at the same time as I was unwilling to break up the relationship. My unhappiness could not be magnified further, and I enlarged on his failures, hoping that these would dissolve the bonds of dependency that made my leaving so fearful. Although I recognized that love was not a sufficient vocation and understood that a career held more promise for satisfaction than marriage, this strong feminist vision did not lessen the intensity of sexual and emotional attachment nor the hysteria at its loss.

Too proud to plead with Iqbal for shelter, I stayed with Karmal and his roommates, young Indian men who tried to cheer me up and saw that I ate occasionally. A few nights before my departure for the United States, I had a nightmare. At first I imagined I was lying on a cement floor which was borne up in the air by a layer of clouds. I felt simultaneously the cold hardness of the floor and the soft fleeciness of the clouds. Then the strongest fear came over me—the fear of being alone. I could not wake up out of this fear. As I whimpered in my room, Karmal heard me. "Hold me," I begged him. "I'm afraid." He must have held me for a long time. The total panic was like an accumulation of the pains of abandonment that had crowded my life, till I no longer understood the difference between abandonment and love, between the abandoned and the abandoner. Gradually, Karmal's thin warm body woke me out of the dream and the panic seeped away. So I have learned to ask for help from strangers.

Boarding the Boeing jet in Kuala Lumpur en route to Bangkok, then to Frankfurt, Amsterdam, London, and Boston, I was numb with misery. Iqbal had not come to the airport to say good-bye, and among the many friends who were there, there was no discussion of when I would return. In the airport lounge, gazing at the batik decorations intended for tourist consumption, I felt already the disconnection of the stranger. I would never see Malaysia again, except through the eyes of a traveler.

# CHAPTER EIGHT

# Black Bird Singing

The white stuff was falling still, dry light bits of brittle snow, drizzling like chemical crystals. Pushed over from the wide avenue and stacked high on the sidewalks, it was in everyone's way, except those who walked on Massachusetts Avenue, risking their exposed sides to upflying wet dirt thrown by the cars and trucks. It was Wednesday morning. I was looking for experience, persons, some tolerable moments in the stretched intolerable February.

Three blocks north of the avenue were Porter Square and the train station, frozen and deserted at this hour. It was usually standing room only in the train, twenty minutes away from the next whistle-stop, and a half-hour's clammy ride to the difficult hilly Brandeis campus. I pushed south toward the town of Cambridge, the warm-air bookstores, bric-a-brac shops, cheap Indian cotton boutiques, the counterculture commerce, knowing I would meet no one except salesclerks and tradespeople. I would shop slowly, eking out each encounter, and buy nothing. There was a story in this for me, but I could not find it.

Massachusetts Avenue drove into the township of Cambridge from the South Shore, hugging Harvard Square like a crooked elbow, before heading across the bridge over the Charles River into Boston. On any day it was dull and utilitarian, an artery for heavy traffic, wheels pounding over potholes bumper to bumper. Students knew its five- and ten-cent stores and doughnut places: one must be fed again and again. The cheap doughy pizzas, muffins, and pastries dissolved in the guts in a thin sugary stream. Winter-pale, I smiled at my reflection in the display glass, malnutrition showing in my dark red gums.

Immigrants in Cambridge had a hard time, especially in their first experience of a blasting blizzard winter. Behind spilling garbage cans and dirty snow hills the sodden apartment houses that smelled like rotting layers of onion skin offered no hospitality. Peeling shingles exposed the rickety construction that gave the New England milltown its disreputable appearance—warehouses and whorehouses for the nineteenth-century working poor, today converted into disintegrating rentals for scholarship students.

I was a true immigrant, shabby, unrooted, poor, and perpetually afraid of losing my way. From the morning I arrived at Logan airport in early September, I had felt two predominant emotions, gratitude and guilt. I did not belong in Boston, but I was relieved to be out of that monstrous compression chamber that had carried me from Kuala Lumpur, across Asia and Europe, and the Atlantic to Boston. I stood in the white Boston airport like a starving crow looking for the Farleys to pick me up and deliver me to my host family.

Professor Farley and his wife were waiting in the arrival lounge. It was only much later that I understood the distance between their Amherst home and Logan Airport. That August afternoon, their pale towering presence was all I knew of the United States. As they drove to my host family's home, I turned my eyes away from the dizzying mountains of buildings that whizzed past us to watch their backs gratefully.

The International Students' Office at Brandeis had instituted a program through which arriving foreign students were matched with a volunteer family to help them through their transition. Thus, after lunch, Professor Farley and his wife left me the first night on U.S. soil with my host family—Emily, her husband David, and their eighteen-year-old daughter Ruth. As I watched the Farleys' white Plymouth pull out of the pine-shaded driveway, the sudden anxiety played against my determination to fit in. I simply had to lie low, play the roles set out for me by people who didn't know me, and live my life within myself. I felt myself an empty-handed transient, dependent on the charity of strangers, without resources, adrift, wholly without community, yet burning with pride and shame, which Emily in her desire to be kind only exacerbated.

"How small you are!" she exclaimed, and yes, I was smaller than her daughter leaving for college next week. "Look," she said, "you can wear Ruth's clothes that she has outgrown."

I took the heavy velour sweaters ungratefully. Full and richly burnished, even to my untrained eyes they were expensive and hardly used, warmer than anything I had carried with me from Kuala Lumpur. But my mind shrank from such comparisons; comparing the Frank Lloyd Wright house set among mountain laurel, dark green myrtle, birches, and towering pines that Thoreau would have apostrophized, with its easy domestic harmony of clear glass expanses, stone-fitted fireplaces, and wood-accented rooms, to the unfurnished room in which Karmal had held me for hours in my panic at leaving Malaysia. I did not wish to compare Emily, barely a generation older, the confident do-gooder, to me, unsettled, homeless, with less than a hundred dollars in my purse.

Emily lived in plenty. In the guest room downstairs, as I undressed for my shower, I opened the closets to find dozens of shampoo bottles, baskets of soaps, stacks of unused towels, enough skin lotions, cleansers, air fresheners, and toiletries to stock a stall along a Malacca night bazaar. Yet the house had the empty appearance of real wealth, where space is aesthetic and not vulgarly material.

"What shall we do for dinner?" David, my "host father," had just returned from his dental practice. Quiet, subdued, he let Emily do the talking.

"We don't have anything ready to eat!" she exclaimed.

"Perhaps I can make you a meal?" The spotless kitchen was sheathed in gray steel—a giant steel refrigerator, twin steel sinks, steel ovens and stoves. I would float in this steel sheath, my labor in return for the velour cast-offs, the hot shower, and bed for the night.

"Oh, would you?" For the first time since the Farleys had dropped me off with her, Emily appeared excited and happy about my presence. "Will you make a Chinese meal? There's only beef chuck in the freezer."

From a steel cabinet smoking with cold air she pulled out a parcel wrapped in waxed paper. The cream-spotted meat was crystalline with ice. I ran warm water from the gleaming spigot and the beef thawed into a shapeless mass. Slicing it as thinly as possible, I made a mound of half-frozen beef chips. Slathered thick with soy sauce and stir-fried with chopped garlic, the dish was the success I could not be. We ate around the kitchen table like an amiable family.

Even silent David grew expansive. "You know, we are really connoisseurs of Chinese food. Boston has some good restaurants, but your stir-fried beef is better than anything we've had."

I was passing for a Chinese chef, I thought deliriously. In my life with Iqbal, my cooking was barely to be tolerated. America, I saw immediately, had no discrimination. Frozen mushy beef here became a gourmet meal; a heavy-handed worse-than-ordinary attempt at cooking a culinary feat. The elegance of a home, where the mouth does not know the fine from the crude, was clearly not to be trusted.

The next morning Emily took me to Brandeis, where I found the Housing Information Board. Emily came out of the international student adviser's office and read my neatly-blocked notice: "International graduate student looking to share an apartment either with male or female roommates. Please call International Student Office and leave a message."

"No, no!" she exclaimed, distressed. "Your notice gives a wrong impression. People will think the worst."

To please her, I rewrote the notice to read "looking to share an apartment with female roommates." But the student adviser already had a prospective apartment for me, one with a young married Canadian couple in a wood-frame house two miles away from the campus in Waltham.

That afternoon Emily drove me to meet Jason and Brenda Clinken, both short, broad-beamed, very pink with red-gold hair.

"Oh gee! It would be nice to have you as a roommate," Jason said, blushing with pleasure. "I'm an anthropologist, and I'd like living with a foreigner."

"How sweet to have you share the house with us!" Brenda's voice was always pitched an octave higher than Jason's. She looked like an overweight schoolgirl, but she extended her fingers toward me as graciously as a school principal. "I'm sure we'll get along very well. You'll see, Jason and I are very friendly people, aren't we, Jason?"

"W'you say? Oh, yes, yes." Jason's laugh was shy, although it rumbled from a large chest and tight trousers. "As you see, we have a lot of room. You'll get the front room, and we'll share the kitchen and living room."

Emily didn't press me when I refused to stay a second night in her home. She'd bring my suitcase over, then call me in a week or so, she said.

From the first, Brenda treated me as if I were a half-wit. "Oh, are you writing poetry again?" she'd ask, looking up from her knitting. "I don't know why you waste your time. You should take up something more useful, like basket weaving."

Over the years, other Americans have made similar judgments on my choice of work, and I have not always successfully ignored them. At Brandeis, overwhelmed by Oscar Handlin's *The Uprooted*, I thought of writing my dissertation on American immigrant literature. When I approached him tentatively with the idea, Philip Rahv, a stocky, irascible, and remote professor who spoke with supreme authority, although indistinctly, as if his mouth were full of spittle, said with final irony, "There are no good immigrant writers, they write only sociology. And all this attention to black writers! There are only James Baldwin and Richard Wright, and even they are limited." He was unapproachable and so, it seemed, was the literature that I faintly glimpsed would speak most to me. More than a decade later, another Jewish professor wrote a confidential letter flaying me for my lecture on two Chinese-American writers, Frank Chin and Maxine Hong Kingston. If Chin and Kingston were the best I could come up with in Asian-American literature, in contrast to the splendid literature of China, he wrote, then the field had nothing to say for itself. More recently, a Chinese-American historian, debunking literary scholarship, said, "You literary types just read a few books, then write an article, whereas we historians have to spend years gathering empirical data before we can write anything." In her mouth, "empirical" rolled out like "superior," "reality," and "truth." In an evaluation letter, she lectured the reader on the moral gulf between empirical scholarship and interpretative analysis, and deplored the state of academe in which the latter stood on par with the former. Many Americans, it seems to me, are quick to condemn what they don't do, to judge what is different negatively. Something about a society whose founding principles are articulated on an arrogation of ethical superiority has given rise to a morality of intolerant standards: "we" are always better than "you." It is ironic that Americans of non-Anglo background who have struggled so hard to achieve excellence on American terms are sometimes the most self-righteous about defending a chimeral ideal of the good, whether it is seen in basket weaving as opposed to poetry, Chinese literature against Chinese-American literature, or history against literary criticism. The most grudging gatekeepers are often those just admitted into that city on a hill.

Jason told me the second evening that he and Brenda were nudists. "We're from Calgary, you know, and we love the cold. We think our bodies are healthiest when they are exposed to air. We never catch colds, and we never get sick!"

Brenda nodded her head sagely beside him. "Now, you mustn't mind if you come across Jason or myself sitting around buck naked in the living room. We don't think there's anything to be ashamed of with our bodies."

Her body was very white, dotted with pink pigment, and red-gold hair hung in a bush covering her mound and peeked from under her armpits. So much white-pink skin! Her stomach folded in layers over her thighs as she sat on the one large armchair, legs tucked primly under her, knitting and watching television in the living room. Jason's skin was ruddier, his round belly firmer. A red hairy bush like hers hung over his genitals, a baby replica of the tangle of hair which grew luxuriantly over his face. His pale blue eyes and small partially visible lips were those of a young boy, although his laugh was like a hearty Jesuit's. He usually sat on the couch facing the television, a book on his lap.

Their nakedness was intrusive. Walking home from the fall semester's seminars, I worried at the evening's prospects of watching television in the company of Brenda's white folds and Jason's flaming pubic hair. I kept to my room till they went to bed. Then I crept out and turned up the thermostat from sixty to sixty-eight degrees. Even then I shivered under three sweaters and my blanket, sitting up all night with a pot of black brewed coffee and a box of corn flakes, writing poetry spitefully, writing against Brenda's daily clicking knitting needles, her condescending green cat-eyes set above the pendulous swinging white breasts with their brown staring nipples.

I was taking a creative writing seminar with J. V. Cunningham, a man with a notorious reputation for refusing students he did not find worthy. I had written poetry from the age of ten. Was there something that could be taught about writing poetry? Cunningham was a dour teacher, sour-faced, with the shivering hands of an alcoholic. He sat at the head of the seminar table and, choosing his words with extraordinary care, offered a few directions. "Bring in a poem you have written," he asked the first week. "This is not a poem," he said, returning a sonnet I had written on reading Coleridge's "Rime of the Ancient Mariner." Stunned, I sat through the period, looking not at him but out of the window at the rapidly darkening afternoon, the tossing bare branches warning me of the cold blowy walk ahead of me later.

Only 5 P.M.., the day was already gone by the time I left the seminar. The glorious flaming plates of maple leaves had by now turned into sodden masses on the sidewalks. Again the sea-blue morning skies had deceived me earlier, and I had walked out of the house in sandals. Now my toes crisped with pain as I shuffled-ran past the rows of unlit frame houses. "Fuck you!" I said to Mr. Cunningham as the cold burned my ears. There were more ways to be a poet than sit still beneath his judgment. I read Robert Creeley that night, and copied his lines on orange paper which I taped to my walls.

"Now, why would you turn up the heat?" Jason laughed reasonably. Groggy from lack of sleep, I stared at him from under the sheets, the blanket, and the cheap chenille cover that I had found in Woolworth's. I could have been naked when he walked into my bedroom unannounced. "Brenda and I really cannot tolerate a hot house. Jesus, the temperature was nearly seventy degrees this morning! You know, that's like living in a hothouse."

The only place where I could sit in the department was in a small room converted into a student lounge. My loneliness was conspicuous in the empty room as I tried drinking the foul instant coffee from the plastic cone that tipped precariously on its flimsy holder. I lit a cigarette with fingers lashed over the handle and dropped the match just as Jeff, another graduate student, walked in. Furiously he stomped out the quick flames that left a brown singe on the carpet. "Hey, you've got to be careful!" He gave me a wary look then left hurriedly.

I stayed up later and later, writing on the orange notepaper I had bought on sale from Woolworth's, which I haunted on Saturdays. During the seminar, I sat as far away from Cunningham as I could, turned in my poems, and expected nothing. One day, looking at me, he noted that sonnet sequences were a traditional form that could be well adapted for contemporary occasions. In his minuscule handwriting he dropped brief comments, "nice," "perspicacious," "elegant." I felt a tide turning under my feet, but the distance I had measured outside that window one afternoon remained.

Into December and January, it was cold, then colder. I could not believe how cold the world could grow and still be a world to live in. I bought ugly pink-sprigged thermals, wore three pairs of socks, covered my face with synthetic mufflers, learned to blow my breath out before breathing in my own warmth. I dreamed of geese force-fed till their gullets burst, whose rich crimson livers appeared on gilt-edged servers as *foise grasse,* and woke up a vegetarian. Apples, bananas, yogurt, cereals, and above all the craving for sugar. I tried bars of Mars, Mounds, Peter and Paul, Babe Ruth, Snickers, Bounty, and liked them all.

I refused to eat with Jason and Brenda, who boiled kettlefuls of eggs, peeled them, and pickled them in vinegar and tea. "It's important to have protein," Jason protested, holding a tea-stained egg between his fleshy fingers. "Besides, we bought all the eggs on sale. This egg is only five cents!" He put the whole ovaloid mass into his mouth and chewed vigorously. "It's delicious."

I dreamed of the Strait of Malacca, of the gentle salty warm water in which I had rocked as a child, murmuring, "The sea is my mother, the sea is my mother." One evening, desperate with cold, I ran the grainy old bathtub full of hot water and sat soaking in it, eyes closed, pretending it was grains of sand I felt running under my body and the water barely up to my chest the vast mobile expanse of a tropical sea.

"Hey, I have to use the bathroom," Jason said, pushing the door open. "You don't mind, do you?" I sank as far down as I could into the tub and shut my eyes. Close to my right ear, his urine hissed into the toilet bowl. "Jesus, it's hot in here. How could you sit in this heat for hours?" When I didn't answer, he left. Later that night, Brenda, still dressed in her librarian turtleneck and skirt, looked up over the moving needles and said in her polite principal's voice, "May I say something to you? You can't get too prudish with us. You know, a pussy is a pussy. It doesn't mean anything."

In November the Farleys called to invite me to Amherst for Thanksgiving dinner; a friend driving up from Boston would bring me up with him. Mr. Farley took me for a walk through the woods in search of trillium for a friend in Japan. I crushed the acrid oil of a winter mint leaf between my teeth, gathered dark orange berried vines of bittersweet, and spied wrinkled raisins deep in sprawling wild raspberry canes. Mr. Farley clipped armfuls of piney hemlock for twining around bent wire hangers. "Nature doesn't mind if you take just a little," he said in excuse. The bird feeder in the yard was busy with nuthatches and chickadees fluttering to and fro. Mrs. Farley took me down to the fruit cellar to pick a jar of pickles for Thanksgiving dinner. The stony space was lined with plain wood shelves on which she had stored her jars of homemade jellies, relishes, and pickles. The furniture in the large Victorian house looked as if each piece had been in its place for decades. After dinner, the ample linen napkins, still clean, were stored away for the next meal. Their company was quiet and undemanding, but this Thanksgiving had nothing to do with my shifting, shabby life as a graduate student.

For an international student, U.S. graduate education is often an obstacle course through isolated terrain. In 1969 and 1970, Brandeis, already worried about its association with the radical philosophy of Herbert Marcuse, who had retired from the university in 1965, was reeling from the notoriety of students linked to the Weathermen Underground, bank robberies, and bombs. Its most famous graduate, Angela Davis, had been arrested in connection with the attempted prison escape of the Soledad Brothers. Faculty and administration, responding to parental fears and a drop in enrollment and donor money, were rapidly de-escalating the political activism on campus. I had arrived just in time for the deep freeze.

The massive indifference I faced in the department was not personal but systemic. Irving Howe, whom I had come to study with, had left for The City University of New York. Coming without prior U.S. mentors, with no alumni ancestry, I was seriously invisible. It did not occur to me that the professors were racist or that my "foreignness" made them uncomfortable; they were just as indifferent to Jewish and other students, although a few students did become attached to individual faculty "stars" and enjoyed close relations with them—conversations, coffee, dinners, special seminars. But such attention was unique, given against the grain of institutionalized neglect, dependent on a mysterious nexus of interests: personality, class, ethnicity, persistence, a lucky break.

I was provided with a first-year adviser, Mr. Harts, a sixteenth-century scholar. He was gray and lean with a friendly formality that reminded me of Professor Farley. For a few weeks I sat outside his door during his office hour, only to find that he was not available. When he finally met me, he asked with a smile, "What are you doing here? You should be married. What do you hope to get out of Brandeis?"

For a moment I was unsettled by his questions. No one in Malaysia had ever asked me why I was continuing my studies or suggested that I should give them up for marriage. No one except myself. I was shaken that he should so boldly voice what I had been struggling with in silence. I racked my mind to answer as truthfully as possible. "Well, I want a Ph.D., and my university back home only offers master's degrees." Even to me my answer sounded weak, but Mr. Harts did not challenge me further. Instead he glanced at the folder of poems I had brought with me and suggested that I bring it with me when we have our second meeting at his home in Cambridge on a Saturday morning.

I was careful to set off early that morning as I found Cambridge still a disorienting town of disjointed streets, gaps, and unnamed alleys. The house was a lovely New England Victorian, white with green wooden shutters, in a row with other Victorians. The side street was empty and peaceful after the week-end throngs at Harvard Square. I rang the bell and waited, pleased to have the poems with me, pleased that I was finally connecting with my adviser. The door opened suddenly and a middle-aged woman began screaming at me, "Slut! Whore! You're not coming in! Get out of here, you whore!" Her gray hair uncombed and tangled, she glared wildly at me, then banged the door shut.

Trembling I looked down the street and was relieved and anxious to find all the front doors still shut, and no one looking out of a window in response to the screams. I felt conspicuous in my short green dress, unclean, as if her words had splattered me with feces. I was confused and fearful at the same time. Would she would come out with a knife? Had I rung the wrong doorbell? But it was the number Mr. Harts had give me. Had she mistaken me for someone else? Where was Mr. Harts, and why didn't he come out to tell me there was a mistake? What if I had the wrong address and Mr. Harts was waiting for me somewhere else?

Wandering aimlessly toward Harvard Square I ran into another graduate student. "What are you doing?" Jay asked, at which I burst into tears. "Well," he said, at the end of my tearful account, "we'll just go back together and see if you've made a mistake on the address."

I stood behind him, my eyes red, crumpling his wet handkerchief in my hand, as he rang the bell on the same green door. Mr. Harts opened the door as if he had been expecting me, "Oh, you've come for our meeting."

"She got lost, and there seems to have been some kind of misunderstanding," Jay explained very calmly. "Well, I'll leave you for your meeting."

I followed Mr. Harts into a polished gleaming living room with soft rugs and leather chairs. He offered no explanation and I said nothing about the woman. He spoke briefly about courses I should cover, and after about ten minutes it was evident our meeting was over. The inexplicable accusations, his silence on the matter, and my utter confusion form a design that characterized the bizarre U.S. culture I had entered.

Gray houses, wood-shingled, derelict, fronted the side streets of Waltham. In the winter chill, they looked like frozen decaying garbage, the cold preserving the structures, the decay visible yet suspended. One could choose, instead, to walk on Main Street, past the painted low rectangular concrete structures before which cars regularly pulled up, then drove off loaded with bulging brown bags. In the A&P, long banks of fluorescent lighting illuminated heaped-up gleaming packages of bright red beef, pale fat-wrapped sides of pork, whole chickens frozen to stony condition, and tubes of processed meat all of equal dimension. Hundreds of maroon-flushed apples with starred bottoms, hard and shiny as candle wax, waited to be gathered. Everything was in containers, even these apples in their waxed coats. Butter came in separate oblongs, covered in gold paper, then contained further in cardboard boxes.

The supermarket was as large as the Petaling Jaya wet-market in which I had shopped for Iqbal's dinner-parties, but in the entire air-controlled space crammed with hundreds of tins of fish and beans, bottles of oils and sauces, boxes of cereals and grains, scores of soaps and detergents; the aisles narrowly lined with towering stacks of paper, fluids, plastics, metal goods; hissing cold giant iceboxes stuffed with gallons of ice cream, shrink-wrapped Boston cream pies and frozen cheesecakes, there was not a single scent of ripeness, a welcoming softness to suggest salivary delight, a tang whether sharp or sour promising kitchen smells and steaming dishes. The bananas were hard greenish yellow; onions in three-pound nylon sacks appeared scrubbed clean. If there was nourishing sweetness in all this warehouse of food, one would have to tear through unyielding metal, thick polyvinyl, pounds of cardboard; and the sweetness jacketed in the shapely banana was so mixed with the bitter gummy chemicals of its premature harvesting that my stomach heaved in disgust even as my teeth frantically chewed to keep ahead of my ravenous hunger. For the first year in the United States I was always hungry, a hunger that rebelled against American food.

I wrote letters to Iqbal every week. After Christmas, he called to wish me a happy birthday: I was twenty-five. His voice came from some place so far away I despaired I would ever see him again. Stupidly I said into the mouthpiece, "You sound Malaysian!" I had remembered him as American. Now, from Massachusetts, I saw that his American self was a fantasy, my memory of him already distorted, another fantasy. He laughed, a laugh that still managed to boom across the underwater Pacific lines. "I love you," he said, and I held on to what was not promised in his words: faithfulness, waiting, meeting.

But his letters stopped after that call. January, February, March. I lingered at card shops, searching for the perfect message to start up the engine of our relationship. Images of bare black branches against a white sky. A man and a woman etched against an open window (but they were white!). A moon hovering over water broken into panes of light and shade. Purple mountains. Cheerful yellow-splashed love messages from Sister Corita. I began to think of my letters as calls to my shadow, slipping into another universe in which mysterious forces guarded my other psyche. They were not lost, not unread. I sent copies of my new poems, buying lavender notepaper, writing on brown wrapping paper, writing around the margins of the heavy oversized cards. I stopped asking for my mail when I got home.

I was always hungry, but I never shopped at the A&P again. Instead I fed coins into vending machines and chewed the slippery fudge centers of handfuls of chocolate bars. My clothes became too tight, and I wore the same pair of tight blue jeans every day. One night, around 3 A.M., the coffee pot almost empty, dizzy with hunger, tired of writing poetry, I looked into the small mirror in my bedroom and saw my mother's face. It was pale, pudgy, deeply unhappy. My hair hung long and limp like dead moss. With a fury of revulsion, I found a pair of paper scissors and cut it from waist-length to just below the shoulders. But my mother's face continued to stare at me out of the mirror. To come so far, and to find myself swallowed by my mother!

The next day I threw away the candy bars. "Yes," I said when Maurice, a philosophy graduate student, invited me to his housewarming party in Cambridge. My heart pounded as I searched for the apartment that Saturday afternoon. When I arrived, there were groups of people in every room, in the kitchen, the different bedrooms, the study. Only the living room was empty. An incense stick burned and from the speakers poured the familiar raga of Ali Akbar Khan that Iqbal had loved. I walked through the apartment smiling vaguely at no one. "Ah, my poet!" Maurice said, taking me by my hand, then releasing it to speak to someone else. I returned to the living room where someone in a white shirt, his brown hair still wet from a shower, was picking a guitar softly.

"I'm looking for a housemate," he said, his expression changing from doleful to cheery when I sat down beside him. "I have an apartment in North Cambridge. Where do you live?"

Gerald was a songwriter, not yet recognized. "You must move in with us," he insisted when I told him I was taking the train back to Waltham. "Neil and I can't afford the rent by ourselves. Besides, you don't want to live in Waltham. It's a dump. Everyone lives in Cambridge."

And so I told Brenda and Jason that I was leaving the next month. I took down my wallpaper of orange poems, gave them my orange-painted door-top desk, packed Gerald's old Volkswagen with my two suitcases and with boxes of newly purchased books, and moved to a walk-up two miles above Porter Square. A songwriter would help me unbecome my mother. Gerald was as different from Brenda and Jason's deluded rationality as I could hope for.

The first week I hardly saw my two new housemates. I wandered through Harvard Square, marveling at the intense claustrophobic desire of browsers standing heads bent for hours in the secondhand bookstores. I spent two weeks' groceries on a seventeenth-century leather-bound copy of Milton's sermons and wrote on the margins recklessly. It seemed to me that all New England's centuries had seeped into the paper dust over the hardcover books by authors that no one wanted any more: William Vaughn Moody, Van Wyck Brooks,

Vernon L. Parrington, Joseph Wood Crutch, John W. Aldridge. Books by Irving Babbit, Carl Van Doren, William Dean Howells, and other Anglo male names were always among the reduced piles by the doorways. I had arrived in Cambridge to study American literature in time to witness its dissolution into something else. Or perhaps the unsold secondhand books were like the disinterred bones of vanished folk, like the ancestral portraits my parents had set up on the family altar, that could only gaze, features fixed, at the commotion of the living. Around me, students carried copies of *Steppenwolf,* quoted Marx and Alice B. Toklas, and baked marijuana into their brownies.

Neil stayed in his room most days and came out to retrieve his small jars of cottage cheese from the refrigerator. He was all bones, his elbows sticking out like those of famine victims, his cheeks gaunt with hollows. An M.I.T. student, he never went to the university during the two months I stayed with them. The only word he said to me was "Hello."

The second week, Gerald came to my room and asked for a date. I refused. "You're a witch," he said good-naturedly.

Then it began to snow. I tried going out on the second day. The sidewalks were slippery, piled high with frozen snow, and the air was filled with flakes, dropping, dropping. Wearing cheap rubber boots I slipped inch by inch toward Harvard Square. After about an hour, still miles from the square, I gave up and slowly slid back to the apartment. The third night, I knocked on Gerald's door for company but he was out. Sitting on my sagging bed, I called my host family. There was no reply. I dialed the Farleys in Amherst and, as the phone rang and rang, I imagined the map of the United States as I had sketched it in countless exams, now no longer a drawing but a territory of vast snow drifts, and myself holding a telephone without a voice on the other end.

There is no pain as bad as the pain of isolation. At the corner of my mind someone stood up to scream. But I carefully put the telephone back in the living room where it remained silent for weeks. I crawled under my chenille cover and curled up to touch my toes with my fingers. "I am a baby," I thought, "and babies need to sleep," and I lay in that position all night, unsure if it was sleep or consciousness I felt.

The morning was bright, the sky empty of white stuff. I dressed in my thermal underwear, shirts, sweaters, pants, socks, coat, muffler, cap, gloves. Swaying through the snowy mounds like a fat explorer, I caught the train to Brandeis, then clumsily slipped around the campus, fat arms stuck out for balance, looking and looking for someone. The drifts had forced everyone indoors. Finally I entered the Castle cafeteria, desperate for others, even if they were only strangers, even if only to breathe in their bodily smells. The small round tables were crowded and noisy. Sitting in their coats, people were eating soup and hearty sandwiches, talking with their mouths full, and the air was hazy with cigarette smoke. I bought a blueberry yogurt and sat by the door.

Adam Bulcovich, still writing his dissertation after ten years at Brandeis, asked, "May I sit here?" I knew he was married with children. Putting his bowl of soup on the table, he leaned over and looked at me. I saw my mother's swollen face in his eyes. The yogurt tasted like nothing I had grown up eating. I forced myself to keep swallowing each sugary-sour blue spoonful.

"Something's the matter with you," he said. There was a muffling distance between his voice and my body. I was sweating under the layers of clothing. "Come with me." He got up and took me by the elbow.

Obediently I waddled beside him out of the cafeteria, across the quad, to the Heller Building. He said something to a secretary and then to a woman in another room. I sat across the desk and looked at the woman. The sign on her desk said Dr. Helda. My throat was burning with something withheld.

"Do you wish to cry?" she asked.

"It's shameful to cry," I mumbled. I remembered my brothers' jeers. I had come all the way from childhood without crying. Not when Father beat me, not when I woke up and found my body scarred, not when I left Malaysia. A jagged hook was lodged in my throat. Someone had slashed me from ear to ear, and I was choking on my bile.

"It's only human to cry," she said as she handed me a box of Kleenex.

The pain moved upward, it burst out of my nostrils, spilled out of my eyes. It was hot, like water from a long-heated kettle, and it wouldn't stop running. I licked the water as it splashed over my face, so much of it that Kleenex after Kleenex shredded from the flood. It was almost an hour before I stopped crying. "I'm sorry, I'm sorry," I repeated. "I don't know why I'm crying. It's stupid. It's just that I'm such a failure."

Adam had brought me to the Crisis Intervention Center. Dr. Helda was the first of women strangers in the United States to help me learn what my mother had never taught me. It is all right to cry. Carry your own key, even if it is to a temporary home. After you have painted yourself into a corner, you can always get up and walk out of that corner. Living is an achievement.

Gerald was having a hard time selling his songs, and when he was home in the apartment, he wanted me to listen to his songs. "You can be my inspiration," he said, beaming on the one afternoon I politely sat beside him as he strummed his guitar. His songs were tuneless, or rather they all sounded like a generic version of James Taylor's "Fire and Rain," and the lyrics were about ordinary disappointment, in language that made much about the disappointment. So much in the apartment was about wrong choices. Neil struggling at M.I.T., Gerald struggling with his songs. And myself?

I wanted a prophecy, a fortuneteller to tell me my future. "Come in," Professor Cunningham said. As usual, he was grim and uneasy, all at the same time. He did not welcome company. Instead he stood stiffly by the window, his tenseness holding me by the door. "What do you want?"

"I want to know what you think of my poetry."

He made an unreadable gesture with his hands.

"I know someone who's in his forties" (I was thinking of James puffing on his pipe and dazzling his students with rhetoric), "and I don't want to end up like him with only yellowing pages of unpublished bad poems."

He looked at me reflectively. Then in an impatient hoarse voice, he said, "You have talent, but what happens to it depends on you."

I had not expected that much from him. I never asked him again about my poetry, although I continued to send him some of my poems through the years, until his death in 1985. Instead, I worked with him on my dissertation, learning to appreciate him as a taskmaster whose parsimony was a form of respect for necessary boundaries.

I was drawn to Cunningham's aloofness because it maintained these boundaries when all around me strangers kept pushing them down. As I tried to overcome the isolation of the foreigner in New England, the first boundary to be tested was the use of my body. One day in the kitchen Gerald came up behind me and hugged me, pressing his body against mine forcibly. When I pulled away, he frowned. "You really are a witch," he said, this time with an emphasis. "You've bewitched me, and I can see that this is what you do to men." "Witch!" he taunted me, whenever he saw me leaving the apartment dressed up.

Fearful, I began to lock my bedroom door at night.

To escape from Gerald's knowing smiles, and pleading the necessity for library proximity to finish some incomplete papers, I asked the International Office to arrange for me to spend the spring break in a dormitory. All the students had fled home or to warmer havens, and I roamed the deserted campus, a solitary walker among stiff bare lilac bushes, heaps of weeks-old snow still mounded over hillsides and shrubbery.

That week a letter—the last he would write, it said—came from Iqbal after months of silence. He was with another woman, he wrote, someone he was able to feel responsible for in a way he had not been ready for with me. His Berkeley sickness, his letter said, was over. Like the snow, my feelings were old, cold, and brittle. I walked everywhere, unable to sit still, to read, or to write. Here were fake Danish sofas with ancient coffee stains on their orange covers in empty lounges. Here also were gleaming glass doors opening to locked offices. The parking lots were empty, the dormitory corridors silent, the narrow paths between library stacks clear. The university, the huge physical conglomerate of brick, glass, concrete, plush, fabric, metal, and vegetation, its heating and lighting dynamos humming still, offered a strange solace, an empty-handed gesture in which I could stay suspended, feeling and not feeling, sheltered yet homeless, solitary yet not absolutely alone.

In April the snow thawed, and the Commons turned into sticky mush under the boots of hundreds of revelers at the Renaissance Festival. Long velvet skirts dragged in the mud. Pasty winter-pale faces blurred into masked apparitions, sequined, feathered, beaded masks under which long arched noses and moist red lips wriggled.

Emily and David had taken me out to a Chinese dinner with an astronomer from Harvard the week before. The cornstarch-thickened oily sauces paraded on my tongue like so many freaks. I could barely speak all evening, a disappointment to everyone.

The Renaissance Festival, with its jostling costumes, masks, bedraggled pretend splendor, its changing stream of actors, voyeurs, passers-by, snackers, shoppers, schleppers, sellers, the students and the residents, strangers moving among strangers, was where I chose to look for the way out of my corner. When people smiled, I smiled back. Someone spoke, I answered. Flyers were handed out for a dance at the community center. Later that evening I wandered into the center. In the dim hall to the whining acid energy of late Beatles, bodies whirled singly, motion and sound taking the place of a human partner.

"So, I was hoping you would show up." Prematurely balding, a wispy blond mustache hiding a sensitive mouth, Luke was gentle in speech like the Farleys. We had talked briefly above the din at the Commons until the moving crowds had separated us or until my restlessness had allowed him to drift out of sight. Everything about Luke was pale, his light blue eyes, his white skin without the spotty ruddiness of Jason and Brenda, his thin yellowish hair. A slight tremble ran through his body, like a continuous current discharging a psychic energy.

Luke could not be ruthless. His extreme sensitivity to others was like an antenna, a radar that could not be switched off. It was as if his consciousness were constantly flooded with information which it had to interpret.

In one evening he intuited my fears, my isolation, my pride, and my need to be alone. "Listen, I have just moved to a new apartment on Beacon Hill. I'm away on assignment a lot, and I need a housemate. You will be by yourself most of the time. Think about it." He gave me his work number. He was a reporter for a major newspaper in Boston.

When I returned to the apartment that evening, Gerald was awake. "Where have you been to, witch?" he asked, as I came out of the bathroom. His eyes and his large teeth gleamed in the semi-dark.

The next day I called Luke at work. He sounded jubilant. "I'm leaving this afternoon for a story in Cincinnati. I'll leave the key under the rug, and you can move in whenever you like."

Luke's apartment perched like an aerie on Beacon Hill overlooking the white-sailed yachts skimming on the Charles River; but until I moved out of the apartment to the Castle at Brandeis, I was never comfortable with myself.

One problem was keeping busy. Living in Luke's apartment, I looked for ways to affirm that I was not living off him. I insisted on buying the groceries and preparing meals on the days when he was home from assignment, but doing the laundry, dusting, and cleaning still left huge gaps in the day.

Each morning, I took long desultory walks. Beside the rushing trucks and cars by the entry to the turnpike, I found greening privet hedges and carried back a branch, the furled leaf-buds like an oppositional message from the cold hard dirt. As the weather grew milder, I sat on benches beside Swan Lake in Boston Commons, always aware that my Asian body gave me away as a foreigner. It was as if I walked inside an invisible bubble, and all downtown Boston hubbubbed around me, visible but out of my reach.

I saw a sign advertising for waitresses in a window of a bar at Copley Square, and walked in on impulse. The swarthy manager looked me up and down. "Any experience?"

I shook my head.

"What do you say if a customer wants to, you know, take you out later?" When I didn't reply, he smiled. "All right. Come in tonight at seven."

I never returned.

Instead I began sitting in the Boston Public Library all afternoon with five to six science-fiction books each time. I read as if my life depended on it, seriously, unthoughtfully, without a single memory of the books, except some titles and authors. Beginning with Robert Heinlein's *Stranger in a Strange Land* for the sense of the title alone, I went down the shelves of Isaac Asimov's novels and ended with the annual collections of *Science Fantasy Tales*. All the books were about aliens, alien planets, alien systems, alien languages, alien relations, and the dangers, risks, threats, disasters at work in alienness. I dropped the books each night exhausted, sat staring each morning at laughing couples and families as they paddled the garish swan boats over the summer-blue lake, walked around and around Boston at noon, spying on the distant history of still-elegant brownstones whose windows were crowded with spiderplants and wandering Jews, and did not try to make sense of my life.

Luke was very kind. Glancing obliquely at me with his light blue eyes, he would suggest drives to upstate Massachusetts.

We spent a weekend at a halfway house for schizophrenic patients, set among head-high goldenrod and clumps of Queen Anne's lace. The members of the house were young and vigorous, golden-brown in worn dungarees and flannel shirts. We walked down trails bordered by overgrown huckleberry bushes. Round yellow and brown bumblebees hummed in the thick sunlight, and burrs stuck to my blue jeans. Some gnarled apple trees shaded the front yard of the rambling structures, once a farmhouse. I resisted picking the apples, knobbly, dimpled, half the size of my fist. Left over from another time when pruned, watered, and made much of, the trees must have bent low with ripe full fruit, these apples were no longer edible. We sat around a community dining table, drank sassafras tea with clover honey, and listened yet again to a James Taylor's tape replaying "You've Got a Friend." A copy of Maurice Sendak's *Where the Wild Things Are* lay among a sheaf of magazines in the common living room.

How does one make oneself at home? I began to see that I needed to be useful to someone else other than myself. What had preserved me in Malaysia, the struggle for an individual self against the cannibalism of familial, ethnic, and communal law, was exactly what was pickling me in isolation in the United States. In the United States I was only a private person. Without family and community, I had no social presence; I was among the unliving. With Luke I had a parasitic life, attached to his company when he was home, but cast out alone to the Commons otherwise.

In August I applied to be a dormitory counselor at the Castle in Brandeis. At the interview, I was asked how I felt about being on call on weeknights and weekends. The prospect filled me with joy. To be of service! To be necessary to others!

I was careful to reply soberly that of course I would be available, to indicate that I had another life with a friend on Beacon Hill. But it was clear to me that in moving to a single room earned through my work, a room to which I alone held the key, but which was part of a social complex, I had taken the first step to entering the United States on my terms.

The Castle then was a segregated dormitory; the main doors were locked at eleven and men were not permitted in the rooms after that hour. Except for a few occasions when lovers from distant states stayed over, the floors were wholly female every night. At their first meeting with the dorm counselors, the resident counselors, a married couple, spoke not so much of caretaker responsibilities as uncomfortably and vaguely about being there when we were needed, as if we were to be unintrusive, benign parents whose hovering spirits evoked security for middle-class undergraduates.

And, indeed, I found in the sex-segregated dormitory culture—a culture different from the academic, female competitiveness prevalent in the residence halls of Kuala Lumpur—a necessary security. At eleven, after the last reluctant male was turned out, the women came out to shower wearing hair rollers, shower caps, flowered robes, and footed pajamas. We knocked on doors and sat on desktops, idly chatting, a lightness circulating with the cigarette smoke in the certainty that we were all women for the next few hours. Perhaps it was the late hour, the time of midnight snacks when the indulgence of fruit-sweetened yogurt and fudge brownies awoke the comforts of childhood. In that brief period without male presence, I felt how sweet it was to be in a community of women, where one's laughter was laughter and not flirtation, where someone combed your hair to adorn you, not to penetrate, where a palpable affection in the moment, requiring no commitment, possession, or competition, was good enough for the moment.

But such communities are ephemeral. Feeling like a sister is a fugitive emotion in societies where women marry, bear children, and enter their husband's house to work. The recognition of the possibility of sisterhood, however, has remained steady despite the passing of those moments.

One evening, Martha, Elise, and Susan invited me to Martha's room before a lecture by B. F. Skinner. Giggling, Martha passed around a joint. Their concentrated inhalations gave them an air of solemnity broken immediately by their silly gasps. The room was thick with marijuana smoke, and though I refused the joint, I grew light-headed. By the time we arrived at the lecture, the hall was crowded, so we went up the stairs to a second-floor gallery. From that distance, Skinner appeared small and insignificant, his voice through the microphone tinny and affected. The women were laughing and looking for acquaintances among the audience below. A sudden nausea frightened me. I thought I would have to hold on to one of them to maintain my balance, I would have to confess that I could not manage alone. My head spun with the panic of losing control, and I had an image of cards delicately balanced one on the other, just on the point of falling down. Then, as suddenly, I thought, "It's all right if the cards fall down. My friends will help me set them up again." The terror left me. I looked around. Neither Martha nor Elise nor Susan had noticed anything.

The felt insight that there were others who would help, so contrary to my childhood experience of society as indifferent if not actually hostile, came to me through the affectionate companionship of women friends. This provisional sisterhood is neither an ideal nor a concept, merely a repeated experience that I look for, work for, use, offer, and cherish. It's true that women are divided by unequal privileges of race, class, age, nation, and so forth, but across these divisions, of white middle-class women and myself, for example, or young Chicanas and myself now, a rare yet common ground is visible. We understand each other in devious ways: our physical desires and the shame we have been trained to feel over our bodies, our masked ambitions, the distances between our communities and our hungry selves, our need to be needed. We are safe when we speak of women's literature and feminist theory, for here we can talk about common ground without presuming to talk only about ourselves or only about the other. Although some feminist theorists have bracketed the concept of "sisterhood" as an anachronistic embarrassment, it is the only term I can find to suggest not only the necessity for coalition and the work of solidarity but also the sensibility of support that grows when social gender is recognized as a shared experience.

After the limited meetings with Dr. Helda, I measured the world differently. I wanted to see it through eyes other than my suffering ones. Meeting Alice, also a dorm counselor at the Castle, I saw the disparity between us, and immediately envied and desired that difference in her.

Once a worshipping Congregationalist or Episcopalian, Alice was still clear-skinned and friendly, still encumbered with middle-class desires that, like a sweet tooth, nagged for love, security, and marriage. But she was also on speaking terms with Hegel and Marx, and was writing a thesis on Weber and industrial states. Like me, she was a graduate "woman," set aside from the undergraduates we lived with by overhanging career anxieties and sexual confusions, but I saw Alice as mildly fretting under these questions which for me were terror-edged. She drove a huge maroon Buick, a hand-me-down from her parents, and returned for weekends to her parents' home in Connecticut where she sailed with her brothers and father on their yacht off Long Island Sound.

I watched how she maneuvered the new space outside her parents' society, but it was a lesson I could not grasp: her easy sociability, as if she were everyone's equal, given a democratic birthright in U.S. privilege, without the crankiness of people who anticipate slights, condescension, and rejection as their lot. She had odd sayings drawn from a childhood of afternoon television cartoons—"Holy Murgertroyd! Beep! Beep!"—that she threw out as non sequiturs and that made her appear thoroughly mainstream and wholesome, an exotic Episcopalian ad-libbing among the heavily New York Jewish-accented environment of Brandeis. She walked briskly, with determined cheerfulness that attracted notice in the midst of the cultural melancholia of the anti-Vietnam-era campus.

But I could also see how she had wilted around her edges. Only a sufferer would make up a daily schedule that meticulously broke the day into set activities, listing time for meals, laundry, shower, calls home, library, and television viewing. Coming across her discarded schedule pages, I recognized the mania of the isolated. She was ahead of me in the game. She had already learned how to keep busy, how to spend time with people she would will herself to know, how to open her self little by little till her hours were filled with unscheduled life.

Cambridge held no terrors for Alice. She had migrated only from Connecticut, and she walked at home among multitudes of students and faded into their gregariousness like a white and brown wren in its urban habitat. Alice was friendly with Jim, Linda, Bob, and other students, all white and brown-haired like her.

I was only too aware of the precariousness of my privileged relationship with Alice. The summer of 1971, she was living with Joshua, who had brown curly hair, smoked a pipe, and was Jewish, and she offered to share their sublet north of Porter Square with me. Who knows why she decided to admit me into her life? Sharing the apartment with Joshua, she might not have wanted another man in the picture or another attractive woman. She may have seen my foreignness as outside of Joshua's desires. Alice was such a healthy normal American that her impulses might have been unreadable to herself. She acted from an unconscious instinct for self-preservation in which the need to appear open, direct, and gracious was foremost. I was in love with her openness, her Anglo graciousness.

When we became roommates that summer, I felt I was being admitted into an American family, a fortuitous, unexpected, blessed accident. Careful to hide in my room, I spied on their experiment in domesticity: Joshua puffing on his pipe as he read his sociology tomes, Alice baking brownies in a kitchen almost romantic in its scrubbed-down minimalism. Joshua and Alice planning picnics during which watermelon-seed spitting contests were prominently featured. Joshua and Alice returning from the laundromat with their clothes and underwear intimately tumbled together. There were none of the fights, few of the tones of dominance and service that had marked my experiences with Ben and Iqbal.

Like a maiden sister, I was invited where they were invited. To an apartment in Cambridge crowded with walls of records where a researcher of rock music offered Mexican *mole* that he had stewed for three days. To a rental in Somerville where people made ice-cream sundaes and talked about the return of religious fundamentalism.

Joshua and Alice moved among a mating cohort. In the midst of national trauma, with young men contemplating ways to increase their blood pressure, plead insanity, or achieve flat-footedness to avoid the draft, domestic coupling seemed to be the herb of choice for the thousands of migrant graduate students in Cambridge that summer. Everyone was paired, like woolen socks or flocks of nuthatches dispersed in book-lined nests.

I sat by doorways and behind other guests, pretended interest in paintings and shrubs, observed the little clouds in the summer blue skies like an unreal watcher, the scenes and twosome characters before me alternately vivid and gray, not of their world and without any other available to me.

Sitting in Brigham's alone one afternoon and staring at the bottom of my glass sundae dish, I listened to the chatter of Americans caught up in the great adventure of their culture: the war in Vietnam, the Weathermen Underground, the presidential elections, Lionel Trilling's recent lectures. There was no entry for me. Too recent, too raw, I belonged elsewhere; was elsewhere; longed for elsewhere. The United States and I were too provincial for each other. I felt the intensity of our different self-absorptions, had hoped that brisk busy Alice would let me in her world, but as summer was ending I saw, against her pinky whiteness, how hopelessly alien my own body appeared.

"My God, Shirley!" It was as if a ghost from Malaysia had been summoned to Brigham's by the intensity of my longing. It was Sharma, whose party was the first I had attended with Iqbal in Kuala Lumpur three years before, Sharma, on a government-sponsored summer course at the Kennedy School of Government at Harvard, with an African colleague by his side. He glanced at my cut-off blue jeans, my rubber thongs, and the single empty dish, his enthusiasm perceptibly diminishing.

I could think only of Iqbal in his presence, but I dared not ask my questions. Instead I invited them to the apartment, a piece of Malaysia to meet my precariously formed new American family, Alice and Joshua and just-baked brownies which Sharma turned down politely. I could see in Sharma's eyes what he would write to Iqbal, the bohemianism of graduate summer living not suitable for civil servants on the fast track. Sharma was not impressed by Alice's loud talk and direct handshake, or by Joshua's Weberian conversation. Even three years ago, in his Kuala Lumpur bungalow with his handsome saried wife circulating food and drinks, he had appeared grown-up and settled. His tone that afternoon was condescending, suggesting that our lives of inquiry were irrelevant. I never met him again.

His African companion called, inviting me to a movie. After the movie, he asked to come back to my room. Unspoken, his casual assumption that two lonely exiles would have at least that in common. I refused, but that night, facing the stark alternatives, I wrote to my faithful friend Karmal, whose last letter had talked about his attempt to adopt the daughter of the woman he was marrying. I was tired of being alone, I wrote. I was ready for marriage.

CHAPTER NINE

# Two Lives

N o one who has not left everything behind her—every acquaintance, tree, corner lamp post, brother, lover—understands the peculiar remorse of the resident alien. Unlike the happy immigrant who sees the United States as a vast real-estate advertisement selling a neighborly future, the person who enters the country as a registered alien is neither here nor there. Without family, house, or society, she views herself through the eyes of citizens: guest, stranger, outsider, misfit, beggar. Transient like the drunks asleep by the steps down to the subway, her bodily presence is a wraith, less than smoke among the 250 million in the nation. Were she to fall in front of the screeching wheels of the Number Four Lexington line, her death would be noted by no one, mourned by none, except if the news should arrive weeks later, thirty thousand miles away.

A resident alien has walked out of a community's living memory, out of social structures in which her identity is folded, like a bud in a tree, to take on the raw stinks of public bathrooms and the shapes of shadows in parks. She holds her breath as she walks through the American city counting the afternoon hours. Memory for her is a great mourning, a death of the living. The alien resident mourns even as she chooses to abandon. Her memory, like her guilt and early love, is involuntary, but her choice of the United States is willful.

For what? She asks the question over and over again. At first, she asks it every day. Then as she begins to feel comfortable in the body of a stranger, she asks it occasionally, when the weekend stretches over the Sunday papers and the television news does not seem enough, or when the racks of dresses in the department stores fail to amuse. Finally, she forgets what it feels like not to be a stranger. She has found work that keeps her busy, or better still, tired. She has

160

found a lover, a child, a telephone friend, the American equivalents for the opacity of her childhood. The dense solidity of Asian society becomes a thin story. At some point, she no longer considers exchanging the remote relationships that pass as American social life for those crowded rooms in Asia, the unhappy family circles. And were those rooms really that crowded, the family so intensely unhappy?

By 1971, it seemed I had learned something—the something Alice enacted for me that summer: women could not live alone in society.

Unknown to me, however, hundreds of counter-Alices in Cambridge had tried and were tired of marriage and were beginning to see their salvation outside of coupling with men. The consciousness-raising groups that sprang up among academic women in the Boston area may have first organized only blocks away from the apartment where I wrote, as it were, my letter of resignation. For me then, these consciousness-raising groups held no historical significance beyond a metropolitan faddishness. Instead, struggling for a footing in U.S. society, I was bedeviled by the super-fragmentations that attend alien status in the United States.

In my second year as a dorm counselor, I moved from the annex of the Castle to the main Castle building. A folly imported stone by stone from some impoverished European countryside, the Castle was a massive walled edifice impossible to keep warm and the curious landmark in a campus fast filling up with sleek contemporary glassed architecture. To live in the Castle gave one some cachet and a great deal of inconvenience.

Helen, Roz, Wendy, a half-dozen or more of the undergraduate women who had shared a corridor with me the previous year, had left the Castle. They had left for apartments in Waltham with new boyfriends or, tired of the Castle's deep-freeze and ancient electrical outlets, had moved to cheerful new dormitories across the campus. Alice did not return to the dormitory; she and Joshua were by now a fixed couple. For a twenty-five-year-old alone, the fall days stretched minute by minute into early dusk and lengthy evenings. It was impossible to break out of the solitude, for the undergraduates had their own intertwining mating circles, their extended study groups.

Now and again I ate with Julie and Carol, five years younger, and listened absently to their stories of men who let them down and mothers who were never available. They had beautiful blue and green eyes and privileged lives. Julie stocked her small refrigerator with yogurt she stole out of the dining halls, and kept herself warm with a long suede coat. Her father was a doctor, but she was greedy for a life of her own. She wanted not to live with him, just as she wanted not to eat in the dining hall. I wondered at the loneliness she sought, the dignity with which she opened the refrigerator door to choose a blueberry or strawberry or vanilla yogurt cup from the array within the cold compartment.

Carol of the long green eyes, however, was always looking for a man. Everywhere we walked there were men, and she moaned that no one, no one ever really wanted her. Men were too timid, they didn't like big women, they found her sense of humor too Midwestern. Someone didn't call, another had a girl back home, she couldn't tell if this one was interested. Her eyes changed from olive to slate gray to tawny cat's eyes. Her father bought her a shiny red pick-up truck, but she cleaned the houses of professors, scrubbing their toilet bowls, to pay for the gas. If I had her eyes and her pick-up truck, I wouldn't be complaining, I thought.

It was the waste of time I minded most, a sludgy feeling that took over October and November. In September, almost a year after my arrival at Brandeis, Father had written to say he had been diagnosed with throat cancer. He was seeking medical care in Malacca. "Don't come home," his letter ended, "I don't want you to interrupt your studies."

I told no one. Food stuck in my throat whenever I thought of Father. The thought was like a fishbone, sharp and nagging. I couldn't speak of him.

Another short letter arrived from China without a return address. I read it over and over in the safety of my room. "I am doing well," it said. "My white blood cells have gone up, and I am feeling stronger." The small black-and-white photograph that fell out of the envelope showed that he was lying. The shirt draped over his body like a sheet over a child, although his face was old and sad.

For a few months, the letters came from China without a forwarding address: he was staying near the clinic in Canton, noted for its cancer cures. He wrote irregularly. Like a careful student, perhaps because he was lonely, he sent the laboratory reports on his white blood count. His letters were optimistic to begin with. The white blood-cell numbers had improved; he was enjoying this Chinese city he had never seen before, visiting parks, zoos, and museums, with a new friend also undergoing treatment at the clinic. Then a letter arrived complaining of homesickness. He wanted to be home with the family; he missed Malaysian food.

When Thanksgiving came, the Castle emptied out. Julie and Carol returned to Brooklyn and Missouri. On Friday I picked up a letter from my mailbox. The rice-paper-fine aerogramme rustled as I spread it out to read the ball-point print that smeared across the crumpled blue surface. It was a letter from Second Brother, and I was immediately afraid, for Second Brother had never written to me before. "We buried Father two weeks ago," he wrote.

I stared at the words and calculated the time. Two weeks ago, and a week for the aerogramme to cross the world to reach me in Massachusetts. It was unimaginable that Father, the source of whatever drove me, that total enveloping wretchedness of involuntary love, my eternal bond, my body's and heart's DNA, had been dead for almost a month. The world had a hole in it, it was rent, and I would never heal.

Maggie came knocking at my door just as I finished reading Second Brother's letter. An orphan left with a trust fund, she was slowly completing her graduate studies, while spending most of her time volunteering to help with the animals in the zoo. She wanted to know if I had had any pumpkin pie yet for Thanksgiving. Would I go with her to the cafeteria for a piece of pie? I was still holding Second Brother's blue aerogramme in my hand.

"My father's dead," I said to her. Why was I telling her this? Would I have said the same thing if the janitor had knocked on the door to fix the radiator? "He died two weeks ago."

"Oh," she said. "I'm sorry." I could see that she was. Tall and big-boned, Maggie was deep water, quiet-spoken, all reserve.

I paid for my pie and coffee at the cafeteria and watched her eat. She left the crust and scraped the brown gooey filling carefully with her fork till it was all gone. My throat hurt. Then I returned alone to my room. I knew Maggie would never visit me again, I had been too painful for her.

At first I didn't cry. It wasn't Father's death that drove hardest at me; it was that he had been dead for more than two weeks already, and I hadn't known all that time that he had gone. "We didn't think you should come home," Second Brother wrote. The grief and the guilt lay beyond tears. Months later, in Brooklyn where I was sharing a studio apartment with Charles, the Brandeis graduate student whom I would later marry, I woke up in the middle of the night my face drenched with tears. I had wept in my sleep for Father.

A month after the news of Father's death, Second Brother sent me a package of papers from Father's belongings. Father had kept all my old school record books, annual school certificates of achievement, examination diplomas, yellowed letters of recommendation from high school teachers, and Malaysian citizenship documents. On an unmailed aerogramme sheet, Father had scrawled in a shaky hand, "I want you to come home now."

My brother also sent me a diary Father had kept in the last weeks of his life. Only a few pages were filled, and all the entries were addressed to me. In the early entries, he wrote he was hopeful he would recover, and he did not want me to return home because it was so important for me to continue my studies. In the second to last entry, he asked that I hurry home; he didn't believe he had much time left and he wanted to see me. In the very last entry, addressing me as his dear daughter, he wrote that although he knew I would do so, still he asked that I promise to take care of my brothers and sister, Peng's children. The entry was very short and the handwriting erratic. My father had willed his children to me.

The day I received the package, I emptied my bank account and sent the few hundred dollars in it to Peng. With it, my letter promised that I would send her as much as I could each month. For a long time, every U.S. dollar rang as precious Malaysian currency for me to remit. A ten-dollar shirt? I paid for it and guiltily counted the groceries the money could have bought for Father's family. I disapproved of my growing consumerism. The pastries that gleamed, sugar-encrusted, at Dunkin' Donuts, which I eyed longingly, would buy copybooks for my half-brothers. For the next few years, I carried my father's ghostly presence through department stores and restaurants. His sad smile was a mirage of poverty. I saw my half-siblings ragged and hungry whenever I glanced at a sales tag, and every month, I made out a bank draft to Peng and mailed it out as an exorcism.

An exorcism I could not explain to Charles, my American husband. How could one eat well if one's family was starving? For Chinese, eating is both material and cultural. We feed our hungry ghosts before we may feed ourselves. Ancestors are ravenous, and can die of neglect. Our fathers' children are also ourselves. The self is paltry, phantasmagoric; it leaks and slips away. It is the family, parents, siblings, cousins, that signify the meaning of the self, and beyond the family, the extended community.

In writing the bank drafts I remained my father's daughter, returning to Father the bargain we had made. This is the meaning of blood—to give, because you cannot eat unless the family is also eating. For years, I woke up nights, heart beating wildly. Oh Asia, that nets its children in ties of blood so binding that they cut the spirit.

In my second year at Brandeis, I had met Charles, one year ahead of me in graduate school, who was also writing his dissertation with Professor Cunningham. Our conversations grew, and soon he was driving every weekend from New York to Massachusetts to visit me. After Father's death, we decided I should join him in Brooklyn, and in November 1972, increasingly committed to each other and beset by visa and work permit uncertainties, we married in the New York civil registry. Charles was the stable center that finally brought me calm.

I wrote much of my dissertation in the New York Public Library Reading Room. For months I ate my lunch on the library steps by the giant lion statues, then returned up the massive stairs to the second floor. In the green-shaded glow of the reading lamps I turned the knife-cut vellum pages of volumes of genteel nineteenth-century poetry, some unread for decades. I typed my chapters on a portable Olympic in our Brooklyn apartment from notes scrawled into bound notebooks.

After three years, my Wien fellowship had run out, and there was still the monthly draft to Peng to be accounted for. Fortunately, I received a teaching fellowship at Queens College for 1972 that saw me through writing the dissertation. Teaching composition classes was all that was expected of the fellows, and aside from a couple of meetings when we were introduced to each other and a few bored department members, we were mostly left to our own devices. Intellectual life was reduced to reading composition texts and banal essays.

For all its status as a leading college of The City University of New York, Queens was a commuter, working-class institution. I wanted to give, but my Queens students were not interested in what I had to give. The composition classes were filled with sullen freshmen who resented a writing requirement that appeared removed from their urgent career goals. I spent hours reading their compositions, pondering and writing long commentaries in response to their short paragraphs, but none of my students found their way to my office to talk. The best relationships I could cultivate were with students—Marcy, Robert, and Angela—who lingered after class. An uneasy restlessness disturbed me, and I felt the absence of mental and emotional exchange as my shortcoming.

What could have been achieved in our brief interactions? Why had I expected so much of myself? Freshmen at Queens were not looking for a Socratic figure when they signed up for English 101. Besides, with my long straight Chinese hair and accent, I was not any young American's image of Socrates. It must have been discomforting for some of them to find a "foreign" graduate student explicating Thoreau and the dull mysteries of the argument paper in their first experience of higher education. The only Asians many students might have met were waiters in restaurants, with whom often they had had to communicate without English.

Angela was different. Already in her late forties, she was a first-generation Italian who had decided that she wanted a career as a social worker. Her husband was a union carpenter, her sons and daughters all grown and working. She saw me as a model, a non-Anglo commanding attention in a college that was homogeneously Anglo-American and Jewish. "Come for dinner," she asked repeatedly, "I want my husband to meet you." She made a feast of breaded mushrooms, lasagna, and veal, in a kitchen that was wallpapered with golden fleur-de-lis and laid with linoleum, and the dining table was crowded with tall muscular sons and talkative daughters. Her silent husband, Angela explained, was only comfortable speaking Sicilian. "She is my English professor, and she likes my writing," she said to him, and he poured some red wine into my glass. "Eat, eat," she commanded. "I am so proud to have my professor come to my home."

Following Angela's example, I gave a dinner party for my students. An hour late, Robert and Marcy arrived. As it became clear that no one else was coming, their presence grew excruciatingly more embarrassing. After some long silences, they left—Brooklyn was too far away for Queens students, they assured me.

Alone, I froze the leftover chicken and brownies, enough to feed twenty guests. Wrapping the chicken in foil, I thought of how frozen food had repelled me as a child: Malaysians insisted on freshness in their food—chicken slaughtered just before steaming, long beans freshly picked in the morning, fish freshly netted from the sea. Frozen and thawed food was *pantang*—taboo, not for human consumption, gone bad. Standing barefoot in the cold kitchen, I jammed the freezer full of packages.

A wind had started up, and dark branches waved outside the kitchen window. We had cleared the backyard of the rented Brooklyn brownstone of ragweed and broken bottles; but the neighbor's tall ailanthus sent shoots into our yard, like strong stubborn weeds that could not be put down. Standing between the freezer and the yard, I knew I was learning about living in the United States.

After the abortive party, I gave up trying to find intellectual commonalities with my students. These connections were there to be made, but not in the confines of fifty-minute periods devoted to outlines and thesis statements.

One day I ran into Alan, who had been a year my senior at Brandeis, in the corridor of the English department, an office three buildings removed from the cubicle I shared with three other teaching fellows. Like me he was writing his dissertation, but unlike me he was a junior faculty member. My husband Charles, tall and bearded, had also found a full-time position at another CUNY campus. Talking to Alan, I was struck by how much he resembled Charles; indeed, how much he resembled the department chair who had interviewed me for the fellowship. My officemates were all women, two traveling in twice weekly from Nassau and Suffolk, and the third a New York University graduate student living in the West Village. In response to the expanded demand for such classes after the inauguration of the open admissions policy, women made up the teaching ranks of temporary composition instructors, while the few literature positions were filled by men whose suit-clad broad shoulders crowded the English department offices.

What can one say in the face of all the evidence that U.S. academics then gave preferential treatment to white males who looked and talked just like themselves? I said nothing, but set my mind to completing the dissertation and returning to Malaysia with Charles. At least there I would have a real position in the university, and I would be able to teach something more than composition.

In 1973, after completing my Ph.D., I wrote to my old Head of Department in Kuala Lumpur. Gracious as always, Dr. Wismal replied promptly offering me a position. I longed to return home as the native daughter made good and to teach in the English seminar room where I had sat through lectures by British men. I saw myself driving past the campus roads where I had wandered as a confused young woman with Iqbal, lighting up a cigarette in the Senior Common Room where I had once had to buy a sandwich through its kitchen door. But Dr. Wismal also wrote that my American husband would never find a position teaching English at the university. "We are in the process of nationalizing the university," his letter pointed out. "There will be no positions available for non-Malaysians."

Could we try nevertheless to find work in Malaysia together? Charles, born in Brooklyn and raised on Long Island, was willing to teach in Malaysia for a while, but he warned me that he could not live anywhere else but in New York. "New York is the world," he said. "Once you've lived in New York, nowhere else counts."

Malaysia and New York were incompatible. I weighed my choices: returning to Malaysia I would be assured of a university position, but it would mean separating from Charles and entering a life of difficult singlehood. I had to choose not only between countries but between two kinds of commitment: the commitment to a lonely celibate career teaching English in a Malay-dominant university at home or to a shared life of literary studies, albeit in exile.

In the meantime, my savings were running out, Peng's children were still in school, and I had to find more money to send to her. In June, I applied for a job at the Abraham and Straus department store near Brooklyn's Fulton Street. On the form I was careful not to note that I had just completed my doctorate at Brandeis. For three months until I found a position teaching in a community college, I went into A&S every morning at 9.30 A.M.. and worked as a checker in the housecoats department. My duties were the simplest, to count the items customers carried into the fitting room and to give them a ticket with the number on it.

The first day I picked up the housecoats from the fitting room and returned them to their racks, but Fanny and Dotty quickly put a stop to that. Fanny was the regular cashier, a small proud plain woman in her early fifties. "No, no," she said, annoyed and upset at my ignorance of store hierarchy, "Dotty's the one who puts the clothes away. You have no idea where anything belongs, and everything will get mixed up!" Once I learned to sit in my place, silently offering tickets to customers, she became graciously remote, ignoring me for whole hours, except to smile and excuse me for lunch.

Large and slow moving, Dotty was an even more gracious woman, teaching me in a gentle southern voice as much of the store's arcane policies as I could wish to learn. Moving slowly from dressing room to racks, her arms full of house frocks and aprons, she was a constant presence in the department, like a black wave moving through an ocean of clothes. "No, I cain't sit down," she'd say, looking without any rancor at me fixed on my chair by the dressing room. "Mr. Simpson, he look out for me. He don't like it when I sit. I just keep moving, hangin' these dresses. And I like to move. Always something new to see. I buy some good things seeing something new like that."

It was terrifying to see how much Fanny and Dotty bought at the department store. A&S employees received a 20 percent discount on everything the store carried. The saleswomen talked about the jewelry on sale, star sapphires and diamonds; the down-filled coats and boots, crystal vases, sofas, chandeliers. In the United States even the lowliest dressing-room clerk could shop like a tycoon. Fanny and Dotty bought on credit; each month their salary was docked by a percentage that they owed the store. But they didn't mind. Fanny came in every morning made up with fresh pancake and lipstick, in new high heels, and suits, groomed like the wife of a Long Island doctor. Dotty, in her loose skirts and blouses, was quieter, but even she flashed fingers ringed with gold and stones, showed off a new winter coat, her dark hand smoothing the fur collar like a lover's dreamy caress.

I felt I had entered an unreal world, one constantly lit and with Muzak playing every moment, where desire was bright and seemingly solid: a good wool dress, a jar of bath oil, or a ruby and sapphire ring. Customers came in every day, some days more than others, walking as in a trance, browsing in circles, fingering and picking up and carrying away. Above the Muzak— "raindrops falling on my head," "strangers in the night"—were the squeak and clack of hangers, hour after hour. Women moved one housecoat after another on their circular racks, studying frocks varied by pink or blue polka dots, by lace or rickrack, alpine flower or yellow daisy print, by collars or boat-necks, three-quarter sleeves or sleeveless, straight shifts or tucked bodices, fabric-covered buttons or elastic bands, zippered, ribboned, pleated, short or long, from size two to size twenty-four. All kinds of women bought these housecoats— respectable housewives, daughters shopping for mothers, women for their sisters, their aunts, their mothers-in-law. Housecoats were big in Flatbush and Red Hook, all over Brooklyn where there were Italian-American, Jewish-American, Polish-American, and West-Indian families.

It was always happy land in A&S. Only people with money came, and they came to find and claim and take away. For a few weeks I too went to the different counters during my lunch break, looking and looking for things to want. But my purchases were disappointing, only a passing physical attraction. The crystal bowl turned garish in our Brooklyn brownstone, the beige suit was too short and too tight. Besides I needed to send money to Peng, so I stopped shopping and took to reading during lunch.

"A college girl!" Fanny sniffed. "You should be doing better than a check girl!" and grew more distant, and even sweet-natured Dotty stopped talking to me. I was relieved when September came and I could quit to take up a teaching position in the South Bronx.

That summer, between my days at A&S, I had mailed letters of inquiry for teaching positions to institutions within a fifty-mile radius of New York City. I had decided to stay with Charles in the United States, with fifty miles as the commutable figure between work and house. It was a difficult decision, but millions of people make such decisions every year. In California, for example, Chinese children attend private schools while their "astronaut" fathers and mothers live out of satellite apartments in Taiwan and Hong Kong, checking on their children's progress in weekly telephone calls. Like these parents and their children, guilt and apology dogged my decision to remain in the United States, and for over a decade, I did an emotional shuttle run between Asia and the United States, voluntarily displaced.

In my first few job interviews, I wore a green and yellow patterned Malay gown, a *baju kurong,* placing my foreignness in view, and determined not to be perceived as American. I took a long train and bus ride out to Elizabeth, New Jersey, past the stinking oil plants and giant gas containers, and waited for the English department chair to evaluate my abilities to teach American literature to the college's white working-class students. I walked down to the basement of Hunter College where an African-American administrator, regally wrapped in a green and purple head cloth, questioned me about my political position in seeking greater support for blacks in The City University of New York. In an office in a Pratt College brownstone, the department chairman asked me to recite my poems. Professor Cunningham's letter of reference had praised the elegance of my language, and the chairman wanted a demonstration. How does one measure discrimination?

As an alien resident, I feared I was already asking too much. Too much acceptance of my British colonial accent, my brown color and Asian features. Too much tolerance of my difference: not white, not Jewish, not black, not Puerto Rican, the four groups whose needs and words filled the columns of the *New York Times.* A non-American, I could only hope to fill the interstices, foreign to all and mutable, like a small helpful glue.

I finally found a teaching position at Hostos Community College in the South Bronx, a college with a black and Latino student population. The Queens College teaching fellows congratulated me, but not enviously: Bertha said she had not applied for the position—she could not contemplate teaching in a Puerto Rican college. When I met my office-mates a few years later, they were still teaching composition classes as adjunct faculty.

New York City had set up Hostos Community College to pacify the militant Puerto Ricans who had seen open admissions benefit everyone but themselves. The two-year college was a prize to the heavily Puerto Rican borough, a resource to develop its young people for skilled jobs in the hospitals and for transfer to four-year colleges. It was also a holding pen that kept black and brown students out of the established campuses of The City University of New York, until such time as a  few of them, after years of lower-division education, were permitted into the four-year colleges.

As a gesture of community solidarity, Hostos was located on 149th Street in the Bronx, across from the classic Federal Post Office, and only a few blocks away from miles of burnt-down shells of brownstones that the slum landlords had leveled for insurance money. Its site made Hostos accessible to the city's Latino population, but also fearfully intimidating after dark to almost everyone, for it was located in a police precinct popularly known as Fort Apache because of the Hollywood-Indian-and-cowboy-style shoot-outs that occurred frequently along its derelict streets.

Twenty years later, it is still difficult for me to make sense out of the experience of teaching college English in the South Bronx. Americans are bombarded with pastoral images of higher education, a sentimentalized distortion of the Socratic teacher circled by young men and women listening to his perambulations, embowered within an attentive Nature—trees, blue skies, and warm autumn clouds. Campuses promise verdant spaces in which the tranquil spirit may track paths of inquiry, to produce social beings calibrated to degrees of civilized society. How to satisfy the demand from black and brown Americans for a share of this promise?

In 1972, more blacks and Puerto Ricans were graduating out of the city's high schools. Since its inception, The City University of New York's free tuition policy had attracted immigrants to New York. Now, challenged on the deficient representation of nonwhites among its students, the university implemented an open admissions policy. I was a beneficiary of the civil rights redress. For the three years I taught at Hostos Community College, I was conscious that my position was earned on the backs of black, brown, and working-class activists. It took over an hour on the subway to get from my Prospect Park home to 149th Street and the Grand Concourse where the doors to the three-story, cinder-block college building were guarded by uniformed security. But the distance between my townhouse and the college was more than miles—it was the distance between an already secured middle class and a dispossessed class, between someone already marked with entry, no matter how tenuous, into U.S. privilege and those who were still denied entry.

My department colleagues, chiefly white Americans, also did not live in the Bronx, but came in from the suburbs of New Jersey and Westchester county, or from the doormen-guarded enclaves of Manhattan's West Side. Like me, many were fresh Ph.Ds, anxious about family responsibilities and bills. We were liberals, committed to helping our brown and black students succeed, and because we were scholars in the South Bronx we were more deeply conservative about our criteria of academic success than teachers at the four-year state colleges. The credits for the college's English courses were transferable to the four-year colleges and needed to satisfy their requirements. No sentence fragment escaped our eye. We were determined that our Spanglish students know how to use a semicolon, understand the difference between a thesis sentence and a supporting sentence, and never misspell "their" or "separate." Of course we taught Hemingway's "Hills Like White Elephants" and Shakespeare's *King Lear,* selections found in every anthology.

Besides, nothing in our doctoral training prepared us for the *terra incognita* of open admissions. "Irrelevance" was a bogey which we firmly ignored. Else, what was the point of our credentials? How else to explain why we English Ph.Ds, rather than someone else, should be teaching at Hostos? If not Shakespeare, who should be read? If not English, what language should be taught? Puerto Ricans and African Americans had compelled The City University of New York to open its doors to them, but the doors opened onto bleak cinder-block walls. The results of their struggle for equal opportunities were programs in English as a Second Language, entry exams, remedial writing, introductory courses in composition and English literature, and exit exams.

For three years I believed I had only to work very hard to help my students. Still stinging from the absence of contact with my students at Queens College, I was eager to make Hostos students my community. I came in to teach five days a week, arriving early at 8 A.M. and staying till 5 P.M., and when I was not in class, I was in my office teaching students one-on-one.

From the beginning, it was clear to me that Hostos students could not master the complexities of English literacy in the classroom alone. I read Paulo Freire, and asked how my working-class and welfare students were being served by the college. They believed that college classes would see them out of their tenements and into jobs in the city's offices. Certainly, arriving on time, completing assignments, analyzing arguments, sharing readings, some proved their malleability. But many of them sat silently through the class period, their anxious eyes giving them away. The readings were incomprehensible. Despite the expensive textbooks, they did not understand the distinction between a phrase and a clause or a metaphor and a simile. The failure to understand caused tremendous anguish: they apprehended an immediate relationship between this failure and a future at the bottom of ladders.

Responding to the long lines of students waiting to meet me for individual help each day, I set up a writing center, first with senior students as paid assistants, then through a federal grant, with two Columbia University graduate students available for consultation. Patiently we handed out drills, discussed individual paper assignments, and explained what English idioms meant. The Writing Center became a drop-in place for students.

Students brought poems they had written, poems which we praised extravagantly because they showed a visceral engagement with the English language that signified more than a second-language relationship. I encouraged the publication of a student literary journal, naively titled "Upstairs" to underline the economic and social mobility that brought the students to the Writing Center. Soon I was coming in to work on Saturdays as adviser to the student yearbook. Evie, a welfare mother, lean, dark, and street-wise, learned to crop photographs. William, tall, broad-shouldered, and just one year out of the army, his dark physique offering me a grateful shield through the Grand Concourse crowds, was a willing editorial assistant, more good-natured and gentle than anyone I had met. Perhaps they shared with me the belief that even if we were not saving the South Bronx, we were doing something ethically worthwhile. The work on the students' journal and yearbook felt right in a way that struggling to explain Byron and the English Romantics did not.

I invited my yearbook students, a half-dozen of them, to a party in our rented brownstone duplex in Brooklyn. I made rice and curry; Lucinda, a shy and graceful African American, barely twenty, brought a southern dish her grandmother made—vanilla biscuits, banana slices, and a pudding mix. William brought beer, Evie brought plantain fritters, and Josefina, a Peruvian Indo, brought matte tea from the Highlands. They were all on welfare, except William who was on veteran's benefits. Lucinda had just gotten pregnant; she was going to raise the baby with the help of her grandmother.

After weeks of working together late into the evenings and on Saturdays, they had grown closer to me than had my father's children in Malacca. When I left Hostos after three years to teach in a suburban community college, it was these students I remembered and missed. They were tough yet naive. They talked about being evicted from apartments, speaking to their children's truant officers, being interviewed by the welfare worker, but not one ever made up an excuse for not completing an assignment on time. They were honest in a way that other students, looking out for number one, are not.

In 1974, after my first full year of teaching in the South Bronx, I returned to Malaysia for the summer. Second Brother was teaching at Universiti Sains in Penang, and for a strange space of three months, living with him and his wife, I experienced a simulacrum of another identity.

Returning to Malaysia almost without thought, I was glad for the undemanding familial routine, a contrast to the difficult five years in the United States. For the short time I would be with Second Brother I had no wants and no struggles. It was easy being a dependent in my sister-in-law's house. Their home, kitty-cornered between vacant green lots and older houses constructed in the 1950s, was airy and cool, pierced with windows and lattices, possessing the air of colonial buildings built before the advent of air conditioning. On weekends, I biked down the avenues laid out by eighteenth-century British administrators who had named the outpost Georgetown after their monarch, and who had envisioned an orderly seaside town like Brighton with healthful breezes blowing for recuperating British soldiers and their families en route or returning from India. For more than two centuries, Penang island, separated from the Malaysian peninsula by a channel that was a short ferry ride span, had preserved this air of quiet pleasure at being away from any center. I biked past royal palms unthreatened by motor traffic, and read under *casuarinas* by the sea wall as if in a time warp, under a cellophane wrap, neither child nor adult. My sister-in-law's maid took care of laundry, meals, and house cleaning. There was no urgency to earn a living, only a simple reciprocity to work on Second Brother's manuscripts.

From Monday to Friday, I accompanied Chien to his office at the university, which sprawled over a secluded height overlooking the Strait of Malacca. He gave me a little desk right by the door and set me to work editing his master's and Ph.D. dissertations on the economic history of British colonialism and peasant agriculture in Perak and in the Federated Malay States. He had done the research during his graduate years at the Australian National University. Oxford University Press had offered to publish his thesis, and his first book later won the Library of Congress Harry Benda Prize for Southeast Asian history.

Copyediting was a challenge, taking over someone else's ideas and language and refining them, like a kind of intellectual domestic work, in a home that is not one's own. Paragraphs that tangled arguments, sentences that wandered away, ill-fitting grammar, thoughts that deserved a better position or more attention: the manuscript had all the marks of dissertation writing. Crammed full of original data dug out of colonial archives in London and Amsterdam and conclusions that proved false the claims of the benefits of plantation agriculture and British rule to the indigenous population, Second Brother's dissertation was an exciting document. Revising sentences and paragraphs, I could complete no more than ten pages each day before the sense would dull for me.

Hearing my frustrated sighs, Second Brother would take me out to lunch at a roadside Punjabi *roti* stall. More often I wandered alone across the university, reveling in its tranquil torpor. Unlike the single barrack of Hostos Community College, Universiti Sains covered verdant acres. Maroon bougainvillaea spilled over low walls, and trees of golden showers and flame-of-the-forest tossed their ferny leaves and brilliant yellow and scarlet in the afternoon breeze that blew inland from the cooler South China Sea. The sky was almost always an intense cobalt blue, after the blue of the surrounding sea. Standing anywhere on the campus I could see the shadows of cumulus nimbus in the distance following the white giants as they slowly drifted in the vast glowing ether. In contrast to the frenzied roar of the New York subways, the campus, hardly a few years old and still new with fresh paint, held a tranced silence.

A visiting Australian professor, red-haired and red-skinned from the tropical sun, invited me to teach a creative writing course with him. A scholar of Indonesian literature, Harry addressed the students in fluent Bahasa, for the national language of Indonesia came from the same Malay linguistic stock as the Malaysian national language. I had not used Bahasa Malaysia since studying it at seventeen for the precollege examinations, so I lectured in English. It was another of those international cultural ironies that befuddle simple identity equations. Harry had just translated a collection of stories set in New York City by an Indonesian writer. "If you could read this and check the American idioms," he said, "I would be ever so grateful." He had never been to Manhattan, had to guess at the speech of New Yorkers from old Hollywood movies, and thought of me as an American.

Perhaps that was what I was becoming, even as I reluctantly counted the days before my return flight to Kennedy Airport. I wrote from this space of undetermined self short lyrics that might seize on senses that were rapidly displacing themselves. Then, in Kuala Lumpur during the last week in Malaysia, Ashok Kumar, a Heinemann editor, suggested that I consider submitting a volume of poems. I returned to Brooklyn in August uneasy yet alert to the dilemma that, as a writer, my audience, like my emotional resources, was still rooted in Malaysia.

My life in the United States was a continuous hardship. Enduring the hour-long, jolting, shrieking ride back and forth each day from Brooklyn to the South Bronx; the tension of hyper-vigilance whether walking through 148th Street and the Grand Concourse or scurrying through the tunnels of the Grand Army Plaza subway station; the physical labor of negotiating a loaded shopping cart over cracked pavements and falling garbage containers. All this and water roaches the size of mice, rats like small mastiffs, mildew that required daily attention, hundreds of barely literate scripts each month to read and grade. In two years, our Brooklyn apartment had been burglarized twice, the woman who lived in the apartment upstairs had knocked frantically at our door one afternoon after she had gotten herself out of the closet into which a rapist had locked her before fleeing, and Charles had been mugged in Greenwich Village one evening after leaving a chess competition.

New York held little pleasure and all too much terror. What then, besides Charles's career, was keeping me in the United States? A promise of unlimited opportunity? A social disorganization that offered individual rights, the carrot of possibility, in contrast to Malaysian realpolitik, where I would always be constrained as a racial Chinese? Clearly I had chosen an ideology of social and political freedom with all that it meant of isolated and isolating material struggle in the United States. That ingrained stubbornness the Irish nuns tried so hard to beat out of me kept me striding along dirty underground stations, pushing for something yet in the future.

Augusts are dangerous in New York, even in a middle-class neighborhood like Park Slope. Forgoing movies and restaurants, and buying our furniture from the Salvation Army, Charles and I had saved for a down payment on a house. That summer, while I was in Penang, Charles had found a three-story town-house with a limestone-hewn facade and cherry-wood paneling which we could afford because it was in a block of mixed tenement buildings and unren-ovated brownstones. In late August, sweating, dirt-streaked, we hauled out loads of broken furniture and garbage left behind by the previous owner, and scrubbed away a generation of grubby fingerprints and kitchen grease. So I was unprepared to see us as class enemies of the tenants who hung out of their windows in the large tenement building right across from our home.

An unemployed cook and his wife and five children lived in the second-floor apartment directly facing our parlor windows. Their cousins lived on the floor below, including a car mechanic who did repairs for his friends on the weekends. They and many of our other neighbors were Puerto Ricans, like the students and colleagues I worked with in the South Bronx. Feeling a bond of recognition, I had introduced myself to them.

Encouraged by our friendliness our neighbors began to sit on our stoop, talking loudly till late at night. They left their beer bottles on the steps and played their radios loud as they repaired their cars before our door early on Sunday mornings.

Working in the South Bronx all week, I knew it was morally incumbent on me to accept their different cultural ways. After all, their apartments were too small for their large families, and they baked in them during the Indian summer of late September. Our garden duplex just for two of us must have appeared a shocking expense of space.

Private property makes no sense to people who possess none. What could be more inviting to cooped-up tenants than a shady high stoop, clean and empty, with a view of the leafy park? How could I object to their sitting on it, since I never used it myself? And the plane tree in front of our door that had simply shot up after my assiduous watering, what good was its shade if no one worked under it and enjoyed its green scent?

Seeing my distress at the noise, Charles went out one afternoon and asked the stoop-sitters to leave. Thirteen-year-old Davey decided he was being picked on and flourished a large knife. We called the precinct, the patrol car arrived, and weeks followed of court papers and police visits.

In the meantime we petitioned the Historical Preservation Society and received permission to put up an iron gate in front of the stoop, its curlicues and wreaths a replica of nineteenth-century wrought-iron styles. The cook stopped smiling at us. He leaned over his window and stared across the narrow breadth of the street into our windows with hostile attention. Reading in the parlor, I would look up and find children's eyes trained on me. Faces in windows followed me as I left for work in the morning, and appeared in the openings as I walked home at night. If they could not challenge my legal claim to private property, they could still unsettle my privacy as a person. Derisive laughter and Spanish phrases drifted across the dividing border of the street.

More and more uneasy, I began to despair at my middle-class hypocrisy and fears, at the disparity between my political valuation of my Puerto Rican students and my discomfort with my Puerto Rican neighbors. My life in New York was both too thin of community and too dense with people, too busy with work and too empty of activity, too isolating and too much under surveillance. The very complexity and fragmentation of social organization overwhelmed me. It was not as if the municipality offered a way for me to relate to the cook and his children. An approach on my part, fractured by our different language skills, would have been fatally marked as condescension.

"Of course these people hate you!" Tom said on his visit to our home. "You represent a totally different class from them. Look at what you have, books, records, sofas, carpets. They hate you each time they look right into your windows."

Tom was a registered socialist and union organizer. He also owned a brownstone, but in a block of working-class homeowners. On our street, the brownstone owners ranged on one side, our garbage cans neatly lidded and out of sight under benches, facing the row of tenements with their broken street lamps and brawling parties.

In spring 1975, in response to increased confrontations over street parking, Esther and her architect husband sent out flyers to begin a block association. Only the brownstone owners turned up for the meetings—West Indians, Polish, Jews, Asian, many of us young professionals. We discussed how to get the city to do more garbage pick-ups, how to get the fire inspectors to move on the violations in the tenements, how to get the landlord to repair the broken windows and pipes in his buildings. Unspoken was the understanding that the tenements were our problem. We could not live safely in our homes until the tenants were safe in theirs.

Esther suggested that the newly constituted association hold a block party at the beginning of the summer. It was a way to bring out the older home owners who did not feel comfortable with the younger professional activists, and the renters who resented our newly constructed black iron fences, the fancy gates, and window grills, signs of boundaries that kept them on their side of the street. For one day we would mingle out on the street as equals. Or at least the street would be common territory, a public space rather than a dividing line.

The block association introduced me to U.S. politics. It was a peculiarly Western social phenomenon: people with nothing in common beyond property interests drawn together to secure these interests. Knowing nothing of each other, with no sense of common background or cultural concerns, our first meeting was itself the first move to the formation of a community. In Malaysia, despite my parents' disintegrating social ties and despite the colonial disruptions of Asian traditions, I had never doubted that my thoughts and feelings, violently alienated as they were, signified within familial and communal histories. They made sense to me as a Malaysian. In Brooklyn, I was bemused by the way in which community relations followed after class identity, and actions resulted from class interests. We would probably never have been invited into Esther and Steve's home if they had not been concerned about the deterioration of the block; and we would never have spent time with Susan and her husband Roy, both social workers for the city, had they not just bought the brownstone within sight of the problem tenement building. In the Malaysia of my childhood, stratified by race, religion, and long-standing familial bonds, historically existing communal identities so dominated political action that new formations of civic identity were difficult if not impossible. In contrast, the necessity for political action in the United States, I discovered, could create community where none existed before, thus contributing to the continuous fresh construction of civic identities.

But the community offered by such block associations is as transient and unstable as its members. Related to them by little else than an agenda for security of property, I was never able to feel comfortable among these strangers. None of us came from the same region, had attended the same schools, knew the same people, worshipped the same religion, or even shared the same food customs. Esther and Steve were members of a synagogue; my husband was a nonpracticing Jew. Susan was an undefined Eastern European; her husband an undefined white ethnic. Marly had come from Barbados, his bleached-blond wife from the working class in Britain. Anna had grown up in Red Hook among an Italian-American community. No one knew the landlord of the tenement building, but most of his tenants were African Americans and Puerto Ricans. The only thing we shared was contingency: we all lived on the same block and shared the same air space, looking out into the street.

We advertised the block party with flyers that Esther's children stuffed into mailboxes. I filled boxes with unwanted paperbacks and textbooks, lamps, old dishes, high heels now disdained, bell-bottoms and outgrown dresses, plastic chairs, and unwanted canning jars. Because the previous owners had left behind a store of three-inch pots, I planted tomato seeds which sprouted leggy leaves in time for the warm Saturday July morning. Too late we realized that only our side of the street held the white elephant goods, the cupcakes, chili, lemonade stands, the rows of potted tomato plants, and boxes of paperbacks. We were carrying out of our brownstones the material excess of our middle-class status, while across the street the cook's children, together with rest of the brown and black tenants, eyed us suspiciously.

Esther sent her children to set up their face-painting table by the tenement door. For the first half-hour we basted our shish kebabs and ate each other's sesame noodles and potato kugel. Then Jose crossed the street with a swagger. His wife wanted to know the price of a tomato plant.

"A quarter," I said, "and five for a dollar." Of course, he knew that the money from the block party was to buy trees for the block? And the lamp? Fifty cents.

Jose went back across the street. In a few minutes his wife came over beaming. The tomato plants were the first to go, as well as the baby dieffenbacha and spider asparagus and coleus. In their tiny apartments, the women longed for those house plants that pressed against our brownstone windows, reminding them of their gardens in Puerto Rico.

We were firm with our prices. No, we were not offering charitable cast-offs. Sneakers were another quarter, chairs a dollar, jars fifteen cents each, shirts and skirts a dime or a quarter. Everything was sold or given away by evening, including hunks of brownies and slopping paper plates of beans and noodles. Next year, our neighbors assured us, they would prepare fried plantains and roast pork. Their children would run games like ring the bottle.

But we never invited them into our homes. The wives and children remained on the opposite side of the street, and occasionally we nodded at each other.

The block association members donated some money and bought a half-dozen trees with the proceeds from the block party. The sidewalk was dotted with open ground where trees had once stood. We made a show of it, all of us in the block association with spades and buckets digging the holes and carefully tamping the tree balls into the Brooklyn soil. Each time I brought a bucket of water for the tree in front of my house I carried a bucket of water for the new sapling across by the cook's window.

I watched as the children stripped the tender leaves and as the men leaned against its slender trunk. Each evening the man down the street walked his dog up to the sapling and whistled while it pooped. In a few weeks the tree was dead.

The tree in front of our house sprouted tall enough so that the branches waved over our heads and threw shade over the sidewalk. After the block party, having successfully crossed once, Jose and his friends continued to cross the street. The men brought out folding tables and chairs and sat under its shade smoking cigars and playing cards. They stared at me as I walked past them and through my iron gate into my fenced-in front yard.

Father had also set up a table under the tropical cherry tree in the common compound in Malacca. Night after night he and his friends had played noisy mah-jongg, breaking repeatedly into comic obscenities and curses. Even when the stakes were hot and high and they became grimly silent, the clash of the tiles rocked monotonously through the early hours of the morning. Awake, I read on and on, fast turning the pages to keep ahead of the falling mah-jongg walls, going through three and four novels a day.

I had not thought of this male world until the poker players kept me awake past midnight with their jovial chatter. But unlike my childhood tolerance, I was now unforgiving. I resented the loss of my sound space, my air space, my adult space, all the power I had struggled for in order to escape my father's house, and I was angry with myself for my resentment. I feared I was becoming a racist. Instead of admonishing the men for the bottles of beer left reeking by the side-walk and for their late-night rowdiness, I kept the door locked all the time and stayed in the back rooms, brooding over my increasing intolerance.

It was my failure, not theirs. Their street was a public square; my street was a private loneliness. Their loud quarrels and laughter isolated me in a way that silence and books could not defend me. I did not want their music in my home, but it was impossible to shut out the blare of their radios. Why could I not learn to love this culture of the island and the street? It was clear that I did not hate it, for I loved its expressions in my Puerto Rican students. It was that I loved my own culture, the culture of the interior world, more.

Coming home from the South Bronx, I was stricken with exhaustion each evening, for there was no escaping the South Bronx at home. The sounds of beer fights, the broken bottles, the raucous epithets and dizzying music were right outside my door.

Soon my unhappiness with my tenement neighbors began to affect my work at Hostos. I felt out of control and violated. As the city's budget crisis grew worse, my students took to the streets to demonstrate against the threat of closing down the college. I took my turn carrying the pickets in front of the Board of Higher Education building at 89th Street.

"The People! United! Will Never Be Defeated!" we chanted, balding professors and mild-skirted professors mimicking the revolutionaries in El Salvador.

I could not hold together the middle-class mortgage and the South Bronx communalism, the desire for writing and books that I felt as a mourning and the material noise and violence that had seized my life. My final year teaching at Hostos held an edge of unreality, as I retreated from the contradictions.

My work at Hostos was constantly fraught with the tensions of my identity. My liberal white colleagues felt themselves motivated to help their working-class non-Anglo students, and they never questioned that they were the best people for that position. It didn't seem to matter that they were white and Jewish and that they came from upper- and middle-class backgrounds. They seemed endowed with an unself-conscious confidence that they were fully empathetic with their ghetto students, that they were asking the right questions and would arrive at the important solutions.

I had no such faith in myself. Over and over again I wondered if my hours of intense teaching were helping or actively harming my students. Of what value was it for Puerto Rican and black students, already in their late twenties and thirties, to figure out the difference between a main clause and a dependent clause, so that they would be able to write complete sentences rather than fragments? Were we setting up obstacles to lengthen their social dependency and lowly economic status and to justify our salaries and professional rank? Should a grammatically correct five-paragraph English essay test stand between intelligent adults and the decent jobs they needed? Why were we counting errors in spelling and mechanics as one criterion of ability? Why five errors and not ten? What does it mean to decide that a paragraph does not have a main idea sentence? Is all written English formulaic, and is teaching English the teaching of a series of formulae? Why are the rules and expectations of English composition both elementary and fundamental to college success? Is an educated person a writing person? What does it mean to be a writing person?

I fended off my uneasiness with the forms of education at Hostos by keeping myself extremely busy. The whirlwind of work, I was convinced, was ipso facto productive. Setting up the Writing Center, producing grammar and idiom exercises, I was meeting students' need for special help. Our students were called nontraditional: closer to thirty than twenty in age, many had children cared for by grandparents; some were also illiterate in their mother tongue.

Almost all of them had grants or student loans and aimed for vocational degrees as lab technicians or radiology assistants. On the third floor student dental hygienists practiced on other students.

Hostos was the first full-time employment for many of us. Anxious to prove we were intellectuals, although not elitist, we desperately needed reassurance that we were college rather than high school teachers. In numerous meetings we pushed each other to teach harder, write more memos, send out more grant proposals. Ever more technical language marked our progress: teaching strategies, diagnostic tests, instruction modules, evaluation sheets, mastery learning, assessment and accountability studies. We exhorted our tough ghetto students to express their feelings, but only in acceptable grammar. The contradictions were unbearable.

Carlos registered for an English as a Second Language course in my third year at Hostos. Tending toward chunkiness but handsome with vulnerable yearning eyes and a soft face, he was clearly troubled and highly intelligent. He could have been a poet if he were not in the South Bronx. His compositions followed no paragraph rules. They sprawled page after hectic page, and they described his circle of feelings.

"I am singing today because the subway is so white the light is good instead of the darkness with the many rats which I always hated when my mother left me in the room alone. I want to do good in college. I am tired of being put away. It is good to walk outside and see the stars even if they don't always shine and Bachio is standing outside the building with his people giving me the bad looks . . . ."

Uncomplainingly he filled sheets of grammar drills, marking the apostrophes, the periods, the quotation marks correctly. These were social skills he was mastering in returning to the South Bronx from wherever he had been "put away" before. We talked in class, myself encouraging his flights of prose, excited at finding a student who wrote without a required assignment and as he wished.

A few weeks later, his eyes began to turn upward in the middle of an exercise. "I'm bugging out! I'm bugging out!" he hollered, his unkempt curly hair seeming to spring out of his skull. We worked carefully around him as he lowered his head and glumly studied the grain of wood on his desk for the rest of the period. He began handing in essays written at home, long incoherent passages:

"The sword is coming out of the East and it will cut down the hordes before it. The star that shines will not bring peace but war. There will be blood in New York and chaos overtaking Adam will throw the seeds of the future into the ocean with the fish and the fire . . . ."

Sitting with crossed folded arms he stared impassively at me as I wrote homework assignments on the chalkboard. He rejected the worksheets passed around the classroom. I imagined he saw the division within me, between the grammarian and the writer, and disdained my grammarian's role.

Invited for a social tea with a famous psychiatrist who had trained with Piaget, I took Carlos's essays with me on a whim. As his guests were leaving, in the whirl of winter coats and mufflers in his Central Park apartment, I showed the psychiatrist the crumpled pages.

He read and reread the cramped careless handwriting, then fixed his serious Swiss blue eyes on me. "You must be extremely careful with this individual," he said. "He is violent and losing control of his feelings. He has confused you with other things in his life. You have touched him, and so you have overwhelmed him, and he is on the edge of doing harm to you. Avoid him at all cost."

A twentieth-century fortuneteller. A medical opinion. But I was the gypsy scholar and these were the dreaming spires of New York City.

The next week I pretended that Carlos was not present in the classroom. No drills came his way, I made no eye contact, and asked for no compositions. He was invisible, and sat heavily nodding at the desk. Whatever the reason he stopped coming to class.

I began to question my ability to help individual students. Some afternoons, weary of repeating the rules of subject-verb agreement or explaining the necessity for topic sentences in paragraphs, I would leave the building at three and take the subway down to Bloomingdale's. The streets around Alexander's and Bloomingdale's were always dense with shoppers and pedestrians. The crowds shifted and moved like enormous animals, one swaying downtown, another undulating across a green light, nervous segmented trunks that paused for trucks and surged around corners. The city was a rackety booming noise, full of body heat even in the coldest weather, when mufflers and ski masks, padded nylon parkas and boots, slushed on curbs and salt-encrusted pavements. I would buy a giant knotted pretzel, warm and burnt black, and stone cold in patches, and chew on the tasteless hard mass, licking the crystals of salt sprinkled on it like a mindless cow, while I walked up and down Lexington Avenue. Manhattan, how shall I love thee, I wondered. New York, city that had launched a nation of immigrants. I stared at the Haitians, the West Indians, the Colombians shopping in Alexander's, at the indistinguishable whites gliding up and down the Bloomingdale's escalator. I also was one of these masses.

That third year, I looked forward to summer when I could stop taking the Lexington to the Bronx, could stop hurrying up the flight of steps from the subway into the concrete block where the guards stood by the door, where my students waited with the books they could not afford for an education it was harder and harder for me to believe in. I never went back to teach at Hostos. After three years of the South Bronx I moved to a suburban community college twenty-five miles from the city.

I left Hostos because The City University of New York was threatening to close it down during yet another budget crisis. At least that was the catalyst for my leaving. Teaching at Hostos was transforming me, and I was not comfortable with the changes. I had chosen not to return to Malaysia, because, among many other reasons, a new government had implemented a Malay monolingual constitution. To confess to an attachment to the English language and its literature as the motivation for professional study is to open oneself today to the scrutiny of the tough-minded and the incredulity of materialist philosophers. A blind attachment to English and its colonial past reveals vulgarly the colonialist formation of the colonized subject. The very integrity of the decolonizing intellectual must drive her to critique her own ideological formation and so to jilt her first loves. The dominant narrative today stages a culturally free subject who, in the moment of nationalist independence, must disavow the music of Lord Alfred Tennyson, the inscape of Father Gerard Manley Hopkins, and the modernist distemper of T. S. Eliot's *The Waste Land*. After the disillusionment of the May 13 riots, however, I had no nationalist idealism to imagine. The cultural parochialism that took shape in the aftermath of the riots in Malaysia, which includes race-based quotas, communalist politics, and separatist race-essentialized cultures, was absolutely anathema to me. I did not leave Hostos for the white bread of the suburban community college merely because of the city's budget crisis. I left because I could not reconcile English literature and the deprivations of black and brown students. I believed that Hostos students deserved better and more, and I did not believe that teaching them English grammar was what they deserved. More to the point, I left Hostos because I was edgily depressed, hating my engagement in the colonialist versions of higher education.

That summer I stayed in Brooklyn among my books, but not in the backyard of the brownstone that we had bought. It had been taken over by a pack of stray cats. The stink of cat urine made it impossible to walk in that small open space without choking. The little peach tree, the grapevine that had crawled in from the garden next door, oozing dark purple Concords over a tilting arbor, the tiny patch of rosemary and thyme that I had so proudly picked last summer, none of these were possible for me in my third summer. Instead I brooded in my narrow study overlooking the wild cats as they yowled and stretched in the August heat.

In August, in response to an invitation to interview for a position, I took the train from Grand Central to North White Plains Station, then walked a mile or so to the college. The station was empty of people, but its huge parking lot stretching on every side was crowded with cars of every color and size. I looked out over the shining steel and chrome and polished reds and blacks and electric blues. It was uncanny, so much power on show, becalmed, the belongings of Americans who didn't have to live in tenements or straighten their thoughts into five-sentence paragraphs.

I was going crosswise. The road to the college campus was steep and cars careened through it, so I had to keep to the rocky side, scraping by the roadcuts. It was not made for walking, despite the thick summer vegetation and the white birches and sumac that grew above the rock faces. This countryside had been formed by the automobile with everything else that it offered of convenience and security for the individual.

The teachers who interviewed me spoke in modulated and good-humored voices as they looked me in the eye and asked, "Do you believe you need a doctorate to teach here?"

"No," I replied truthfully. I had learned at Hostos that it was not subject matter but relations that counted in student learning.

My answer, that effective teaching was a different matter from doctorates earned, was a popular response. There were warm encouraging smiles, a general relaxation of mood. I liked these people. They didn't ask me about my politics or about my background. They asked instead how I constructed a writing syllabus, whether I was prepared to teach four courses of composition a semester, how I felt about not teaching any literature classes. I liked the fieldstone walls, ungated, that bounded the campus. I liked the acres of beech and oak, the mowed football fields, and the multiples of tennis courts that bordered the low classroom buildings, dispersed like afterthoughts around an expensive estate.

"All this belonged to Mr. Hartford, the man who began the A&P supermarkets," Dr. Spacino, the Academic Dean, said. "This administrative building was his country home. It's got a secret room with a hidden door in the library paneling, and had bathroom fixtures made of gold."

I didn't like the fake library shelves, book spines turned impressively outwards with no word on them. I was beginning to feel shabby in my old batik skirt and brown top. It was going to be a long walk back to the train station.

"How does the college feel about an Asian teaching here?" I asked, meaning here among Mr. Hartford's custom-made blue and gold medallioned carpets, among the comfortable pleasant white middle class.

He reached into his jacket pocket, took out a black wallet, and flipped it open to the colored snapshot of himself with a fair-haired woman seated beside two smiling Asian children. "This is my family," he said. Later, he told me that he had a third child, a biological child born after the Korean adoptions.

I remembered the photograph when the offer came from the college. It promised that I would belong, on that campus, among the goldenrod and Douglas firs of hilly Westchester County. It was the first time a stranger had confirmed my Asian identity as a familiar rather than a foreign self. I wanted to believe that photograph, the simplicity of his reply, and its blessed indirection. I couldn't drive, and commuting to the college would take up almost five hours each day till I finally overcame my fear of the Brooklyn-Queens Expressway and the Triboro Bridge. Still, I decided, the inclusive portrait that Dr. Spacino carried in his jacket pocket, the acceptance of Asian difference, was worth the upheaval, the financial disadvantages, the move to yet another community of strangers.

In 1976 during my first year at the suburban community college, I commuted from Brooklyn to White Plains and continued living in the brownstone, but as if in a cloister. I took the driving test in the fall, and by the winter I was navigating down the dark double-parked streets, merging into the Brooklyn-Queens Expressway, and flying across the Triboro Bridge, onto the Bronx River Parkway to emerge out of White Plains into the college's wood-shaded lots. The traffic was always bad, no matter what time of day it was. Moving in a fog of carbon monoxide fumes behind trailer trucks that reminded me of tyrannosaurus rexes, I drove petrified, my face up close to the windshield. One day, snow falling in sheets, the car skidded coming onto the Triboro. I chewed Rolaids like Lifesavers. I could not afford a gas attack negotiating the notorious curves along the rutty expressway. I worried about my body until I learned that hemorrhoids were common in the United States.

But there was the new pleasure of maples reeling by, scarlet and gold and burnt brown. White houses with green shutters and expanses of emerald lawn. Gray Canadian geese in V-shaped battalions flying across speckled November skies. The smell of cut grass, like a cool potion of chlorophyll. Each time I stepped into the car, shut the door, and turned the key, I imagined I was entering a different house, a house not under hostage to the cook, the mechanic, the gamblers, the listeners of salsa, and their children. It was enveloped by the roars of a frenetic world, but it was a silent house. I never turned the radio on. Sometimes I talked to the car-house, I hummed and sang aloud. I did not mind my neighbors as much; there was always the fifty-mile drive each day to the green world of Westchester County.

Anticipating the noise and brawls, Charles and I decided to leave the street to our neighbors for the summer in 1977, and to travel to India and then to

Singapore and Malaysia. Charles would be meeting my family for the first time, a visit that also coincided with Third Brother's wedding in Singapore.

Third Brother's house in Geylang was noisy with the clacking of mahjongg tiles and irrepressible prewedding joshing. Every room was crowded. No one wanted the separation of hotel accommodations, preferring the dormitory-style crammed family reunion, with Beng sleeping in the car one night to find some quiet, the women sharing one room and talking late into the night, and the men throwing themselves on the mats in the living room after they had exhausted themselves gambling. Only the wedding couple were permitted the privacy of a bedroom.

I brought a manuscript of poems with me, for Ashok had arranged for me to meet Edwin Thumboo, a poet, editor, and professor at Singapore University. Calling for a taxi and glad to escape the twenty-four-hour Lim community, I arrived at the Bukit Timah campus that Sunday morning.

Thumboo, sitting behind a large desk in his office, knocking the ashes off his pipe, reminded me of that British colonial academy that I had fled just a few years ago. Unlike the British professors, he was dark-skinned, the son of a Tamil father and Hakka mother, and he was welcoming. He had just edited an anthology of poetry from Malaysia and Singapore, and coincidentally had included a couple of my poems that he had found in an Australian journal. Mindful that he had come to write in his office, I stayed for a scant half hour, but left with a sure sense, for the first time, that such a thing as Singaporean/ Malaysian writing existed, and that I was to be a part of it.

The brief meeting with Thumboo, his enthusiasm for local poetry, despite the rather ominous trappings of the important office, the briar pipe, and the British accent, excited me. The conjunction of a national university and poetry provided substance and belief where before I had had only typed pages and a figment of faith. My first book of poems was published in 1980 with an introduction by Thumboo.

Gershom is my good-luck American baby. Two weeks after I left Northern Westchester Hospital with him in my arms, I received my copy of *Crossing the Peninsula,* published by Heinemann, a British house known for its English-language series from Africa, and now planning to repeat its success in Asia. When I received a call from John, the chief editor at the U.S. office in New Hampshire, I thought he had called to tell me that the book had received a Kuala Lumpur prize.

"No, no," he said, speaking more loudly over the static, "your book has won the Commonwealth Prize."

I had no idea what the prize signified, but was relieved that someone thought well of the poems.

"You have been invited to London to receive the award from Lord C.," John continued. "We will try to get you a ticket through Malaysian Airlines, but I'm afraid that that may be difficult to do. You know, Malaysia is tricky about writing in English, so it may not be possible to get you a sponsor in Malaysia."

It had not occurred to me till then that since only writing in Bahasa Malaysia was considered national literature, my book might not be admitted into official existence. How strange to be a poet without a country! And yet how inevitably it had come about that it should be so. The prize, like my poetry, was going to be both substance and shadow after all.

"The awards ceremony will be a significant occasion," John went on. "There'll be all kinds of newspapers and media. You are the first woman and the first Asian to win the prize!"

"But I can't go."

There was a silence at the other end.

"I've just had a baby."

"Well, congratulations! Can't you take him with you? It's a boy, is it?"

"Yes. And no, he's too young to travel with. I'm still nursing. If I go without him, he will have to stop breast-feeding."

At the back of my mind I felt a faint pressure of regret. Fame, if only for a day, was passing me by, and also the possibility of another audience. London of the British whose poems I had memorized and loved: oh, to be there to seize the award and be my own poet for the day. In the snuggly across my chest, my infant son's warm fuzzy head turned hungrily. There was no choosing.

"I suppose someone from Heinemann can arrange to be your proxy. Could you write a poem for the occasion? I was told the Commonwealth Institute would like to have one of your poems read during the ceremony."

I sent a poem to John which began, quoting Conrad, "Master, he dead." It was tortuously political, claiming the English language as no longer a colonial intrusion but a postcolonial free-for-all. I regretted sending it as soon as it was in the mail.

No news came of the ceremony, but a few weeks later a letter arrived in the mail confirming that I had received the prize. My son's birth usurped the birth of the book, one sacred moment making a heresy of the other. Or as paired siblings, the younger of the two shrinking to a runt in the presence of the bonny one.

# PART FOUR

# CHAPTER TEN

# Immigrant Mother

How does one make a home? Sometimes I think too much is made of homes, as if because we equate having nothing with being nothing, we burrow deeper into the stuffing of sofas and beds. Too much can be made of homeland. Stories we tell often take their identity from a piece of soil, and the strongest stories may leave us still standing in the scene of our powerlessness.

Birth changes a place to a homeland: birth land, children, our childhoods, where our parents have buried our umbilical cords, where our children will bury us and will bear their children. There are homelands of the memory and homelands of the future, and for many of us, they are not the same.

I had never wanted children. Although I cannot wish one less than the ten children my father brought into being, for, once born, each child was a body, a cry, a name, and a brother, although I feel blessed to have these many brothers whose faces and voices continue to materialize my father's ghost for me, I had never wanted children for myself.

Peng's baby slept in a cloth sling tied to a spring that was suspended from a wooden beam resting between the door and window frames. His weight pulled the cloth around him, like a cocoon's shroud, and the sling sagged with his bottom. I pushed this cradle up and down and swung it gently to and fro. The spring bounced, magnifying my hand's tug. One must gauge the strength of the cradle's momentum, for it was the gentle swaying motion that rocked the baby to sleep.

But the baby twisted and turned in his sling. He did not want to sleep, although I had fed him a bottle of milk, I had changed his cloth diaper, I had sung every Irish and Scots ballad I knew over three times each and had bored myself, and now I wanted desperately to be out of the room and to climb a tree and give myself up to reading. I bounced the cradle a little more vigorously. "Uh, uh, uh, uh," he whined. I felt the strain on my arm, the enormous power that surged from shoulder to fingers, that wanted to hurl the cradle smack against the wall and crack the wriggling body inside the flowered cloth cocoon. The strain hurt, as gently, ever so gently, I tapped the cradle and allowed the baby's weight to rock it.

Another year. My little brother, the one who grew quiet after Mother left, whose grades in arithmetic and English slipped from A to F in one year, whom I believed I should love as mothers should love their babies, called me a name one afternoon. A crowd of brothers and cousins clustered by the doorway. I was sticky, unbathed, and hungry, always hungry. At eleven, I was many inches taller and fiercer than this small, malnourished seven-year-old. Around us the children jostled and laughed at the name he had called me. Balling my hand into a large fist I hit him as hard as I could in the stomach. His face turned sallow. He buckled at the knees and almost fell over.

The sensation in my chest was like nothing I had felt before. As he wailed, half-collapsed, all the brothers and cousins stared at me. I put on my defiant, I-don't-care-I-am-not-ashamed glare. I've killed him, I thought. I've killed my little brother. My fist stung from the impact.

"What did you do that for?" Beng, my growly eldest brother, asked. And, yes, in all the fighting, yelling, and name calling that went on among the brothers and cousins, no one actually punched, hit, bit, mauled, pulled hair, or scratched. Only Baba lashed out crazily with the cane and the feather duster.

"I mustn't become crazy," I thought, as I backed off from my brothers' and cousins' astonishment. "Crazy like Baba." Only, it was too early for me to apologize. I was afraid of myself, of the ability to hit, suddenly exhibited like a hidden talent.

There is this access to violence in my body, that I have inherited, like an alcoholic gene, and that I have to keep in sight of, vigilant, never to let loose.

Having a baby in 1980 was the best thing that had happened to me. It was the best thing because I wanted it to be so. I was willing to set aside everything else to steep in the transient sensations of motherhood, as if in a fiction, a long pleasurable novel, a romance. In this romance, women had control over actions and outcomes, for motherhood is what women do as a way to make stories about their lives.

The phrase "biological clock" became popular at about the time I worried about not having children. It is a powerful image, inherently persuasive because it evokes a sense of the body as a giant organic timer in which an allotted chronology is inscribed, ticking down to atrophy, to barrenness, to death. One falls asleep listening to the two-tick pulse of the heart, the engine that drives the timing mechanism, and imagines the blood sloshing and sluicing inside the intricate veined network of the womb as an amazing water-clock. Every twenty-eight days or so, it dongs; out rushes an egg. Whoosh! The water-clock opens its locks, releases the tide of blood and fluids that have risen during the last cycle of the moon, bearing the sacred egg out of the treasure cave, down into the toilet bowl.

The image penetrated my dreams. My body felt like a dying dump: either I used it now for the one thing only it could do, or it would never be usable.

We had a routine at the college: every Tuesday and Thursday, three to five of us ate lunch together. I was the only childless person at the table. The conversation was almost always pleasant and inane, circling around baseball and tennis jokes I did not understand, and semi-flirtatious exchanges guaranteed to make each of us feel safely desirable. I left each lunch meeting with a minor buzz, as on those occasions when I had had a glass of wine to help me enjoy a slow evening.

"Do you think it is a good idea for me to have a baby?" I asked half-seriously.

"What would you want one for?" Dennis appeared truly perplexed. He had a homemaker wife and two teenagers and an impregnable philosophy that life was a pursuit of suburban security, and he hated and feared any intimations that his life was insignificant. "You have a full career," he insisted. "You write, teach, travel. You have your wonderful friends. A baby will simply be a burden to you."

I must have looked hesitant, for he continued, "And where will you find the time? You have to leave time for us, you know."

We were a friendly circle of people around the table, yet the intimacy we shared was shallow, founded as it was on the principle of pleasantness. No unpleasant home truths, no confidences that discomfort, no topics that might require instruction or reveal ignorance, no passionate tones that got under the skin. The conversations replayed each afternoon like television commercials advertising deodorants, shaving products, lemon furniture polish, and air fresheners. In my anxiety not to be different, I sleepwalked through years of such meetings, smiling, nodding, keeping my mouth and mind shut, drinking drafts of boredom, hypocrisy, fear, cynicism, and the desire to be accepted.

Early in my career at the college, after I had spoken up against a senior colleague's position, Dennis had asked me to his office. "I notice that you always speak your mind," he began.

"Well, I have a point of view and if I believe something I express it."

"Is it so important to always speak your mind?"

I blinked. "I've never thought of it in that way."

"I try to look around to see how other people will react to what I say. For example, when you disagreed with Elena, you made her angry. She bears grudges, you know, so you've made an enemy. I always ask myself who will be upset with what I say before I say anything."

The culture of conformity. Now Dennis was giving me his home truth: he was possessive of my time, and a baby would disrupt that cozy lunch ritual that had come to mean so much to him.

That fall, I became pregnant. Each morning I woke up with a sour taste in my mouth. No coffee or tea for me. Charles had brought home a book that listed all the suspected foods and their potential mutating effects on an evolving fetus: potato products, wine, beer, cigarettes, aspirin, any medication including cough drops and mouth wash. The list filled an entire book.

For three months, I could ignore the list; nothing made me more queasy than the smell of food. The harsh chemical scent of fried oil. The sewage stink of beef, dead cow in a pan. The rotting odor of fish, penetrating the kitchen wallpaper with smells not just of death but of carrion. The pungency of carrots, stinging with a sharp orange cut. Brussel sprouts, bitter and rank like dark soil. Cabbage bilge water, long stagnant. Hopelessly nauseous in the presence of mayonnaise and tuna fish, I stopped eating with Dennis and the lunch group.

I became an American politically with the birth of my child. I may have been a blackbird, flying into Boston as a disheveled traveler uncertain whether I was choosing expatriation, exile, or immigration. But I had no such doubts about my unborn child. He would be an American child of Jewish and Asian descent.

Native-born children carry the cultural imprint of Americanism in a way that their immigrant parents cannot. If they become encumbered by nostalgia and regret, like their parents, this consciousness of another country cannot undermine the infant primacy of an American homeland. I wanted my child to possess the privileges of a territorial self, even as I had as a young Malaysian. "Out of the cradle endlessly rocking," the folding into and unfolding out of a social space and a people. While all citizens are guaranteed juridically their claim to a place in the United States, not every claim is unquestioned, nor is that place certain. Poverty, skin color, sex, disease, disability, any difference can arouse suspicion and exclusion. I did not expect my child to be safe from these discriminations, but I wished, at least for his infancy, the primal experience of bonding with an American homeland. In this desire, I marked myself as a U.S. citizen, and I finally began the process for citizenship.

Without relatives and with only my college colleagues for a community, pregnancy was a lonely, isolating experience. One morning I had to be in New

York City for an interview with the Immigration and Naturalization Office. The train rattled through the underground tunnels into Grand Central Station, shaking its entire length. On any other morning I would have been absorbing its energy, bouncing with it, waiting eagerly to emerge into the day outside and to merge into the anonymity of coats and boots and shining shop windows.

Now, overcome with nausea, I munched furiously on Saltine crackers. My seatmate pretended not to see the crumbs that fell like dandruff over my black winter coat. My stomach heaved and rumbled. It was aching to throw up, but there was nothing inside, only dry lumps of baked flour like wet cement chuting down to settle my hunger pangs.

The doors opened and everyone pushed out. I was a black fish gathered up in the net of bodies. The bodies carried me out of the train and up the stairs through other tunnels. I could not slow my stride; my legs trundled like part of a centipede's hundred pairs. I had no will in this morning rush hour's masses. Slowly my head was turning dark, and I felt myself lose consciousness. The centipede was rushing down a flight of steps toward the downtown Lexington. Just ahead the subway cars were spilling with other bodies, and a mechanical voice was announcing, "Keep clear of the closing doors. Keep clear of the closing doors." The feet rushed faster, faster down the steps.

But I could not keep up. I sat down on the steps, despite the press of bodies behind me. The river backed up, split open, then swirled around the boulder that was myself. I put my head down between my knees. The concrete steps were black and brown with grime. The dirt had piled up along the backs of the steps, bits of fresh candy wrappers still colored blue and gold, brown filter tips and butts with shredded tobacco falling out. I could see only a little piece of concrete. The rest was filled with moving legs, tan and khaki pants, blue dungarees, suede heels, frayed hems and silk-bound hems, unwashed sneakers split at the sides, white leather sneakers squeaking new, dirt-crusted workboots with soles like floors. No one stopped to ask why I was sitting on the steps of Grand Central Station. I was grateful for the city's impersonality: I could have been sitting by the abyss of the Grand Canyon listening to the rush of the wind among the bent piñon and ponderosa pines. The huge ingrained ugliness of New York's subways appeared as much a force of nature as the Grand Canyon's wind-scrubbed beauty; I was as invisible in the midst of thousands of hurrying feet as a hiker lost on the canyon's red-scarp edge.

On Saint Valentine's Day, 1980, four months pregnant, I stood in a hall in White Plains and swore allegiance to the flag and to the republic for which it stands. There must have been about two hundred others there that morning, more white than brown, and there was a festive mood in the hall as the black-robed justice congratulated us. This is the crucible of America, the moment when the machinery of the state opens its gate and admits irrevocably those aliens who have passed the scrutiny of its bureaucrats—language tests, history tests, economic tests, social tests. Tests that impress with the enormous and amazingly indifferent power of representative Americans to deny you identity, tests that force you to compliance, tests for inclusion that threaten exclusion. So my patriotism on my first day as an American citizen was not unbounded. Scooping a piece of buttermilk pancake from its puddle of maple syrup at the International House of Pancakes where I had gone to celebrate my passage into American identity, I felt alien in a different way, as if my ambivalence toward the United States must now extend inward to an ambivalence toward myself. No longer a traveler, I was included in my accusations of America.

My morning sickness disappeared after three months. I swelled and swelled, fifty pounds above my normal weight, half as much as I was, a red plum tomato in my cotton summer frock. We had moved to Westchester County, fifty miles out of Manhattan, two years earlier, and while Charles commuted to teach in Manhattan, I fell in love with the Westchester suburbs for the first time. The May days were busy with Queen Anne's lace, day lilies, Dutchmen's-breeches, and flourishing sumac. I fretted over a strand of bright orange butterfly weed that had sprung up by Route 100, waving above the still gray water of the Croton Reservoir, just below our white-and-green colonial home. It was too exotic, an endangered wildflower, in plain view, with the red-winged blackbirds flashing among the sumac bushes. Sure enough in a few days the butterfly weed blossoms, winged like palpitating floaters that its milky sap invites, were gone. Some passing human had picked them, robbing the seeds that would have borne more orange wings for the years after.

We practiced huffing and puffing. The gynecologist's receptionist had me down as a *mater primigravida*. The term conjured the images of the Virgin Mary from those faraway convent days: the gravely tragic countenance, the graceful folds of cloak and robes concealing a thickened waistline. A pregnant woman oppressed by secrets, social isolation, poverty, married to a man not the father of her baby, that central story never told directly, the story of woman's delight in childbearing. The narrowing of the story to simply mother and infant, the man far away in the clouds or discreetly in the background, together with the oxen and donkeys. A celibate woman's fantasy, a revenge story for women harrowed by men's demands and commands.

I was lucky. Charles was tender and attentive, but all that deep breathing and panting came to nothing. At almost nine pounds, the baby had to be sprung out of my bony pelvic cage by a scalpel. As the nurses rushed me into the operating room, my temperature rising precipitously each minute and the fetal temperature mounting to life-threatening degrees, I focused on the life in my body. It, he, she was ready to emerge from the container which was myself. The event of childbirth is violent and bloody. As if experiencing her death, the mother cannot change course. She endures and, if she is able and wise, assists in the moment of expulsion. When the anesthesiologist crammed the plastic apparatus into my throat like a giant obscene penis, I willed my body to relax, to float like the lotus yielding its seeds to the light. At that moment I felt the cold swab of the anesthetic-soaked cotton like the curve of a scimitar across my abdomen and lost consciousness.

The nine months of pregnancy had been a slowly swelling swoon into domesticity, marked by giddy strolls through aisles of baby perambulators, crib mobiles, bath toys, terry-cloth books, hooded towels, fuzzy blue, brown, and white rabbits, dogs, lions, unicorns, Smurfs, bears and more bears, an instant cornucopia of infant goods for infant-obsessed Americans. But once my son was born, strenuously hungry and alert, it became clear I could not simply buy him a life.

I had entered U.S. society through the workplace, taking my seat in department meetings and at conference sessions as a colleague. My husband's parents were dead, he was estranged from his only brother, and all my brothers were in Malaysia. It mattered that we spent Easter, Passover, Memorial Day, Labor Day, Hanukkah, Christmas, and New Year's Eve alone, but it didn't matter that much. Occasionally a colleague invited us to a department picnic or a department brunch. But babies do not socialize through English departments. I was tormented by the fear that my son would grow up isolated, as I was, in the United States. I did not wish my son to be lonely the way we were. He was an American, whatever that was, and I wanted him to have the full plenitude of his world, not the shadowy existence of a green-card holder.

The myth of assimilation became a pressing reality as soon as I brought my son home from Northern Westchester Hospital. A child's society is his parents': cut off from the umbilical cord, he is nonetheless tied to the company his mother keeps. Or does not keep, in my case. It may have been important for my imagination to maintain the distance of the resident alien, but I wanted something different for my son. Despite the absence of an extended community, I wanted for him to have a pride of belonging, the sense of identity with a homeland, that which I had possessed as a Chinese Malaysian for a brief time in my youth. I wanted Gershom to be able to run for the presidency of the United States if that was what he wished.

The passage of assimilation began at the earliest age. Anxiously I accepted every birthday invitation that came his way from the Montessori mothers. Together, Gershom and I shopped for Mattel educational toys, boxes with differently shaped mouths and blocks, cobblers' benches, multicolored xylophones, huge plastic contraptions that invited baby fists to punch and ring and pull and pat. I chose the opulent set, the more expensive version of a brand-name product, while Gershom sat in his thrift-store stroller, pointing at each large package within reach. We drove down numerous Yorktown and Somers circular dead-ends, clutching party invitations and directions in one hand. His bottom still padded with diapers, he waddled among pink-cheeked, blond, and blue-eyed toddlers. I sat with the mommies, an alien among a dozen or so white women, an awkward mismatch among the grandmothers furiously snapping Nikons at the cake and chubby faces and the fathers with rolling video cameras. A college teacher years older than the young homemakers with junior-executive husbands, I held my breath and sat very gingerly on the new sofas in these strangers' split-level ranches, where lavish bathrooms were cleaner than the shelters of billions of other humans. I could not afford contemptuous segregation or condescending kinship if I wished Gershom to have a full human connection with America.

Malls and department-store aisles do not discriminate. Everything is for sale to everyone. But women do. Mothers, keeping a wary eye on their scrambling pebble-picking children in playgrounds, do. Fathers, arriving to pick up their toddlers after work, loosening their ties by the Montessori entrance, do. If I could hope to have Gershom pass into Middle America in wall-to-wall carpeted living rooms, we never succeeded in the public playgrounds among anonymous whites.

Weekends and summers Gershom and I set forth to Reis Park, Leonard Park, Muscoot Farm, and assorted town fairs and parades. Cautiously I let him loose in the sandbox, retreated to one side where other mothers stood under the shade of birches and oaks and cast their eyes sidewise on the little spaders and grubbers. There were no homesteaders here, only transient visitors who might or might not return another afternoon. Was it the chip on my shoulder that sounded the alarm? I watched enviously as strangers veered toward each other and began exchanging intimacies of toilet training and bed-wetting. I imagined their eyes were already measuring their toddlers' compatibility, one pink hand patting another pink hand's castle.

My olive-skinned child had dark handsome eyes and thick dark hair. He was oblivious to social slight as he scrambled up the teeter-totter. There was no one to teeter with him. The other children had wandered away with their parents who strolled off deep in conversation. I called out to him, placed my weight on two legs so that my body did not pull the balance down, and planted the illusion that between us we could move the teeter-totter up and down, up and down.

I had approached being alone in the United States as inevitable. It was a lonely society, even lonelier for an Asian immigrant whose train seat next to her usually remained untaken till the car was full. But what I accepted as my position in the United States I felt keenly as unacceptable for my son. A grievance gnawed in me, perhaps the displaced desires for assimilation, a growing anger that, despite his birth here in the United States, his childhood was still marked by the perception of my foreignness.

I began to ask my colleagues, "When did your family come to the United States?"

"Oh, I don't know. My grandfather was a Prussian officer, so I must be third generation."

"My mother came after World War I; got out just before Hitler. What does that make me? A second generation?"

"I came over from Manchester to do my master's at New York University. Never went home."

"Well, I'm not an American citizen. I still have my Canadian passport."

"Of course, my husband's parents are from Sicily. They are horribly traditional."

All these recent origins. All these immigrants. But the stiffness and tentativeness, the distinct charge of distance that marked one as alien and outsider, was directed chiefly to those who did not look white European.

There are many ways in which America tells you you don't belong. The eyes that slide around to find another face behind you. The smiles that appear only after you have almost passed them, intended for someone else. The stiffness in the body as you stand beside them watching your child and theirs slide down the pole, and the relaxed smile when another white mother comes up to talk. The polite distance as you say something about the children at the swings and the chattiness when a white parent makes a comment. A polite people, it is the facial muscles, the shoulder tension, and the silence that give away white Americans' uneasiness with people not like them. The United States, a nation of immigrants, makes strangers only of those who are visibly different, including the indigenous people of the continent. Some lessons begin in infancy, with silent performances, yet with eloquent instructions.

Struggling through the maniacal traffic on the Taconic State Parkway after teaching at the college, I picked my son up from the baby-sitter each evening with a rush of relief, relief that he was still there in the world despite my disappearance for almost nine hours, relief at the end of another separation. I nuzzled his smooth round cheek, no texture as sensuous as my baby's skin, and held his body to mine, his warm breath and growing bulk filling me with the most intense emotions of safety and completion and of fear also.

But the weekends with a cranky baby and a busy husband sometimes stretched long and tense. I could not understand the volatility of my feelings at unexpected moments.

The first week of my son's life I cried easily. My body hurt constantly from this bond, these surges of emotion that physically pulled the milk out of my body. My nipples wept milk each time I thought of this other being, not so tiny at almost nine pounds, already insistent on his own drives, staring unblinking at me, mouth tugging at my breasts, his fists puckered and gradually uncurling ready to push and punch.

We hung a rope of bells above the crib, a mirror, so he could see himself, so he could learn to beat the bells and make a noise upon the world. Gratefully I surrendered myself to his unscheduled feeding, his fretful demands, his nightly wails, the unending rounds of diaper changes, baths, laundries, doctor visits. Satiated with mother love, I had no time for unhappiness.

He was barely two feet tall, and usually I saw him as a vulnerable, weak infant. I was afraid to leave him alone in a room, out of my sight. His slightest cry or fuss would rouse me. Accustomed to nursing on demand through the night, he would stir and wake up crying if I were not sleeping beside him. We dismantled his crib and bought a futon as it was easier for me to lie down beside him to pacify him. His intense dependency was addictive, drugged me so I had to drink jolts of coffee to keep me awake through the day. I was confused by reports that mothers should allow their babies to cry through the night to teach them to sleep alone and by my inability to do so. On the few occasions we lay rigid in bed listening to him screaming, he threw up so violently that we feared he would choke and had to rush in to change his clothes and bedding. Finally, despite the medical advice and the fear that we were contributing to a future pathology, we gave up on our attempt to wean him. In many non-Western societies, babies slept with their mothers till they were older, we told each other.

Why not in our home?

Violence, like racism, imprinted from childhood, can never be totally eradicated. My rage at my baby was all the more terrifying to me in contrast to my usual intimate protectiveness. He was so small and weak, but he struggled to have his way. The shame I suffered when my father beat me was the same shame I felt when I hit my son, only fourteen months old.

Barely walking, Gershom had already learned to say no. "No" was like his fist which waved before the mirror and which rang the bells. He beat us with it. "No, no!" he shrieked, even when he meant yes. It was the lever that pulled his mother back and forth, back and forth. He was terrified when this lever did not work, as if he could no longer see himself in the mirror. With this word he commanded us to turn back from the front door, like a fast rewind of a videotape, and to reenact the earlier scene, erasing the action that had so offended him. He believed time was plastic and recoverable, that he could control events, even to replaying them exactly the way he wanted them to be. When the television cartoon displeased him, he yelled, "No!" then cried because the television set would not replay for him the cartoon he had in mind. He regressed from godlike power to mere human frustration; his rages went on for months.

Like him I too was suddenly enraged. One night, after I had tried unsuccessfully to get him to sleep by himself, I shook him hard, and roared, "Go to sleep, damn you, go to sleep!" He gave me a startled look, then threw up, the white-spotted vomit splattering my face, his sheets, the carpet. Once, hurrying someplace, burdened with his bags, his obstinate weight, I heard him whine. He wriggled, protesting at our errand, and the bags fell. My slap left a red palm print on his cheek, and he wailed. I did not admit my guilt. He was bad, bad, bad. But I remembered my father's anger, and I was afraid of myself.

Then I slapped Gershom in front of Jane and Milton. It was true that Jane and Milton, who came up to northern Westchester every weekend, escaping the West Side, were comfortable people to be around, pleasant because safe. Some weekends they would invite us to drop by their country home, a convenient mile away. Their son, Ferdie, two years older than Gershom, was fascinated by a creature even smaller than himself. I looked forward to visiting their home, a cozy jumble of small dark rooms, set among several acres of brambly blackberries, pines, and overgrown rhododendrons, a wilderness which Jane's grandparents had bought just before the Depression as an inexpensive summer cottage to escape the city's dangerous polio-ridden streets.

That afternoon, the October Sunday streamed blue and gold outdoors. We sat in the one sunlit room, an expanded kitchen, around the scrubbed kitchen table. Gershom was babbling in the highchair while we waited for the kettle to boil. He was familiar with Jane and Milton, and at fourteen months, his confidence was overweening.

The cup of herbal tea steamed up my face, raising a different kind of gold in the kitchen. A placid boredom filled the cluttered kitchen, where every counter space was taken up with brown shopping bags from Waldbaums, packed tight with coffee, sodas, carrots, cabbages, toilet paper, cereals, packages of matzos and bagels, honey jars, and assorted cookies, combustibles that Jane and Milton carried off every Sunday to their Manhattan apartment to see them through the week. Gershom, smiling in the highchair, beat my arm with his fist as I leaned, elbows forward, to inhale the dusky steam.

"Chinese children do not hit their parents," I said. By the kitchen Jane was pouring the water for her tea bag, and Ferdie, his nose dripping from a cold, was tugging at her skirt for an ice-cream cone they had just refused him.

Bang! Again the pudgy fist hit out. It didn't hurt, but I felt myself flush.

"Don't do that!" I warned. "Children should never hit their mothers!"

I suddenly imagined him an adult. There was a panic that if I could not stop him then, make him obey, everything would be lost. "Chinese children must respect their parents," the tape played in my head. A few minutes later, as I listened to Milton, elbows on the table, and blew on my mint tea, Gershom slapped my arm a third time, and chuckled as my elbow gave way. I did not think; my arm flew across the table, and the slap left red finger bruises on his face.

Milton stopped talking and raised his eyebrows. I heard Jane saying, "All right, Ferdie, if you'll come outside I'll give you your ice cream," and the sound of the kitchen door opening and shutting.

Strangely, Gershom didn't cry. Perhaps it was Milton's presence at the table, the adult's sudden wary silence and look of surprise, that stopped him. He lowered his head, bit his lip, then pretended to eat his cookie. I saw a shame in Milton's averted glance. In that moment, I saw through Milton's eyes the scene of my own childhood; it was excruciating. The shame prevented me from picking the baby up; it spoke in a stifled insistent voice, "Chinese children do not hit their parents!" It forced me to stay in my chair sipping the flat mint tea, while Jane and Milton politely talked about Ferdie's ear infections, and led me home, where I cuddled my baby tearfully, because I hadn't meant to slap him.

The shame did not prevent me from hitting him again. Sometimes it was a smack on a diaper-cushioned bottom; or a slap on the hand, sharp enough to cause a pucker and a wail. Each time I felt shame and defiance, mixed with panic: panic that he was not me, he was hatefully not me; defiance against the shame that insisted that what I was doing was wrong.

The last time I slapped him, it was in front of my husband. Not yet two, Gershom was fussing about putting on his shoes. "Hold still while I put on your other shoe!" I said. Sitting on the stairs, he continued to wriggle. His foot slipped out of my hands and the tiny sneaker fell down. As unreflecting and as quick as a branch in a wind storm my hand went up. Whap! Startled I watched the vivid shape on my palm print on his cheek turn crimson.

Charles stood at the top of the stairs, a calm presence. "I'll put your sneakers on for you," he said, and reached down for the baby. A few minutes later we were out of the door, nothing discussed.

The red finger marks on the cheek faded after an hour, but in that silent hour I rehearsed the scene through Charles's eyes, seeing with no excuses my adult size, the actual littleness of my baby, and finally that I was repeating those very scenes of brutality that my father had wreaked on me.

There were no more slaps after that morning, although I continued to struggle with stubborn outbursts of rage, an adamantine insecurity that would turn my child into my enemy were my reason less supported by my love for him. Once started, the cycle of family violence may never end. Only the consciousness of one's own precarious position in the cycle can contain the violence. To change the blow to a caress, the sharp and ugly words to careful explanation, the helpless choking rage to empathy, that is my struggle as a mother: to form a different love.

The consciousness of family as love and violence all in one, and the power to stop the violence, whether practiced by men or women, is, for me, a feminist consciousness. I could only unravel the repetitions of fear and rage by understanding myself as a woman: a girl-child seizing autonomy rather than suffering damage, but damaged still by that premature forced growth, a young woman fearing independence but fearing dependency more.

For women breaking out of closed societies, the break itself is traumatic. Liberation hurts. Feminism must prepare women for struggle not comfort. Women who look for comfort reject feminism's lessons, but without those struggles, we can never move out of our parents' houses.

I did not understand my place as a feminist until very late. In 1982, while my husband remained in New York, I returned to teach for a semester at the National University of Singapore. My son was just two years old, and my mother had been asking to meet him. I intended for the six months to be a private retreat, when my son could be with his grandmother, and I might work out my still unsettled ambivalences with her. However, much of my time there when not teaching became taken up with defining a public sense of a female self.

Unbeknown to me, my first book of poems had brought me public attention in Malaysia and Singapore. Published as part of the Writing in Asia series, it had won one of the most significant international awards ever given to a "local" writer. Still, when the Singapore newspaper, *The Straits Times,* interviewed me, the reporter asked about my husband's response to my success, and the article featured a photograph of me playing with my handsome toddler. Times Books International had also published a collection of my stories that year, a number of which had appeared among the top ten of the *Asiaweek* short-story competition. *Asiaweek* had published both the prize-winning story and an extensive interview. But when some junior college students came to interview me for their newspaper, they wanted to know why my stories centered on women characters. After La Leche Club invited me to speak to its members, the papers carried a short news item about my talk on breast-feeding. It was an uneasy period for me. For all my early struggles and professional visibility, once back in Singapore I was inevitably, inextricably woman. Wife, mother, and breast—I was continuously addressed as such.

There was no escaping gender roles in Singapore, for the public sphere in

Singapore was predominantly male. *The Straits Times* carried pictures of authoritative men: ministers, executives, invited speakers, judges, overseas visitors. The few women in the public domain were repeatedly shown nurturing, sharing, and caring. While Singaporean men were exhorted to transform themselves into militarized rugged individuals, Singaporean women were usually presented as beautiful bodies and loving mothers. Anxiety about the modernization of society seemed displaced on women: the Asian self had to be guarded against Western corruption through the preservation of women's traditional feminine qualities.

During the six months in Singapore, I was approached as a woman writer, representing her sex. My unease came from the struggle to speak as a woman without repeating and also without repudiating the traditional status of women as faithful wives, devoted mothers, and staunch caretakers of elderly parents. Representing women, speaking for the necessity to write as a woman, I was aware that I was speaking revolutionary thoughts out of an inchoate yearning for a world in which women could be free of the constraints of social roles, free to strive, to work, to grow selves outside the mold of gender.

But how could I speak as a woman when I could not even begin to define myself as a daughter? I had come as a visiting lecturer to the National University, exchanging my comfortable home in Westchester County for the bare university bungalow, the nightly whine of mosquitoes, and the transitory and tentative friendships of mendicant professionals, so that my mother might become acquainted with my two-year-old son. I wanted to give my son the memory of his grandmother. He would accept her peering obsessive attention as natural, and his unquestioning acceptance of her love might excuse my estrangement.

Mother had grown old in the five years since I had last seen her. She had suffered a stroke, could no longer hold a job, and was living with Third Brother and his wife in Bedok near the Singapore airport. No longer a modern woman, she dressed in loose trousers and shapeless blouses, her thinning gray hair cropped short, all sexuality gone.

We set up house together in Holland Village, in a bungalow that was part of university housing. Next door the three young children of a junior college teacher from Ireland ran unrestrained. Patrick and his wife were intrigued with my public status as poet. He pressed a copy of Seamus Heaney's poems on me, poetry being our bond, Irish and Malaysian, both our imaginations belonging to a common literary language. But his bright-haired children would not play with Gershom; they already had their secret language of shouts and quarrels which admitted no outsider.

Mother was very happy to be with me. Because of the stroke her mouth sagged to one side, giving her usual unhappy expression an even more discontented appearance. But each time we met friends and relatives, her face beamed with pride. Although no longer paralyzed, her left hand and foot dragged, and she could walk only slowly. So she would hang onto my arm, her round face bright with pleasure. It felt strange to be the focus of such intense attachment.

In the evenings we strolled silently through the neighboring shaded streets. Silently I counted the fences covered with crimson hibiscus, golden gloriosa, and purple morning-glory, gazed at the white and pink plumeria blossoms drooping from their dark waxy foliage. Pushing the stroller with Gershom babbling in it, I wanted to ask Mother how she could have left us, six unfed children, for Singapore. But we never spoke. The walks were a slow torture for me. I felt the Singapore evenings as deep melancholia, and only my son's presence anchored my body to the place.

Returning to Singapore, I had hoped to prove myself a peranakan daughter. It was time to let go of grievances. Mother and I presented ourselves as if without secrets. There was nothing to forgive, for parents can do no wrong. Daily I performed the rituals of ancestral care, taking her for her walks—she slowly shuffling, I patient. Together we waved at neighbors. Shopping at Lucky Plaza on Saturdays, I carried my son on one arm while she clutched the other, as we made our way through the masses of tourists and natives, for shopping was the national sport of the island. Smiling I introduced her to colleagues and new friends, doing what adult children do, winning for their parents those prizes that confirmed their immortality.

But I squirmed in her presence. She was a stranger, dragging bare feet in my temporary rented home, and our relationship foundered on what remained unspoken. Her betrayal was a splinter in my eye. I could not see her except through a red film of pain and rage. I could look at her only sideways, at her gray hair so thin that the pink scalp showed in shiny strips, at her stocky ailing body. I turned my eyes away, and turned my tongue only to the most innocuous of conversations. Certain hurts are amputations, the lost limb unrecoverable.

Each time I looked up from my books, Mother was staring at me. I did not invite her conversation, preferring to treat her with the utmost respect, respect taking the place of love. She had become a born-again Christian. Living with me and without a car, her Baptist church in Bedok was too far to visit on Sundays. Instead she received telephone calls from her church companions. With an open Bible before her, she would read passages of Scripture into the mouthpiece. "Praise the Lord!" she repeated. "Hallelujah! Rejoice in His mercy!" These long conversations with unseen auditors took up most of her afternoons. The rest of the day she cooked for me as if to make up for the years of separation, and gazed fixedly at my every action.

Chattering to the housekeeper who baby-sat Gershom while I was teaching, I would find Mother listening avidly. She hovered over me, always hardly a few feet away, following me from room to room, magnetized by my presence. I read determinedly, forcing myself not to look up. I began taking Gershom alone to busy shopping centers to escape her stares. We never touched. There was no way to begin. She was hypnotized by my life, especially by my conversations with other people, but a long silence of grievances lay between us. I was both her daughter and a stranger, someone she should have known intimately but never did. She wanted to know me as her daughter, and it was too late. Rather it was too soon. Too much the daughter, I could not forgive her yet for abandoning us.

Two years later, I had planned to teach in Singapore again, in order to have Mother with me for the year. I hoped we would learn to talk to each other, that I could speak to her as mother to mother without breaking into a daughter's tears and screams of accusations.

But she had another stroke a few months before my return. When Second Brother called to say she was in a coma, I took a Pan American flight out of Kennedy Airport the next day. Flying into Changi Airport just before midnight, the plane bumped through erratic air pockets, a warning I thought from Mother's unappeased spirit. Sure enough, just after Third Brother had unlocked the gate to his driveway and was gathering my luggage from the car, a messenger arrived from the hospital to say she had died within the hour.

I stayed three days for Mother's funeral. Instead of bringing her body home and displaying it in its coffin as was the ancestral tradition, my brothers, following modern Singapore practice, arranged for the Casket Company to take care of the wake and the cremation. The body was not to be left alone at any time before cremation, and we took turns sitting in the funeral room, one of a number of rooms each dedicated to a different religious observation. The funeral room had glass sliding doors and was heavily air-conditioned, which made it physically tolerable for Mother's numerous relatives to sit and grieve with us.

Mother lay waxy pale and stiff on a satiny bed. Her oldest brother, an uncle I hadn't met in years, was a wealthy businessman, and enormous wreaths of frangipanis and mossy ferns, baskets of giant yellow and white chrysanthemums, tall stands of vanda joachim and tiger orchids, kept appearing in the room. The cards read, "Deepest solicitations on the death of Madame Ong, sister of Director Ong, from the Highlands Cement Company," or "From the Genting Group Company, Limited, for Director Ong, on the occasion of his sister's death," "From Belair Hotels, Berhad, on Director Ong's beloved sister's death," "From Chin, Eng, and Dass, Accountants." I stopped counting after about fifty of these hugely ostentatious bouquets were delivered.

Mother's sister was ecstatic. "Oh, she must be so happy to see all these flowers!" she exclaimed. "How proud we are as a family to get such attention! And to have you come back all the way from New York! Such a loving daughter!"

On the last night of the wake, Pastor Cheng arrived at the Casket Company with almost twenty of his parishioners. He was barely five feet tall, and teetered on platform shoes which added several inches to his height. "God has called Sister Ong home," he said, clasping my hand warmly. "Thank you for inviting us to hold a service for her."

Pastor Cheng had brought a boom-box which cranked out organ music that filled the chilled funeral room with commotion. The parishioners raised their heads and quavered, "We shall meeeet by that beeeautiful shoore." Several elderly women in subdued gray and blue tunics wept as they sang. They had obviously loved my mother. Pastor Cheng stood before his small group of Baptists, waving his arms to the music. Besides the old Chinese women there were young Tamil men, even younger Chinese girls, some Eurasians, some middle-aged Singaporeans in the typical bureaucrats' white shirts and gray pants, what Shakespeare would have called a motley crew. An unlikely community, they gathered around the coffin to say good-bye to Sister Ong. I didn't know my mother. She had found forgiveness with these strangers.

The church members left in a flurry of offers. "Sister June, do you have a ride home?" "Brother Bala, I can drop you off at your house." "Will you be able to make sure that Sister Genevieve gets home safely? Make sure you bring her all the way to the elevator."

The pastor stayed behind to talk. "Your mother was a devout Christian," he said. "She never missed church on Sunday. Sometimes Bala would fetch her to church and drive her home. She was very fond of all the parishioners." He was pleased with himself. Then, smiling broadly, he asked, "When will you be returning to New York? I will be leaving myself in two months. I have been offered a church in Los Angeles, and my family and I have decided to accept the offer."

We did return to Singapore the next year in 1985. While Charles taught at the National University, I spent the year in the Institute of Southeast Asian Studies as a research fellow. In the mildewed rambling structure constructed to lodge trainees for the British civil service in the days before air conditioning, each fellow received a room with high ceilings and its own full bath. Across the street, the institute's new library held a good collection of ephemera and literature on the five countries that comprised the Association of Southeast Asian Nations, ASEAN. I was studying the ideology of nation formation undergirding English-language Singapore and Filipino writing, a particularly exciting time for the research, since martial law in the Philippines was being dismantled that year.

A few months before the Marcos collapse, I went to Manila to interview two Filipino novelists, Frankie Sional Jose and Nick Joaquin.

Manila was like Malaya of the 1950s, with hissing kerosene lamps lighting the ramshackle night-stalls, and miles of seedy concrete buildings, doors open to catch a warm breeze. But the Manilans were frenetic, more like New Yorkers milling through Times Square. There were masses everywhere, hanging on to the seats of the *tuk-tuks,* the motored open vans that gushed out brown flumes of carbon monoxide into the congested streets, reading newsprint books in concentrated *isolatos* in the many city bookstores, and sharing plates of *pancit* and purple yam ice cream in the dim coffeeshops that looked like old American ice-cream parlors teleported to the tropics.

Much of my time in Manila was spent in bookstores and university libraries, collecting materials unavailable at the Institute. Frankie's bookstore, Solidaridad, crowded with shelves of Filipino literature, became an indispensable resource. There, a stream of writers and critics, Frankie's coterie of activists and intellectuals, came by to pick up their mail, to read the latest U.S. journals, and to gossip about the state of politics. Manilans had been adamant that Benigno Aquino, ensconced at Harvard University in rich Boston, could not provide a credible opposition, but his assassination in the Manila airport in 1983 had jolted them out of their cynicism.

The author of numerous novels that imagined the future of a democratic Filipino society, Frankie was never fully convinced that an instant utopia could be created in the Philippines. He and his wife Tessie tried to shelter me from the city's terrors: purse snatching, muggings, gunfire, kidnappings, murders, or simply getting lost in the labyrinthine ghetto streets. His stout aging body housed a skepticism honed by decades of vigilance. Watchful of corrupt politicians, corrupt generals, corrupt corporations, corrupt professors, corrupt Ilustrados, the landed gentry bred on Spanish colonialism, corrupt American diplomats, he was ever tender to the illegitimate, landless, penniless, those blessed only with many children and yearnings.

Frankie's ribald jokes and inside stories of the rich and foolish made my research a live thing, like a submersion into a flowing river. But the poisonous air of Manila clogged my lungs, and I had to return to Singapore, gasping and wheezing, after only a few weeks in the Philippines.

A few months after my return to Singapore, knowing the open violence of the Philippines side by side with its famous hospitality, I was stunned to see Aquino's widow, Cory, dressed in brave yellow colors, on television every night, exhorting the Filipinos to dreams of liberation. And then there was a day of glorious revolution, when the people stormed Malacañang Palace. I finished writing my study on Southeast Asian nationalism and literature in Westchester, under the influence of expectant democracy.

Since Mother's death, I have returned frequently to Malaysia and Singapore to refresh my spirit and my original literary identity. My first community — brothers, dear friends, fellow writers—is now thickly present all over the region. Returning, I am filled with an ineffable sense of completion, a satiety of recognitions. No matter how urgent my struggles to escape childhood poverty and the country's racial politics, I have continued to feel an abiding identity with Malaysia's soil, not only its shining waters, lush growth, and multiracial colors, but even its polluted streams, back lanes, and communal quarrels.

Visiting Malaysia in the summer of 1994 with my teenage son, I noticed how my father's children had taken over the world. Not in power or wealth, but as the generation that carries the past willy-nilly into a differently dangerous future. Beng has for a long time now taken me up as First Aunt to his two daughters. The brother who abandoned his ambition for a university degree to help Father and his siblings, he is the most traditional peranakan in our family, the one who has steadfastly refused to leave Malacca, and the patriarch to whom I willingly pay my respects when I return.

When First Brother drove me into Malacca town in search of a watch repairman, the thick heat and narrow shop-lined streets were still the same. In one alley between two shops whose salesmen had shoved containers spilling bras, cheap silk blouses, and cotton shorts onto the five-foot-way, a gray-haired Chinese man repaired my watch in five minutes, for which he asked a few dollars. The economy of time and price was of my childhood. Across the street another old Chinese Malaysian hunched on a stool, surrounded by awls, hammers, and rubberized sheets, from which he fashioned soles and heels. In fifteen minutes, slicing neatly, he had glued fresh soles on my worn Italian sandals. He had set up his movable business by a shoe store. Beside him, walls sprouted racks of women's dress shoes, each pair adorned with distinguishing buckles, medallions, bows, pleats, the seemingly infinite variety of capitalist invention. First Brother did not think it remarkable to find the watch repairer and the cobbler at work in the age of disposable cameras and disposable shoes. But I did, and my marveling—like a tourist—to find them still in Malacca, which now bustles with tour buses and giant air-conditioned shopping malls, brings home to me the interwoven twinning and splitting of past and present, Malacca and the United States.

Even so do I continue to repair to my brothers' homes in Southeast Asia, mending those ties that had bound me to them—the years of childhood, fighting, singing, talking. Second Brother, a noted historian, now works for an international agency on the alleviation of poverty in Asian nations. Third

Brother thrives in Singapore, with two sons and a family-centered career wife. Fourth Brother helps to manage his wife's family coffee-shop, and Wilson, who had never lived with us, organizes us through dinners, jobs, social contacts, and reunions, constructing as an adult all the family he had missed as a child. Peng's children, looking so much like the rest of us, also form part of our intricate blood-chain.

And Peng? When we first met after Father's death, she burst out weeping, "E sie, E sie!"—"He's dead, he's dead!" and hugged me, the only time we have ever touched. It is Father who binds us together, his ghost still powerful between two women who have shared the longest love for him. Peng lives now contented among her grandchildren, her hopes fixed on her only daughter, born a few years after I had left her house.

Returning, I measure the years through the heights of nieces and nephews. I especially listen to their Malaysian-accented voices, to their longings for equality, their expressions of identity, and their testing of the bonds between parent and child. I would like to think that something of me remains in my Malaysian family, not merely as past but as prologue.

But it is my son who has gone ahead of me into an unimaginable future. At fourteen he speaks and writes a cyberspace language I cannot understand. The tenderness I feel for him is for a wholly beloved stranger, a temporary denizen in my home. When I describe Gershom as a 100-percent American, it is only Americans who disapprove, Americans who, making an equation between essence and face, infer from his features that he has lost his roots. During our visits to Malaysia, my brothers and cousins understand and confirm what I mean: "Hey, you American!" they say to him, teasingly reminding him of his difference.

Gershom's memories include years of July 4th Boy Scout parades and salutes to the strains of "The Star-Spangled Banner," turkey and cranberry sauce dinners, debates over presidential elections and party politics, snorkeling off Catalina Island, marching in small-town band competitions throughout California, and gulping down three burgers in one sitting with his friends in a fast-food franchise. His alienations are U.S.-bred, not foreign-born. He shares nothing of his Malaysian cousins' examination fears, and has seldom felt the full discrimination of monocultural preferences. His confidence in his identity as American is perhaps a tenuous effect, one that can perhaps be shattered by prejudices and racism, but it is a necessary possession. For if Asian Americans are not convinced of their right to American identity, how can they struggle against those who are only too willing to deprive them of those rights?

To my son, the quintessential American consumer, everything that enters his mouth, his mind, his spirit, is American—whether it is sushi, tacos, curry, hot dogs, pizza, jazz, opera, the Beatles, *Star Trek,* computer programs, or roller-blading. Still, his omnivorous culturalism makes him one of those children in the Promised Land whose very privilege must come freighted with responsibility. These years prepare him, I hope, for a broader citizenship with the rest of humanity. Being an American, after all, is not much good if it is not good for something other than identity.

# CHAPTER ELEVEN

# Moving Home

I want you to write a memoir," Florence Howe said.

The exhibition hall hummed around us, cavernous and over-heated, a maze-like collection of flimsy booths resembling many Asian bazaars I had visited. The men and women who clustered around the publishers' display tables clutched briefcases, heavy coats, mufflers dangling from stylish tweed and woolen jackets, and the unmistakable brown-cover convention program, as large as a telephone directory for a good-sized town. Their myriad conversations made a muted noise, like the collected simultaneous proceedings of hundreds of department meetings in a giant conference room, the kind of space that inspires a desire to flee.

I had last met Florence in June 1989 at the airport in Akron, waiting for a flight back to New York after a painful and disruptive meeting of the National Women's Studies Association. Coincidentally we both had had reviews published in a recent issue of the *Women's Review of Books*. She was generous in her praise of my work, and I confided that what I would like best to do is to take up an offer from a university press to submit a memoir. In the meantime, however, it was important for me to continue my critical work on Asian-American literature. Six months later, at the Modern Language Association conference in New York, she remembered our conversation.

Florence was formidable. Her pepper-salt hair sprang vigorously from her broad intelligent forehead, as urgent as her restless mind. Together with a number of contemporary women, she is identified with launching the cause of feminism in academe. She flashed me a smile, dazzling, wheedling, and confident.

I shifted, demurring, "I don't think I have the time." I was on the verge of moving to an eminent research university where, I had been advised, some of the faculty were suspicious of creative writers, minorities, and women, and where I would have to fend off their disapproval by incontestable scholarly production. I could not share this information with Florence who was uncowed by university committees.

"I am so glad for you!" Florence continued. "When I heard you were moving from a community college to a university, I thought, at last, you were being recognized. And I felt others were being recognized with you."

Her outspoken support—even if mediated through class and institutional grids—moved me. It moved me in a moment of ineffability, not mother-daughter, not cross-generational, not cross-cultural, but woman to woman. The recognition of almost impossible sameness between white and Asian woman, or Asian and Chicana, Asian and African American.

Yet, the question remains, What is exchanged in this sharing between women? What reciprocity is unspoken, mythologized, or lost in a moment of cross-sighting?

My move from a community college to the University of California in 1990 was highly unlikely. Scores of minority scholars gleefully congratulated me, seeing my move as a belated admission in U.S. higher education of the significance of ethnic and postcolonial literary studies. My response to such jubilation was knotted with skepticism, scraping against the grating insinuations of inequality. Why did it rankle that my move was universally seen as from low to high, from worse to better, from inferior to superior? Who proffered the recognition?

One of the last unquestioned sites of unearned privilege, negative stereotyping, and class prejudice lies in the unequal status of the university and the community college. Conceived on rationalizations of excellence, external evaluation, and funding for research, the university is symbolically a male territory: its faculty reportedly produces significant research, scholarship, and publication. In contrast, nurturing teaching supposedly occurs in the community college. There, because its standards are domestic and feminized, competitive research and scholarship are irrelevant.

For years I had resisted Charles's advice that I should leave the community college, and that my teaching and research interests would be better accommodated in a university. My deepest socialization in the United States had been through the community college. Coming late to the United States, it was necessary for me to learn about American identities, and the community college offered fertile ground for an immigrant.

Moreover, through all the years of teaching, and since early childhood, there was poetry, poetry which, as Kafka said, is the ax that breaks the frozen seas within. Late at night, after days when I had suffered the panic of disappearing into the nonentity of community college work, phrases, thoughts, images surfaced from that other life of Malaysian childhood and hope. I would get up reluctantly from a warm bed and write, hunched, cold, and happy in an abstract kind of way, as a poem started up in the gray predawn hours. I wrote to know I was still there, somewhere among the accumulating details of numbing reality. Writing offered a nostalgia beyond comfort, the only way to keep alive.

The suburban college to which I moved after three years at Hostos offered better teaching conditions, as basic as the presence of a bookstore, a library, large and clean classrooms, computers, and quiet order. But here I was always haunted by the feeling that the students, almost all of whom were white, saw me first as Asian before they saw me as a teacher. It was not my gender that got in the way but my nonwhiteness. Every semester with each new class, my first challenge was to make my white students take me seriously as a mind and as a mentor.

Many of the community college students resented attention that demanded a reciprocal attentiveness, even with the best of teachers. They came to classes after six hours of slicing bologna and serving meatball heroes at the local delicatessen, or drove from classes straight to the neighborhood 7-Eleven to stock the shelves and count change till midnight. For many of them, English was a requirement like paying taxes or cleaning the toilet bowl, and the mandatory exit exams cued to the five-paragraph expository essay confirmed their experience of writing as a joyless task invented by pedagogues looking for work. They were children of the conservative working class, with few beliefs of their own except for their desire for a foothold in the middle class, a place that their parents now occupied, having bargained a lifetime of dreary labor for the split-level ranch and the enclosed backyard. They had strong feelings, but could not write them down in the ways that English teachers approved; they hated reading books that made them feel dull, and polysyllabic words stumbled on their tongues like rude intruders.

And yet, and yet. Once I got through their dislike of my accent ("She pronounces 'however' as if there is an 'r' in it," a student wrote in a class evaluation), their fascination with my long hair ("Her long hair is very cute," students have written over the years), and their resistance to my "foreignness" ("Although she is a foreigner, she teaches English good," were typical comments), once I could get them to meet me in my office to talk about their writing and their reading, a social amity replaced their detached antagonism.

Most of the actual teaching occurred in my office, face-to-face, as they read passages aloud, confided their hesitant thoughts, and told me stories of their suburban lives. I never had to pretend fascination. They were exotic, inhabiting Raymond Carver's world, where drift, inertia, alcohol, disappointed parents, marijuana, secondhand cars, temporary jobs, and the status of mediocrity, of never being the best, seemed to have convinced them of their insignificance.

Sarah was one of the first to make an impression on me. She did not write prose; the assignments she submitted were a series of poetic outbursts, lamentations of a social devastation that I was sure only a brilliant intelligence could produce. She had been shooting heroin since thirteen. She had run away from home at fifteen, lived on the streets of New York for two years, returned home to her divorced attorney father in Scarsdale, was attending classes as he had requested in exchange for taking her back. She glowed when we talked about her writing.

Halfway through the semester she began to droop. She came to my office often, sometimes simply to sit while I talked to other students. She stopped coming to class, then called from a pay phone to talk.

"My father's kicked me out of the house," she said. "He caught me smoking dope."

"Come back to class," I pleaded. "We'll find an agency to help you. You can make it."

"I can't. I'm sleeping at Grand Central Station. I have my clothes stashed in the lockers."

"Come stay with us till you get a place of your own," I offered.

"You don't know what you're asking. I'll steal everything from you to buy dope. I promise I'll keep writing. Who knows, perhaps I'll still get to be a reporter."

As with so many of my students, I never heard from Sarah again.

Despite the heavy teaching load, the boring repetition of introductory and composition courses, and the hundreds of papers to grade every semester, there were students to be won over to literature and writing. Some were women returning to school after their children had left for college. Other women, tired of keeping house, had enrolled in nursing programs, or computer programming and secretarial courses.

Kathlyn, older and better dressed than I, wrote graceful essays that disdained her classmates' labored outlines, and sent me a thank-you card from Columbia after she transferred. "What are you teaching here for?" she asked me during an office conference.

It always amazed me how many of my students looked down on the college, a contempt that had more to do with pride and prejudice than with reality. The community college was, as Robert Frost would say, a place where if you wanted to go we would have to take you in. The very antithesis of an elitist institution, it was inexpensive and accessible to young and old, poor and rich, white and black, women and men, clever and dumb, successful and failed. An open admissions policy meant that, despite a few restrictions, no one who was determined could actually be refused entry, and this absence of discrimination, a very new paradigm of almost total inclusiveness, resulted in a widespread absence of respect. In the United States, as in many other societies, prestige is signified by exclusivity: how few can be admitted, how many of the masses can be excluded. Here the life of the mind is strenuously ranked, satisfying a cultural craving for class divisions that should appear bizarre in a democracy. The community college was unthinkable as a choice for the brightest and most ambitious of the county's children, and students carried their profound self-contempt into the college classroom.

Often I was most successful with students who had been damaged by prejudice. One semester, I began an experimental beginning writing course which concentrated on journal writing and on reading aloud. Clumsy and childish, Lindy was not a promising student. An overlarge tongue had made her inarticulate during childhood, but she found that she could talk better on the page. Her journal entries read like long intimate conversations, and she became interested in her other classes as well. From writing she discovered sign language classes, and went on to graduate as an interpreter for the deaf.

Michael had no such handicap to overcome in a creative writing course. He was sullen, turned friendly after a few weeks, but remained a classic underachiever. The anthology's selected readings were entirely irrelevant to him; he was interested in none of the assignments. Of course, he could do the work if he felt like it, but since he didn't feel like it, it was impossible to say that he could do the work.

But when we started a literary journal, he began to assert himself. He was good at organizing people, wanted the responsibility of editing the journal, knew a friend who worked in a print shop, and would negotiate for inexpensive publication costs. He would do the layouts, write an editorial. Michael spent hours in my office conferring on the journal and completing his writing assignments. Finally he told me that his father, a high school English teacher, had offered to teach the class desktop publishing, and we could use his school's Macintosh machines for an entire Saturday in order to produce the journal.

When I called Michael's father to make the arrangements, he sounded wary. Michael had never shown any interest in school. He was astonished that a writing class would select Michael as their editor. Was I aware that Michael may not follow through?

Michael's father was distant and brisk when he met us on Saturday morning. I saw his tension: this was something new—sharing his academic world with his son, the two of them wary around each other. But he patiently taught the students to work the desktop program. None of us had ever used a mouse, and many of the students typed with two fingers. With Michael cajoling his fifteen classmates at the keyboard however, we had the journal camera-ready by late afternoon, at which time father and son were sharing smiles.

The next semester, Michael returned to my office with boxes of the journal, fresh from the printer, for distribution to the college. He was no longer diffident or disengaged. "I took a box down to my old school," he said, "the one my dad teaches in, and I gave copies to my English teacher's class. She couldn't believe I was the editor, and that I had written the editorial and the two poems!"

But there were others that no amount of attention could help. I did not recognize Anthony's retardation at first—he was quiet, and when asked to respond, he stammered so painfully that he was incoherent. I didn't question the take-home assignments he turned in, always on time, and always correctly completed. His in-class writing, however, was astonishingly poor; a third-grader would have performed as well. But he brought the essays home for revision, and returned them competently rewritten. His grades see-sawed between F and a reasonable C.

His parents, both school principals, came for a conference with me. He was dyslexic, they said, and needed more time to complete the work than was offered in the class schedule.

A few weeks into the semester I could not avoid the conclusion that his parents were coaching him on his assignments—Anthony was not capable of independent performance. When I failed him for the course, I received a bitter letter from Anthony's father accusing me of grading harshly. Although I did not want to break their belief in their son's normalcy, I could not in the end testify to Anthony's college capability.

Some of the best community college students were never registered for courses. They were retirees, senior citizens who had been young adults during the Great Depression and World War II. Some were from corporate middle management and had never thought of themselves as poets and thinkers. Alone with bedridden spouses, arthritic, they wandered into my class and found a listener. I was delighted to meet students who had read Tolstoy and who were willing to try the sonnet form, and I was still willing to believe them wise.

Gary, retired from General Foods, took up lots of time talking to me, many afternoon office hours when I could have been grading papers. Each time he came for a conference, he was carefully groomed as if for an important job interview. I mused over the irony of our positions: silver-haired Gary, a veteran who had served in Hawaii after the bombing of Pearl Harbor, a relic of New

Englander ancestors, and I, his trusted guide through U.S. culture. He had been writing letters to the *New York Times* editor for years although they had never been published. I suggested he mail his letters to the editor of a local county newsletter, and when one did appear, he was jubilant. It was a fix, and he became a writer, addicted to the next fix. It didn't matter that his letters and postings appeared in print only twice a year. The fact of publication made him a member of the tribe of writers, and gave his fantasies a respectable, public life. His children in distant states now had to take his writing seriously. We discussed places he could submit his work to—church bulletins, little magazines, radio shows. He had opinions the world should be informed of, ideas for poems and songs and high school shows, and my office became his private salon, his old America and my new America together a happiness for him.

Other students also wanted a literary salon, and found it in the poetry group that met weekly in the college. Because we met in Rachel's office, we observed her unwritten rules: no nasty criticism, kindness all around, and above all, supportive comments so that everyone would leave feeling good. Rachel was a superb teacher. She had received more awards for excellence in teaching than any other professor in the college.

After our first few meetings, she walked me to the parking lot. Standing beneath the aching deep blue skies of mild October, she gently reminded me that the students were not so much interested in poetry as in sharing their feelings. "Of course they want to learn from you. And you have so much to teach them. But you can crush them, you do overwhelm them. I know you are only thinking of the poems, but these kids are sensitive. They are just beginning to express their feelings."

Together with Mary Ellen, another poet, I attended the meetings regularly. Sometimes, there were more faculty members than students present. During these Friday afternoons I came to exercise a discipline in self-abnegation, observing, as it were, monastic rules of silence and abstinence. We read mimeographed sheets of students' poems, and only occasionally poems submitted by one of us. Under Rachel's direction we read each poem aloud, sometimes twice or three times. So what if the thought was banal or obvious or trite? Or the lines a series of Hallmark clichés, the rhymes forced, the rhythms a heavy di-dum-di-dum-di-dum? For long minutes I would sit silently, all too conscious that Rachel was nervously preparing herself for another one of my "unconstructive" comments.

Each Friday, I submitted to Rachel's creed: the nurturing of tender young psyches and their protection from the withering blasts of critical judgment. I learned to swallow harsh words. My mind ran, trapped in ever narrowing circles of the prohibited, till I forced myself to blandness: It has an interesting idea! I like the assonance in these lines! That's an unusual use of the word! Having proclaimed approval, I could sit back in silence, eyes down as if in fascination, performing a silent reading over and over again of the wretched stanzas. The poetry group was devoted to students' writing, and I must have sat through more than ten years of utter kindness, the weekly meetings a mortification of intellect and spirit.

Under the eye of Rachel's disapproval I seldom submitted my poems to the group—they would have detracted from students' achievements. Why did I persist in attending these meetings? I believed I had a lot to learn about humility. My British-style education, based on blind merit and intellectual competition, had left me unprepared to teach many of the students who came to the community college, the unformed, unconfident, inarticulate, inexpressive, who may think slowly or badly, and who feared examinations and English teachers. To teach in the community college, I needed to believe in more than academic achievement. Not less but more. That more—the humanity in the humanities, the presence of community in the community college—was something I hoped to learn from Rachel, who was unaffectedly, unreservedly student-centered.

In Rachel's office, we could read and talk about Harry's poems, Harry already sixty when he first came to a poetry meeting, and whose book of poems still remains unpublished today, after his death at the too early age of seventy-six.

Harry had literary ambitions for himself when he registered at City College, but World War II came along, and he signed up for the Merchant Navy. After a few years of service patrolling the Red Sea—"I played cards and saw the world," he reported ironically—he returned to the United States and married a widow with three daughters. At this point, his narratives seemed to disappear into a fast forward of decades of labor: a janitor stoking a boiler room and repairing other people's short circuits; a chicken farmer in Baldwin county, collecting hundreds of fresh-laid eggs every morning, packing and selling eggs, cooking eggs and chicken, till the daughters were grown and scattered, fleeing the hard work. Then he and his wife, cashing in on the acreage, retired on Social Security, into one of the umbrella houses, a handyman's delight, perched above the Hudson River.

Harry's hands were gnarled, his worn shirts and pants always freshly laundered. "No point throwing away good stuff," Harry said, and I felt strongly that way about him. A goodness came out of him, a mild patience visible on his wrinkled face and bent back which his slouching pace only made more emphatic.

Harry symbolized the threat and promise of America for me, for only in America could a poet end up as a janitor and chicken farmer, only in America could a retired chicken farmer remember his ambition at age twenty to write poems that would rival those of Mandelstam, and only in America could Harry find professors to listen and to honor his late-life poems.

"Every Jew in New York in the thirties was a Communist!" Harry said of his young self. He had drunk tea and lemon on the Lower East Side, and written briefly for the *Socialist Worker*. But he voiced no nostalgia for socialism, and I never heard him say the word "capitalist."

A professed atheist, he was the community organizer for his town's Unitarian Church, and every Sunday he and his wife Toni shared fellowship with believers. Harry believed in fellowship, and neither politics, religion, class, or race featured in his feelings. His church gave him an hour each week, and he filled the hour with poetry—all kinds of poets reading their work, and sometimes as a favor to himself, Harry read his poems to the congregation. His poems grew freer as he grew older, shaking off the respect for regularity that had made his thoughts timid.

After I left for California, we exchanged perfunctory cards; Harry was grounded in New York, a piece of New York social history, and I as always a passer-by trying not to look behind. But after four years, he wrote to say he had been diagnosed with liver cancer, and that he didn't expect to have much time left. I wept at the news. All the regret that I had suppressed at leaving the community college, leaving my tenuous, wavering, twenty-year-old relationship with New York, converged upon Harry's illness.

I flew to New York and visited him in Croton on Father's Day, bringing wine and food which I knew he could not eat. For years Harry had proudly presided over a spring lunch for his college friends. That April we gathered at his house, opened his kitchen drawers, set his table, and spoke again of his view, with the black railroad and silver river below.

He called me "sweetheart," a new appellation, and for the first time he spoke bitterly about his life. "Ah, I should have just done what I wanted," he said, his face sadder than I had ever seen. "There was so much of the world I wanted to see." He spoke of himself in the past tense, his frail body worn down by his second fierce bout with chemotherapy, but he was writing every day, taking down the accounts of his battle with his last enemy. As I was leaving, he gave me his cancer poems, poems full of love for language and poetry, bright with the consciousness that his struggle with words was finally to end.

I did not hear of Harry's death till after his funeral. As lovers go, Harry was the gentlest. Like a ghost from another dimension, he never asked of the world what he desired.

I will always be grateful to the community college for giving me work. At least there American higher education made allowance for differences in accents, especially non-European accents. Almost all my colleagues were white, and almost everyone lived in the surrounding well-to-do suburbs. During the fourteen years at the college, I learned to keep a low profile, to appreciate its teaching mission, and to devote myself to my students.

No one made an issue of my Asian background, except for the one occasion when the department secretary called me a "coolie" and the chairperson said she could not take my word for the incident. But the secretary left soon after, and the incident was never mentioned again. Once, during a teaching evaluation meeting, the same chairperson informed me that I was not pronouncing the fricative "s" at the end of "is" correctly and made me repeat it a couple of times after her. Still, my career did not appear overtly uncomfortable. "I never think of you as Asian," one of my closest friends, an academic woman in a neighboring college, said to me as a compliment.

So why did I feel out of joint?

True, the community college culture was determinedly anti-research and anti-publishing. But many of my colleagues in the English department did both. Products of the recession of the 1970s, with doctorates from Columbia, New York University, Fordham, and Brandeis, many of us would have been teaching in four-year institutions had the economy been better, had we not had familial responsibilities, had geography not been a factor, and for some of us had we not been women. Many of us struggled to maintain our research and writing without privileges that support the work of university faculty. But our struggle was ironically undermined by academics of every class.

Some occasions were allowed to breach those class lines. A number of fellowships permitted me entry into the libraries of Yale, Princeton, the Graduate School of The City University of New York, and Columbia University. During the summer of 1978 I jogged past the ancient elms of Princeton, by the heady perfumed honeysuckle tangles, and around the track field, wondering what F. Scott Fitzgerald would have made of someone like me in his green-light vision of America. We twelve summer fellows whom Larry Lipking had gathered for his seminar on the poet-critic reminded me of Matthew Arnold's scholar-gypsies, transient, unsettled, yet seemingly unshakably bonded to an ideal of the university through an imaginary community of scholarship.

My summer at Princeton ended, but my early-morning writing, which had started during those wretched years in Massachusetts, persisted, and I began a series of fellowships which allowed me to write, publish, and do research in Southeast Asia on postcolonial anglophone literature. Fellowships had to be applied for, an act that assumes courage; and once awarded, they had to be accepted, a more difficult act that threatens future problems, punishments, and miseries, for they take a woman out of the home and separate her from husband and children. Campus housing, which winked at partners squeezed into bedrooms with a single twin bed, forbade the presence of children. The ban had something to do with insurance, but more, it said that wombs had no place in the life of the mind. The green and pleasant land of research universities barred babies, all biological attachments. A woman had to check her child at the turnstile before admittance to Gothic halls and reading rooms.

When both my husband and son protested at the prospect of being left at the checkroom, it was always women who gave me permission to do so. "It is you who wants to be at the feminist seminar!" Phyllis, the social worker I had been talking to for three years, noted, when I complained that I could not get my women friends to apply for the National Endowment for the Humanities summer seminar at Barnard. My husband had counseled that I stay home for the summer: I needed rest, he said, and the long drive into Manhattan would be psychically exhausting.

"But what do *you* want?" Phyllis probed. Such a simple question, so difficult for wives and mothers to ask or answer.

Over lunch a year later, I explained to a colleague that I was turning down a writer-in-residency at the East-West Center in Hawaii because it would mean leaving my family for the summer. Iris stared at me irritably through her fashionably-rimmed glasses. "Go!" she said. "Just go." Each time I hesitated, weighing the costs to male comfort and domestic quietude, the apparition of my abandoning mother condensing on the film of my consciousness, I heard Nancy Miller's impatient question, "Well, what are you waiting for?" Women with no responsibility for my private life were sufficiently outside it to give it a metaphorical finger. For women like me, it wasn't male lovers who posed the threat of infidelity. More dangerously and usefully, feminist women reminded me that I also had rights to a separate life, even within a traditional family.

All this research and writing, however, was clearly against the grain of professional hierarchy. For years during the 1970s and 1980s, in the hothouse convention traffic of the Modern Language Association meetings, eyes flicked to my identification badge then politely swiveled away. I was enraged by these visual discriminations at every meeting: Asian, woman, and community college—and the last was decisive.

But not to me. I saw in the bored glances that did not bother to conceal their prejudice the same facial behavior of the British administrators in the Malaya of my childhood. I knew the power of the rejection was historical, situational, defensive, and already in retreat. My very presence that their eyes had to skirt suggested a different vision, less beatific, less exclusive, and less exclusionary.

Borders are policed on both sides. Someone who walks between and in and out of national and institutional borders draws attention to the arbitrariness of divisions and to the vested interests of gatekeepers. There are gatekeepers everywhere, including at the community college.

In 1987, after my fellowship year at the Institute of Southeast Asian Studies in Singapore, I applied for promotion to full professor for the second time in three years. Again I studied the statement of criteria, struggling to decipher the significance of the numerical weighting, numbers whose interpretations mystified me: 50 percent for teaching, 40 percent for college and community service, and 10 percent for professional growth. But for the second time the dean refused to support me. On this occasion he ranked me last among the applicants. Three years ago, the only woman among the college administrators had advised me to confront him: "You have to make him accountable for what he says about you in the deans' meeting."

Confrontation was not something I did well. I disliked my excessive politeness, the obsequiousness that kicked in reflexively when faced with symbols of authority. But I knew she was right. There was something frustrating in my position at the college, although I could not name it. In 1980, after *Crossing the Peninsula* was published, letters of congratulation had arrived from British poetry societies, authors, and presses. Through the years, I had published two more books of poetry, a collection of short stories, and criticism. I had received fellowships and had read and lectured at numerous universities throughout the world, but I remained invisible at my college. My success outside the college contrasted with a profound sense of failure in it. I spent long hours at the Writing Center that I had set up a few years ago, arriving at eight in the morning and closing it at five. I spent time with the tutors I was training, time counseling students who were failing their composition classes. It was as if I had become as stigmatized as my remedial students, relegated to the library basement, doing the cheapest labor for the most needy. Despite my award for teaching excellence, I had never been invited to teach an honors course. Like my desperate students, I was failing at the community college.

But it wasn't sexism that held me back: other women faculty were advancing rapidly. It wasn't racism, for I saw faculty of Asian descent move up the promotion ladder. And I was popular enough with my colleagues and students, both of whom had nominated me for the teaching award.

"I want to know what I can do to improve my record for promotion." Stammering, I tried to find the best words to say across the large desk.

Mr. Gruber stared at me, his round pink face an accusation. "Why do you always feel you have to be first?"

His words stopped me. Was I being pushy, arrogant, unfair? My childish resentment at my father's demand that I always achieve, always be the best, returned in the figure of this white male, nearly sixty, who was rumored to fall asleep behind closed doors, who read the *New York Times* at his desk, and who brushed crumbs furtively from his lap when I came in for the appointment.

My chest tightened. "It's not that I feel I have to be first. I want your advice on what else I can do to help my case next year." My voice was apologetic, properly and sincerely humiliated.

He settled back in his armchair. Short and plump, he was almost lost behind the heavy desk. "Tell me what you have been doing."

I knew he had read my file and had passed judgment on it, but obediently I began, "I run the Writing Center and spend a lot of time tutoring in it."

"That has no visibility in the college. You should serve as chair of Senate committees."

It was true that in eleven years, despite numerous services, I had never been invited to chair a committee. Inexplicably, local decisions moved around me through my colleagues, but I was always outside these circles, never admitted. If it was ostracism I suffered, it was so subtle that I could not name it, except as a deadening of my powers within the college.

I continued, my throat tightening with tension. "I also write a lot and publish." "A little," I added, to avoid the impression of immodesty.

He leaned back and flexed his fingers together. "That counts in a place like Columbia, but not here."

I flushed. No one had ever said it so baldly. "May I quote you on this?"

He stood up violently and pointed his finger at me. "How dare you intimidate me!" His face was red. Almost curiously I noted that his Adam's apple was strained against his neck. "Don't you intimidate me!" he shouted again.

Tears gathered. I was incredulous at the sudden turn in the conversation, and furious with myself for crying. I could not stop the tears. They came from fear and from something else, the moment of recognition of unaccountable injustice, the anger that, at least for this man, all my years of work in the college meant nothing.

"I was not trying to intimidate you," I protested. "It's the first time anyone has told me that publications do not count."

"Yes, you were, and no, you may not quote me!"

The violence of the dialogue repeated in my ears for days. That night I wrote a letter to the college president detailing the encounter. An invitation to discuss it with him arrived a few days later, and because I knew I would cry again at the meeting, I did not accept it. Nothing came of my letter of complaint, nothing except finally my decision to leave the community college for a university position.

"Shirley, you have to understand how people in the college see you," my best friend, Bob, successfully promoted years ago, said to me. "They see this strange woman going to read her poetry in weird places whose names they don't recognize." He was trying to explain my marginality in the college.

Vaguely, I recognized that poetry readings in places such as Princeton University and the Commonwealth Institute at London would be constructed as weird only by people defensive about their own marginalization. In this almost wholly white, middle-class, suburban community, I had feared from the first that either my differences would have to be bludgeoned into sameness or I would forever be stigmatized as different. I had hoped to finesse the problem, engaging in a long painful struggle to pass as an ordinary citizen.

Bob's words underlined the failure of my assimilation in his world and taught me that the struggle was not worthy of my life. I needed to find another, more welcoming America in which poetry, Asia, and woman could be accepted in the same body. Bob's attitude, I thought but did not tell him, betrayed him and betrayed my trust in him. More than Gruber's bullying, his bland defense of nonweirdness persuaded me: my decades-long commitment to the mission of the community college, that sometimes wonderful, sometimes frustrating experiment of skeining gold out of teaching ordinary people, making an intellectual life in the midst of an egalitarian society, was futile.

I began looking for a university position the next year.

A few months after the meeting with Mr. Gruber, I hesitantly seated myself in a hot room at Barnard College. The members of Nancy Miller's National Endowment for the Humanities seminar on feminist literary issues crowded around a couple of battered steel tables, all twelve women warily taking impressions of each other. I had written a proposal that pulled together the aborted starts and fragments of my scholarship on Asian-American women's writing—the novels annotated, the ideas and arguments scattered in unfinished papers, the feminist texts uncritically stacked by my desk.

My public participation as a feminist began with the vision of Miller sitting at the head of the table, beckoning with her keen ear for the voices of the cantankerous others in the room. I saw in her mordant self-reflexivity a critical temper that combined my own nervous subjectivity with a pleasure in the sinewy rigor and turns of the mind that approached the erotic. She displayed both woman and mind in her very performance of self. I did not see the split, the rupture, the ambivalence, and schizophrenic aura that I feared in myself as in the apparently oxymoronic structure of the woman scholar. But I was not looking for the truth of the person. Surely I did not see what it must have cost her to carry out such a performance: perhaps the quarrel of private-public persona, perhaps the shrinking of domestic resources.

Miller was the first woman teacher I studied with in the United States. As an undergraduate I had taken only one course with a woman, a British professor teaching Chaucer and Middle English. The English department at Brandeis University included two junior women professors, but since neither taught American literature, I had not gotten to know them. My years in unprestigious community colleges were more gender equitable; however, gender equity at the community college also masked an active desire for homogeneity which is intrinsically antifeminist. Miller's position of the feminist as teacher enacted a type of activism that I was comfortable with.

Still, woman's performance as feminist teacher within U.S. institutions is fraught with contradictions and bad faith, for such institutions socialize, regulate, police, and domesticate, even as the nuns of my childhood colonial school. Institutions are the housekeepers for minds that do not live in houses, and I am frequently disturbed by the incompatibility between the wildness I value and believe must be valued in women and by the linear cage of academic competition that structures universities. Do wild feminists live in universities? Can they?

I often think that being a feminist minority scholar is what one is reincarnated into for being a male chauvinist in a previous life. It is not a position that affords easy simplifications or rewards. The wonder is that there are any minority feminist scholars at all, for keeping intellectual sight of the multiple contradictions inherent in these conflicting subject positions may be impossible for any human mind. Thus, while I do not believe that individuals can be characterized into races, I understand history as racially and ethnically riven. As an avowed feminist, I have had to learn to trust, respect, and love women; I have had to overcome my sexism, my preference for male buddies because of my preference for male bodies. Scholarship, race, gender, sexuality—I am trying to make sense of volatile and highly political materials even as they appear to be blowing American society apart.

At the same time, contemporary U.S. feminists, especially women of color, are deeply suspicious of do-gooders, especially if they are white. Blake's admonition, "And charity would be no more if we did not make somebody poor," shades any would-be Lady Bountiful in a bleak light. But a girlhood without heroes—without the mother who does good—casts even bleaker shadows. We need women of all colors to jump fences of gender, race, class, nation, and religion, to help us rescue ourselves from the empire of blankness.

I began the seminar almost a decade after the publication of Maxine Hong Kingston's *The Woman Warrior*. Many of the stories of a misogynist Chinese immigrant society in Hong Kingston's fiercely imagined book were familiar to me. What was new was the audience. For years I had been writing to myself, the poems and stories in my desk drawer growing dog-eared and yellow. "Who do you think you are, an Emily Dickinson in Brooklyn?" my husband had challenged me. I thought I was more eccentric than that, a Malaysian woman teaching English and American literature to Puerto Rican and black students in the South Bronx.

"Who is your audience?" a New Zealand professor asked after my first book of poems appeared, the black hole question, the vortex into which all meaning disappears. In my nightmare, I stood before a cheering audience, answering every question thrown at me, spinning the wheel, my hands hot and eager, the arrow circling before coming to rest at larger and larger numbers. Until that final question, the one that stopped me.

After Kingston, I had looked for other Asian-American women writers— so few to begin with: Monica Itoi Sone, Jade Snow Wong, Diana Chang. Then more and more. Hisaye Yamamoto, Janice Mirikitani, Mitsuye Yamada, Wakako Yamauchi, Cathy Song. Almost all of them were from the West Coast, the place where Asia and America merge, thrown together by the currents of the Pacific Ocean. These women, and critics such as Elaine Kim and Amy Ling, publishing in the United States, lit up a different space, one that promised rather than denied community. I wanted to learn another life from them, finally to place Malaysia side by side with the United States, and to become also what I was not born as, an Asian American.

To grow as an Asian-American scholar, I needed more than books and a room of my own. I needed a society of scholars, an abundance of talk, an antagonism of ideas, bracing hostile seriousness, and above all a community of women. In selecting twelve women, nine white, one African American, and two Asian Americans, Miller was assuring a certain kind of summer experience, much of which I missed because I was commuting from a rural town in northern Westchester in my unforgivably middle-class station wagon. I eavesdropped on the other women's talk of baseball games at the Yankee Stadium, off-Broadway plays, picnics at Central Park, and the intimacy of dormitory quarters, yearning to share their summer lives. When I read my poems one evening at Barnard, someone asked, "So, how come none of the rest of us were asked to read our poems?" Then tentatively she answered her own question, "Because we are making space for difference?"

As the weeks passed, we frantically Xeroxed more and more articles, spending our stipends lavishly in mounds of small change fed into the Barnard library's wheezing copy machine: Miller's enormous bibliography of feminist readings loomed, a mine on a fast moving planet that would not turn into our orbit again in our lifetime. We were the late twentieth-century version of the penurious scholar, almost comic in our obsession with acquiring sources, if it hadn't been for our ferocity.

After Mr. Gruber's declaration of intimidation, I dropped out of directing the college's Writing Center, focused on my own research and writing, and sent out job applications in tandem with my husband. During the next two years I received a number of offers from various universities. The call to interview at the University of California, Santa Barbara reached me at the Centre for Advanced Studies in Singapore in 1989, where I was doing research on local English-language women writers. The job description asked for a creative writer who was also working on Asian-American literature and on feminist issues. It could have been written for me. I knew then that, if a community college affiliation would not fatally stigmatize me, I would choose to live and work in California, a state geographically bound to the islands of Southeast Asia in a restless rim of moving plates enclosing the gorgeous Pacific waters.

California is perhaps the closest thing possible to moving home for Asian Americans, whose identity, as any Japanese, Korean, or Chinese national will tell you, is peculiarly American, forged in U.S. history.

Of the two oceans that bathe it, the two land masses that flank it, the U.S. founding fathers could imagine only a nation that looked to Europe, this despite the initiating error of the explorers who believed they had reached the Orient when they met the indigenous peoples of the West Indies. In a restlessly migrating planet, Manhattan island, facing the Atlantic swells, might logically pull in the tall ships from Europe, but Los Angeles, San Francisco, and Seattle were harbors formed for Pacific winds and traders, frontier borders for Asian settlers. A series of exclusions acts, beginning in 1882, foreclosed U.S. potential as a Pacific power and as an Eastern civilization. Asian-American identity can be said to originate in the "barred zone"—the territory west of an imaginary line running between the Ural Mountains, supposedly separating Europe from Asia, a terra invented by the U.S. Congress in 1917 from which no immigrants could come. Under this geographical mythos, people from historically hostile nations such as Korea and Japan were pushed toward a common destiny on U.S. soil.

Only in 1943, acting to counter Japanese war propaganda, and beginning the process of dismantling such legislation, did Congress repeal Chinese exclusion acts and grant Chinese immigrants the right to naturalization, and only in 1965 were the immigration laws changed to place Asian countries on an equal footing with Europe. While in the 1960s there were just over one million Asian Americans in the United States, the numbers are closer to nine million as we approach the millennium. Americans of Asian descent make up over 11 percent of California's population, and California is only now accepting its Pacific orientation, and the contributions of Asians whose national character is never in doubt to themselves. As my son wrote on his desk card for Parents' Night in his elementary school, "Asian-American and proud of it."

Inhabitants of a crossroads territory, in the first state to exclude Asians,

University of California students appear more cosmopolitan than students in other U.S. institutions. In my first three years at the university I taught in the Asian-American Studies Program. To graduate, students are required to complete an ethnicity course, considered by some as yet another nuisance requirement added to physical education and English. Many students who registered for my courses were a captive audience with little patience for the historical and cultural specificities of Asian-American representations. But what surprised me was the enormous goodwill that they brought to the readings and discussions. Lecturing on the century-long history of legislation against Asian immigration, reading aloud the works of writers like Carlos Bulosan, Milton Murayama, and Hisaye Yamamoto, I would look up and find faces, intense with listening. It was as if for many of them, especially Asian Americans, they were hearing spoken aloud something momentously secret, the secret of Asian-American presence in the United States.

Almost invariably, after each first lecture of the quarter, students waited for me at my office door. "How did you get to be a professor?" a freshman Chinese American asked. "I want to be just like you!" a Filipina burst out. Over and over again I hear the refrain, "I want to be like you."

I know these young Asian Americans mean something more complicated than their simple declarations suggest. For many of them, I am the first Asian-American lecturer they have heard. Until this generation, the language of the American imagination that was taught in schools had been European in origin. In just the way spirits are supposed to understand when they have entered the realm of the undead, children of Asian descent looked into the mirrors of poems and stories and never saw their faces. The myth was that Asian-American students excelled in mathematics and in music, symbolic systems that did not need English-language skills, and so it was little wonder that many of them chose business administration, economics, engineering, physics, computer science, or medicine in the universities. But I saw in my students a long deprivation of imagination—poems, stories, images, feelings held in abeyance because correspondence between literary images and self-images seemed impossible.

Even students from other groups were startled by my presence. "You are my first Asian-American professor," they said, intrigued, sometimes suspicious about my qualifications. One Euro-American student, anxious about grading policies, asked querulously if Asian Americans held an unfair advantage as they, of course, knew more about the culture and history covered in my lectures than he did. He was surprised to learn that Japanese Americans are generally as ignorant of the history and community values of Filipino, Vietnamese, and Korean Americans as he, or that third- and fourth-generation Chinese Americans share few cultural practices with the recent immigrants from Hong Kong, Taiwan, and the People's Republic of China. "Besides," I replied, "do you believe you have an unfair advantage over Asian Americans in a Shakespeare course? Or in a course where you read Hawthorne and Melville?"

"I didn't know Asian Americans wrote novels," a student bound for law school confided, "and such wonderful novels!" She wanted to take another Asian-American course with me, but I found she had never read anything by a Jewish-American author. "My parents didn't want me to grow up burdened by a Jewish identity," she explained. "My grandparents had come from Europe after the Second World War, and my mother wanted to leave all that sort of thing behind." Yet in a few months she would be marrying another Jewish American, in a ceremony performed in a Conservative synagogue his family had belonged to for decades. I persuaded her to do independent studies on Jewish-American literature instead. Together we arrived at a reading list, and for the first time she read Anzia Yezierska, Abraham Cahan, Saul Bellow, Bernard Malamud, Tillie Olsen. The books were different, but her dilated gaze of recognition was the same, not of race but of extended humanity.

Like their Euro-American, Jewish, black, and Hispanic peers, Korean Americans, Japanese Americans, Vietnamese Americans, Sri Lankan Americans—students whose families come from mutually alien Asian societies—are all affected by the university's enormous intellectual machinery. These Asian Americans carry the same credit cards, learn the same computer languages, watch the same television shows, and aspire to work for the same Fortune 500 companies as their peers. But together they are turning the nation inexorably into our planet's first world-civilization—both west and east, north and south, and something else so inimitable that every other nation has lost some of its brightest and youngest to the United States. If the United States were to remain only a Western civilization today, it would be set on an irreversible decline.

Setting out from a nation that denied people like me an equal homeland, I find myself, ironically, making a home in a state that had once barred people like me from its territory. The United States, despite instances of still invidious discrimination, is now ideologically where Malaysia may yet be someday. The U.S. Constitution, endowing every citizen with equal rights without regard to race, gender, religion, and national origin, protects individual freedoms, of speech, religion, public association, from the tyranny and prejudices of the majority. These are precious protections that humans long for, for love and plenty can only be assured when there is freedom from injustice. Yet I am always conscious of speaking as an immigrant, from a short hopeful personal past, and of the voices of others whose lives still bear the consequences of a U.S. history of genocide, war, racism, and other violences, who speak to less sanguine emotions.

National transformation promises no security. California is a dangerous state: in four years I have seen civil insurrection, fires, drought, earthquakes, landslides, and floods, catastrophes that level equally. Famous writers like Maxine Hong Kingston have lost their manuscripts in Oakland fires, Hollywood stars like Barbara Streisand have sold their fragile collections in anticipation of a Los Angeles earthquake. Life is simultaneously unspeakably splendid and terrible in California. The pathetic fallacy does not operate here, where even the homeless feel blessed by a natural landscape that admits everyone, as cheap as common dirt and beyond human pricing. In Santa Barbara the sun shines from a brilliant sea-blue sky on hillsides fragrant with wild mustard, sour grass, and sage; the surf beats its creamy foam against hundreds of open coastal beaches, a continuous delight, even if the earth were to roar and buildings pancake, floor on floor, even if ash were to rain from exploding homes in hidden canyons.

I write this on the morning of my fiftieth birthday. A mile away the waves of the Pacific Ocean are in an unusual swell. A northern storm in Alaska has pushed the waters between the Channel Islands and the coast of Southern California into long slow motion. The waves run from the horizon shoreward, cresting higher and higher, as tall as fifteen feet, and as they break where the ground suddenly turns shallow, they form tubes in which surfers race, rushing at fearful speeds, within cells of crashing water. My life rushes me toward a shore, in full motion; only my skills keep me on my feet, not drowning.

How do I reconcile these two different yet simultaneous images—the ropes that my mother and father have cunningly woven, invisible like spirits and ghosts, that tie me to the ancestral altar table which presides in every Confucian home; and the crashing surf that knocks me off my feet and throws me onto a beach, which is never the same from moment to moment?

The dominant imprint I have carried with me since birth was of a Malaysian homeland. It has been an imperative for me to make sense of these birthmarks; they compose the hieroglyphs of my body's senses. We tell stories to bind us to a spot, and often the stories that make us cry knot the thickest ropes. I imagine Baba's spirit breathing over the small Malacca knoll where he was buried, overlooking green paddy fields and leaning coconut palms. I have taken a little of him with me to California, not enough for him to haunt me, wanting to go home, but enough to kindle the joss of memory. Baba is never dead to me, as should be the case with filial piety. Parents do not die; they merely take on the form of ancestral spirits, tenacious in their power, keeping you a child forever in your first imagination. With such ghosts, it has taken me a longer time to leave home than most immigrants.

To give up the struggle for a memorialized homeland may be the most forgiving act I can do. Everywhere I have lived in the United States—Boston, Brooklyn, Westchester—I felt an absence of place, myself absent in America. Absence was the story my mother taught me, that being the story of her migrant people, the Malacca peranakans. But perhaps she was also teaching me that home is the place where our stories are told. Had I more time to talk to Mother, perhaps I could have learned to forgive, listening to her stories. In California, I am beginning to write stories about America, as well as about Malaysia. Listening, and telling my own stories, I am moving home.

CPSIA information can be obtained at www.ICGtesting.com
Printed in the USA
LVOW11s0856280716

497820LV00002BA/18/P